ARCTIC ARCHAEOLOGY

GARLAND REFERENCE LIBRARY
OF SCIENCE AND TECHNOLOGY
(VOL. 1)

ARCTIC ARCHAEOLOGY
A Bibliography and History

Albert A. Dekin, Jr.

GARLAND PUBLISHING, INC. ● NEW YORK & LONDON
1978

Library of Congress Cataloging in Publication Data

Dekin, Albert A.
    Arctic archaeology.

    (Garland reference library of science and
technology; v. 1)
        1. Eskimos—Antiquities. 2. Indians of
North America—Antiquities. 3. North
America—Antiquities. 4. Archaeology—
North America—History. 5. Arctic
regions—Antiquities. I. Title. II. Series.
E99.E7D36   970'.01   75-5120
ISBN 0-8240-1084-1

This book is dedicated to students of arctic archaeology, in hope that their studies may be aided and their understanding enhanced by its contents.

CONTENTS

I. Introduction

This bibliography and history is designed to lead to resources for the study of Arctic archaeology and to an understanding of how these studies contributed to our present knowledge. It is a heuristic device for scholars and is designed to facilitate their access to a widely scattered literature. It is not designed to synthesize our present understanding of Arctic archaeology, but to provide steps to such an understanding. This particular combination of historical narrative and extensive bibliography is seen as being the most useful to the serious student of this field. Its organization facilitates access to both citations and the literature itself, while avoiding the problem of stark lists of entries with all-too-brief annotations.

The uses of this book are as diverse as the researches conducted in the Arctic, but two avenues appear to be the most advantageous. The first is via the space–time frame inherent in the historical narrative, wherein the researches and researchers are chronicled. This may prove a useful introduction to the field. The second is via the bibliography itself. Optimum use of the bibliography portion per se requires some knowledge of who has worked in the North. This knowledge may be gained from the historical narrative or may be acquired from other sources (courses, lectures, articles and other publications).

The bibliography which forms the major portion of this book was compiled between 1965 and 1977, being the by-product of my scholarly development from undergraduate studies at Dartmouth College through graduate work at Michigan State University. Systematic efforts at particular dimensions of the literature were conducted in 1970 for a

1

chapter on the development of arctic archaeology (Dekin 1973a) and in
1974 in support of my dissertation research. During this work, it became
apparent that the "arctic small paper tradition" was a thing of shreds
and patches, access to which was difficult for all but the most persistent or those fortunate to have access to the relatively few extensive
libraries and archives. There were also rather few critical assessments
of developments in Arctic studies, and few syntheses of general understandings. Bibliographies themselves were few and far between and were
often uncritical catalogues or listings varying in the scope and coverage.

The bibliography sneaked up on me gradually, until I found myself
to be a bibliophile. I was extremely fortunate to have access to libraries
with extensive Arctic collections. These included the Stefansson
Collection in the Dartmouth College Libraries System, the Library of the
Arctic Institute of North America (when it was in Montreal), the Elmer E.
Rasmuson Library (with its Skinner Collection) at the University of
Alaska, Fairbanks, and the Library of the Institute of Arctic Biology
at the same institution. Access to collections was facilitated by the
interlibrary loan network of the State University of New York, and the
collaboration of kindly colleagues and students, for which I am extremely
grateful.

When I turned to a more systematic search for sources, numerous
colleagues provided assistance in the form of reports, citations, confirm-
ations and partial bibliographies of their own and of their students. I
fostered the habit of turning immediately to the bibliography of a newly
received publication and of checking its contents against my files.
However, as this process continued, the pace of Arctic research and

2

publication was increasing, and I found it more difficult to keep pace
and to digest contributions to the literature on an expanding international base. Late in 1976, I stopped trying quite so hard, and concentrated my efforts on cleaning up the loose ends of what I had collected.
This meant that the years 1976 and 1977 are somewhat less complete.
Unpublished research, which is difficult to determine except through the
professional infrastructure and newsletter columns, perhaps is most
complete through the early 1970's.

Other bibliographies were of particular assistance, including the
Arctic Bibliography published by the U.S. Government printing office and
more recently by the Arctic Institute of North America. Bibliographies
by Donahue (1973a) and Workman (1972, 1974) were joined by those of
Clark (1975c) and Stothers and Dullabaun (1975) and have provided useful
sources of citations and served to corroborate and correct those obtained
from other publications and files. However, by far the most useful
source has been the published literature itself, as it depicts those
sources found useful in the conduct of research. This bibliography,
then, comes most directly from the actions of Arctic researchers and
their contribution is immeasurable. I would hope that any utility which
this compilation has is sufficient compensation for those scholars,
librarians and fellow students of human behavior whose gracious assistance I value. Looking to the future, I would appreciate being apprised
of omissions which could be included in future editions.

The writing of any history of Arctic archaeology is an exercise
often made interesting by what is omitted as well as by what is included.
I have chosen to chronicle research and publication. I have slighted

3

the personalities and personal development of archaeologists which, while being of interest to the understanding of directions in which the discipline has been drawn, are of far greater scope and of potentially far less value than their results. I have also restricted the tendency to dwell on the winds of intellectual change which blew into the Arctic, except insofar as they contribute towards significant changes in research interests and results. Recent histories of the development of North American archaeology have covered this aspect in great detail, and I will only discuss it briefly in introduction. I have also reduced the treatment of historic archaeology in the North and have not sought complete coverage of the significant European literature on the proto-historic/historic Norse occupations of the Eastern Arctic. But at the same time, I have attempted to include the literature of what some have called the sub-Arctic because it so often relates directly to studies of the tundra and the sea.

In writing this narrative, I had the greatest difficulty with the last section on Current Trends. Perhaps this is because it is always difficult to determine where we are going by looking at our wake or perhaps it is because the publication of results lags uncomfortably behind field work. It was most frustrating to declare "Hold, enough!" However abrupt the transition from present to future, I hope that this book eases the intellectual development of future students of Arctic archaeology and provides a foundation from which they can place themselves in a dynamic and evolving discipline. May they see their development as continuation from the past.

4

The development of Arctic archaeology parallels the development of the rest of anthropological archaeology in North America. Early archaeological work was based on data gleaned from what was basically ethnographic research. With the realization that problems of ethnic origins and prehistory could not be answered by ethnology and trait distribution studies alone, archaeologists began field excavations and expeditions. This was the pioneering era of archaeological research when each spade or trowel thrust revealed exciting and often unexpected artifacts and cultures. From about 1935-40 to about 1960, there was an expansion in the number of Arctic investigators and in the number of sites excavated as well as an increase in the number of archaeologically-known cultures. There was a corresponding increase in the number of research problems. Much of the archaeologist's interpretive energies were expended on problems of general chronology, utilizing new dating techniques which were developed during this period, and on problems of the general relationships among cultures. Since about 1960, our knowledge of Arctic archaeological data has increased dramatically. We have escalated both the number and the complexity of archaeological problems. In recent years, the increased importance of the anthropological aspect of archaeology has resulted in an increase in cultural-ecological studies. However, many Arctic archaeologists are slow to approach the analysis of social change and cultural processes involving prehistoric Arctic cultures. Presently, we are in the adolescence of anthropological archaeology in the Arctic. I eagerly anticipate its maturity.

The concept "Arctic" may refer to geography, land forms, latitude, climate, biota, historic and prehistoric cultures, cultural adaptations and cultural traits. Comparative problems arise because no two of these

5

variables have strictly coincidental distributions. My Arctic region consists of Alaska, the present tundra regions of Canada and Greenland and parts
of the coasts of Quebec, Labrador and Newfoundland. In this summary, it
should become apparent that changes in climate and in the distribution of
relevant archaeological cultures through time may make the heuristic area
that I have defined inappropriate and that we may wish to discuss data from
outside this region.

Several characteristics of Arctic archaeological field work distinguish it from such research in more temperate climes. Permafrost, or ground
which is below the freezing temperature, is both a help and a hindrance. If
cultural deposits have been frozen since they were deposited, the preservation is remarkable, and includes pieces of clothing, bone and ivory artifacts,
butchered animals, and often the inhabitants' last supper. However, excavation must proceed slowly as the exposed surfaces melt, so that vertical
progress in excavation may be extremely slow. Melt water accumulation and
muddy sidewall slump often impede careful excavation. Alternate freezing and
thawing and solifluction may confuse or obliterate stratification (see Corte
1963).

Many sites are not and have not been permanently frozen and so are
easier to excavate, but the recovery of perishable materials is low. In a
region where most of the ground is permanently frozen below the thin surface
"active zone," the most important factor in determining whether a site is
frozen or not is local site drainage. Generally, well-drained sites are
within the seasonally active zone and thus the degree of preservation is
lower in such sites.

In addition, Arctic sites are widely scattered, transportation and
logistics problems are endemic (and expensive), living conditions are

generally rustic, insects are voracious, cold rains or summer snows are not uncommon in certain areas, the excavating season is short, the land area to be covered is vast, and the investigators comparatively few. In spite of, or because of, these factors, Arctic archaeology is becoming one of the most fascinating and dynamic areas of American archaeology and the story of its development follows.[1]

---

[1]Other books and articles on the history of Arctic archaeology are: Larsen 1953; Collins 1954b; Larsen 1961; Harp 1964; Taylor 1968; Bandi 1969; and Dekin 1973a. Most dissertations contain critical reviews of prior research and useful summaries of the state of knowledge at that time.

II.   Explorers and Ethnographers

Arctic archaeology began as the incidental by-product of exploring, whaling and ethnographic research in the mid-to-late eighteen hundreds. As early as 1765 (Cranz 1767) historians had been speculating on the Siberian origin of Eskimos and their peculiar culture. Subsequently, ethnographic data (Rink 1887; Murdoch 1887, 1888) was used to try to solve this problem which has continued as a major problem in Arctic archaeology to the present day. Rink and Murdoch (for different reasons) saw Eskimos as originating in the Arctic interior. Thalbitzer, a linguist, suggested in 1904 that the Bering Sea region was their homeland. Steensby (1917) proposed in his classic "An Anthropogeographical study of the origin of Eskimo Culture" (published and translated into English, like so many important papers of this period, in the Danish journal Meddelelser om Grønland) that there were two cultural strata—the Paleoeskimo and the Neoeskimo. The Paleoeskimo were adapted to sea ice hunting and lived in snow houses but originated from the inland Indian cultures in the Central Arctic and spread both west and east. In Alaska, there was a subsequent transition under the influences of Pacific cultures (Japan) which led to the Neoeskimo development of open sea kayak hunting and the umiak. Investigators were trying to solve essentially archaeological problems with data and techniques of ethnology.

Small archaeological collections from Greenland were obtained by Koldewey in 1869-70 (1873), Ryder in 1892 (1895), Amdrup from 1898-1900 (Thalbitzer 1909) and the Denmark Expedition of 1906-1908 (Thostrup 1917; Thomsen 1917), but the artifacts were believed to be of no great age. Solberg (1907) attempted to justify a stone age of some antiquity in West Greenland using data collected from what we now know as sites of Sarqaq and Dorset cultures (see Collings 1953a), but the antiquity of these finds was

8

disputed and as late as 1931, Mathiassen still considered these finds to date after Norse contact with the Greenland Eskimos (1931a:196).

In the Central Arctic, the explorer and whaling captain George Comer returned to the United States with artifacts found in 1900 on Southampton Island in western Hudson Bay which were described by Boas (1907) and thought to relate to recent Eskimo populations. The exploitation of the Central Arctic lagged behind the Danish exploitation of Greenland and the Russian and United States exploitation of Alaska so that our knowledge of this area also lagged. This exploratory period of Arctic archaeology was prolonged in the Central Arctic.

In the Aleutians, the French ethnologist Alphonse Pinart recovered several relatively recent skeletons and grave goods in 1871 from a cape on Unga Island (Pinart 1875). From 1871-1874, the geographer and naturalist William Dall undertook excavations of supposed Aleut village sites and burial caves during his spare time from his U. S. Coast and Geodetic Survey activities. He also visited the cave reported by Pinart and his excavations on 6 Aleutian islands resulted in a 3 stage sequence of Aleut subsistence and culture, mainly defined by stratigraphic differences in midden composition of food remains (see Jochelson 1925 for a description and critical evaluation of Dall's work). Although these elaborate interpretations have not withstood the scrutiny of subsequent excavations in 1909-10 by Jochelson (1925), Dall's 1873 excavation of the Amaknak cave and other sites was the earliest excavation in Alaska to take careful note of location and relationships among artifacts and to note and record evidence of stratification (Dall 1875a). Dall also reported on the recovery of "mummies" from a dry cave in the Aleutians by ship captain Ennig of the Alaska Commercial Company (1875b) thus pointing out the peripheral yet informative nature of Arctic archaeology during this

9

period.

Aleut origins were also considered at an early stage in our knowledge of Arctic archaeology. Jochelson reviewed the literature in 1925, noting that the Russian Veniaminoff as early as 1840 suggested a theory of Mongolian origin which was supported by other explorers (Jochelson 1925:111). Dall in 1877 (95-97) pointed out that the great sea distance and poor transportation potential of the Japanese and Ainu, etc., mitigate against the Aleut migrating from the west.

During this early "Explorers and Ethnographers" stage of Arctic archaeology, artifacts were collected from various parts of the Arctic. Most of the data then available to attack what I consider to be essentially archaeological problems (origins of Eskimos, Aleuts and Athabascans) were ethnographic and the available archaeological data had to be forced into an historic model of the distribution of Arctic cultures (i.e., sites excavated in the Eskimo territory were Eskimo, albeit earlier ones). The "culture areas" at the ethnographic present were presumed valid in the archaeological past. Unfortunately this assumption persists today. This early period generally ends about 1910-1920 with the dispatch of several expeditions to the Arctic with the expressed purpose of doing ethnographic and archaeological work. We then "knew" the recent history of the Aleut and Eskimo of Greenland. However, just around the corner were some reassuring and some perplexing finds.

III.   Expeditions and Pioneers

In the Eastern Arctic, ship captain George Comer, who was taking supplies north to the Crocker-Land Expedition of the American Museum of Natural History, was iced in and forced to winter in Northwest Greenland from 1915 to 1917. He took advantage of this opportunity to continue his archaeological activities and excavated fifty-three sites around Smith Sound. He observed a dichotomy between recent sites and some earlier sites which Wissler, who reported these finds in 1918, attributed to pre-contact ances- tors of the Polar Eskimos. Iron drills were found in many of the sites of both periods, but were made of meteoric iron in the earlier period and of Norse (?) iron in the later period. An important site on Wolstenholme fiord has been called Comer's Midden (Wissler 1918:112) which contained an abun- dance of bone, antler, and wooden artifacts with few stone remains and a surprisingly large amount of whale bone in the lower levels. There was no clear evidence of stratigraphy so that stages in the development of Polar Eskimo culture could not be defined, but these lower levels were recognized as important and different. The Second Thule Expedition of Knud Rasmussen in 1916-1918 also collected at Comer's Midden and at other sites in the Thule region.

The years 1921-1924 saw perhaps the most important archaeological expe- dition in the history of the Eastern Arctic. Knud Rasmussen's Fifth Thule Expedition, with Therkel Mathiassen as archaeologist, excavated extensively ". . .at Repulse Bay, on the mainland, N.W. of Hudson Bay, at Ponds Inlet in northern Baffinland and in Duke of York Bay on Southampton Island" (Mathiassen 1925:206). The most important site was at Naujan on Repulse Bay, where, in 1922, Mathiassen excavated winter houses, meat caches, graves and kitchen middens. Considerable age was almost immediately attributed to this

11

site because of the location of the house ruins ". . .at an elevation of from
12 to 30 m above the sea, at a distance of 100-150 m from the shoreline; from
some of the houses, it is not possible to see the sea now" (Mathiassen 1925:
206) because of the isostatic rising of the land. Mathiassen named this rich
Eskimo whaling culture the Thule Culture (1925:212; 1927:89) and cited other
occurrences of this culture at Comer's Midden, at sites reported from Northeast Greenland by Thomsen, Ryder, and Thalbitzer and from scattered locales
in West Greenland, Baffin Island, and as far west as Barter Island west of
the Mackenzie River and Point Barrow, Alaska. Mathiassen concluded that the
Thule Culture was ancestral to Polar Eskimo and Central Eskimo but that "The
Thule-culture is much more recently related to the recent-Point Barrow-
culture than to that of the recent Central Eskimos, and there is some reason
for the theory that its home [hence, that of the Eskimos in general] is to be
found in Alaska" (Mathiassen 1925-215). Mathiassen also excavated sites
transitional between Thule and Central Eskimo at Kuk on Southampton Island
which were probably ancestral to the Sadlermiut Eskimo who all died in
1902-03 from diseases brought by whaling vessels. Some of the previous collections of Captain Comer, as described by Boas, were now thought to relate
to these unfortunate people.

        The interest in Arctic archaeology generated by the Extensive re-
searches of the Fifth Thule Expedition led to the establishment of an archaeological survey of Greenland in 1929 headed by Mathiassen under the general
auspices of the Ministerial Commission for Scientific Investigations in
Greenland. Investigations were conducted by Mathiassen and Helge Larsen in
West Greenland (Mathiassen 1931b), Mathiassen and Erik Holtved on Disko Bay
in West Greenland (Mathiassen 1931a), Degerbol at Scoresby Sound (Mathiassen
1934b) and Mathiassen at Angmagssalik in East Greenland (Mathiassen 1932),

12

Helge Larsen (1934) in Northeast Greenland, Mathiassen and Frederica deLaguna in Northwestern Greenland (Mathiassen 1930a, 1930b), and Erik Holtved in the Thule District (1944). The earliest occupation of Greenland was felt by Mathiassen and others to be the Thule culture which was subsequently modified by Norse acculturation as documented by sites excavated at Inugsuk (Mathiassen 1930a, 1930b). This Inugsuk culture then evolved through several minor stages to become the Eskimo culture found by whalers, but it also survived in isolated regions of East Greenland until these people became extinct in the late nineteenth century (Mathiassen 1935:418; see Amdrup 1909).

Perhaps the most important interpretive progress in the Eastern Arctic during this period was the isolation of Cape Dorset culture (now simply called Dorset) by Diamond Jenness in 1925 (Jenness 1925). A rather extensive collection was presented to the National Museum of Canada by Major L. T. Burwash of the Department of the Interior who had collected at Cape Dorset on southwest Baffin Island and had purchased artifacts from Coats Island. Having little provenience data, Jenness was forced to rely exclusively on the attributes of the artifacts in the collection. Many of the bone and ivory artifacts fit Mathiassen's typology of Thule harpoons, but a large segment of the collection had much darker patination, showed holes that had been incised and not drilled, or were previously unknown forms of chipped flint. Jenness suggested that this Cape Dorset Culture preceded Thule culture in the Cape Dorset region but he still felt that an earlier culture in this region was yet to be found (1925:437) and that the modern Eskimos descended from some post-Thule inland ancestors (1925:428; 1923).

Dorset was not immediately accepted as a valid culture and Mathiassen considered it to be merely a peculiar local variant of Thule (Mathiassen 1927:2:165). In 1927 and 1929, Jenness and W. J. Wintemberg discovered

13

"pure" Dorset sites in Newfoundland (Wintemberg 1939:83; 1940). Henry
Collins cautiously endorsed Dorset as Pre-Thule Eskimo (1935), but Mathiassen
continued to be skeptical of the Eskimo nature of Dorset ". . .But are these
people who left their traces on the coast of Newfoundland Eskimos at all?
The culture seems to have strong Indian connection" (1935:422). This view of
Dorset as having been influenced by southern cultures has a long and varied
history lasting nearly to the present day (see Meldgaard 1962:95).

William Strong was a member of the Rawson-MacMillan Subarctic Expedition of the Field Museum of Natural History in 1927 and 1928. He excavated
coastal sites in Northeastern Labrador concluding that these predominantly
lithic remains were related to archaic cultures in the northeast and were
left by races of an earlier Indian population (1930:127) although Junius Bird
considered them to be remains of Dorset Eskimos (1945:180). Apparently a few
artifacts from the Hopedale coast were Dorset, but the majority of the sites
explored represent northeastern archaic cultures.

In the Western Arctic, the Jesup North Pacific Expedition of the
American Museum of Natural History from 1900 to 1902 supported Vladimir
Jochelson and Bogoras in their surveys of Siberian and Aleutian archaeology.
The Stefansson-Anderson Arctic Expedition supported Diamond Jenness's
scattered excavations from Point Hope, Alaska to Coronation Gulf in central
Canada. On Victoria Island in 1911, Stefansson made the first discovery of
Eskimo pottery and in 1912 he dug the Birnirk site at Point Barrow (some of
the artifacts were described by Wissler in 1916). In 1914, Jenness excavated
on Barter Island (see Stefansson 1914) (these data have been analyzed by
Edwin Hall - personal communication 1970). Most of these sites were later
thought to relate to the Thule culture (Wissler did not regard the Birnirk
material as being particularly distinctive). William Van Valin excavated

14

dwellings and charnel houses (?) in 1918 at Point Barrow which J. Alden
Mason later described and attributed to the Thule culture (Mason 1930) although
Collins later contended that most of the materials belonged to the earlier
Birnirk culture.

In 1924 Knud Rasmussen, of the Fifth Thule Expedition, purchased collections made by trappers or Eskimos as he travelled from the Mackenzie Delta
to Point Hope and East Cape, Siberia (Mathiassen 1930c:395; 1930d). Again,
most of the finds were of Thule-related cultures but some unusual chipped
stone artifacts hinted at mixed samples and future complexities.

The first good systematic excavation in the Bering Strait area was
done by Diamond Jenness of the National Museum of Canada at Cape Prince of
Wales, Alaska and on the Diomede Islands in 1926 (Jenness 1929:78). The
upper levels at Diomede contained cultures bracketing Russian contact in the
area (including a Thule variant) but the lower levels, called Old Bering Sea
culture, contained ivory objects inscribed with fine scroll art work unlike
any previously found in the Arctic. Jenness thought that these were con-
siderably older than the overlying Thule culture (1929:86; he seemed to have
had a knack for finding Thule precursors; see Jenness 1928, 1940).
Mathiassen attempted to derive the complex Old Bering Sea decorated harpoons
from the simpler Thule harpoons, but various evidence from stratigraphy and
beach ridge sequences on Saint Lawrence Island reversed this sequence
(Collins 1932:109; 1937:311).

Henry Collins of the Smithsonian Institution conducted excavations on
Punuk Island and Saint Lawrence Island from 1929 to 1930 (assisted by James
Ford in 1930) (Collins 1929a, 1929b, 1932, 1937). Collins's 1937 report on
the Archaeology of Saint Lawrence Island is an important landmark in Arctic
archaeology and the most lucid statement of the status of "Eskimo" archaeology

at that time. This monograph was awarded the gold medal of the Royal
Academy of Sciences and Letters of Denmark in 1936 winning the competition
for papers on Eskimo origins (Collins 1937:iii).

Otto Geist (with Ales Hrdlicka in 1926) and Froelich Rainey also
excavated on Saint Lawrence Island from 1926 to 1935 sponsored by the University of Alaska and assisted by the Public Works Administration (Geist and
Rainey 1936; Rainey 1941). Geist discovered a large mound on Punuk Island
in 1931 and excavated it in 1934, with Ivar Skarland, discovering the Okvik
culture which was the earliest culture yet found in this region, underlying
Old Bering Sea (Rainey 1941). The stratigraphy and seriation of this important series of Bering Strait excavations established an eight stage continuum
(Ackerman 1962:34) from Okvik and Old Bering Sea through Birnirk, Punuk,
Thule and on to Prehistoric, Recent and Modern Eskimo cultures. The largest
differences and most important criteria for distinguishing the early stages
of this sequence were in their art work. Generally, all of these cultures
were called "Eskimo" and the supposed Asiatic affinities of Okvik and Old
Bering Sea reinforced the hypothesis that the Eskimo way of life was a product of the Old World (Collins 1954:297). James Ford, sponsored by the
Smithsonian Institution, undertook excavations in the Point Barrow area in
1931, 1932, 1936, and later in 1953 (Ford 1959). He excavated at the Birnirk
site and the related Nunavak and Kugok burial sites. A lack of funds delayed
final publication and analysis until 1959 when Ford reported evidence of a
developmental sequence from Old Bering Sea through Nunagiak to Birnirk and
Thule, with some evidence for a later return migration of Thule culture from
the east, bringing back such cultural traits as snow knives, half-moon soapstone lamps, ice picks, and certain projectile point styles (Ford 1959:242)
(see Taylor 1963 for a more precise statement of Thule origins in the

16

Western Arctic).

The Stollman-McCracken Expedition of the American Museum of Natural History to the Aleutian Islands in 1928 carried Edward Weyer as archaeologist and Junius Bird as scientific assistant. They excavated an unusual Aleut burial from near Unalaska Island which contained four well-preserved bodies in a driftwood sarcophagus (Weyer 1929:235) and trenched a midden at Port Moller, Alaska (Weyer 1930). The midden contained several compact layers of shell, fish bone, and sea urchin spicules similar to strata found in previous Aleutian excavations. Very few interpretations could be made on this site which did contain one piece of baked clay and harpoons, one of which is similar to one of Mathiassen's Thule harpoon types. At that point, the only conclusion that Weyer drew from this site was that it was both similar to and different from sites previously excavated by Dall and Jochelson.

Frederica deLaguna excavated sites at Cook inlet in 1930 and at Prince William Sound with Kaj Birket-Smith in 1933, establishing three stages of Eskimo culture (Kachemak Bay I, II, III) (deLaguna 1934) which led to a late phase of Chugach Eskimo in Prince William Sound (deLaguna 1956). Through this sequence, chipped stone gave way to ground stone (slate) and "eastern" cultural influences became more important. This prehistoric "Eskimo" (Collins 1964:102) sequence seemed to have more in common with Aleutian sites than with those excavated in the Bering Strait region.

At this point in time, our knowledge of Arctic culture history had several locally-derived archaeological sequences which were only loosely tied together. North Alaska and the Eastern Arctic had a good cross-tie as did the North Alaska and Bering Strait sequences. The Aleutians and Southwest Alaska were somewhat vaguely related, but relationships were not particularly firm. The period of Expeditions and Pioneers saw archaeology emerge from an

17

ancillary part of an expedition to a respectable research endeavor. Field
work during this period concentrated on data-gathering, culture-history sequence and only rarely on the answering of theoretical questions or problems.

There was some confusion in the use of concepts such as Eskimo or
Aleut. What did it mean to call a culture Eskimo? If we meant a historical
relationship, how far back could we meaningfully push the concept Eskimo?
Where did pre-Eskimo end and Eskimo begin? Unfortunately this confusion
continued.

IV.   Chronologists and Prehistorians

This period began with a continuation of archaeological surveys and
scattered research reports, and ended in the middle of several extensive projects. Junius Bird of the American Museum of Natural History excavated sites
of recent Eskimos in the Hopedale area of the Labrador coast in 1939 finding
evidence of an extensive Eskimo occupation along this narrow coastal strip
(1945).

In 1938 J. Kenneth Doutt acquired an archaeological collection from
Eskimos in the Belcher Islands of Hudson Bay and donated this material to the
National Museum of Canada (described by Jenness 1941). This material was
supplemented by grave goods acquired from Eskimos by George Quimby in 1939
from the same region when Quimby was an assistant on a University of Michigan
geological party. Quimby's study (1940), in consultation with Jenness, suggested that the artifacts were from a distinctive Eskimo culture which was
the result of Dorset-Thule acculturation (although Taylor later suggested
mixture of sample--not culture; Taylor 1968:2). Both Quimby and Jenness believed that this culture, which Quimby named Manitunik, persisted until the
historic period.

Sites of the Dorset culture were reported by Douglas Leechman from
near the northern tip of Labrador in 1935 and from near Cape Wolstenholme on
the southern shore of the Hudson Strait in 1936 (Leechman 1943). T. C.
Lethbridge excavated Thule and Dorset sites in 1937 on Devon Island and adjacent Baffin Island discovering several sites containing both Thule and Dorset
artifacts (1939:222-223).

Graham Rowley excavated at Abverjar near Igloolik in Foxe Basin in
1939. This site was one of the first excavated sites to contain an extensive
collection of Dorset artifacts uncontaminated by Thule artifacts, thus

19

reaffirming Jenness's 1925 typological separation of Dorset and Thule cultures. Rowley suggested that the Norse had seen Dorset remains (or people?) in Greenland and that the recent Ipiutak finds at Point Hope might prove to be the Dorset ancestral culture anticipated by Jenness in 1925 (Rowley 1940: 498-499).

In 1951, Deric O'Bryan excavated a late Dorset house on Mill Island in Hudson Strait sponsored by the Arctic Institute of North America and the U. S. Office of Naval Research (O'Bryan 1953). He considered the few Thule artifacts found in the otherwise Dorset context to be evidence of Dorset-Thule contact and he dated the site between 1000 and 1500 years ago.

As a result of these and other investigations, Dorset culture came to be considered a culture of some antiquity in the Northeast. Speculators suggested similarities between the Dorset culture and the early pre-pottery Indian cultures of the Maritime Provinces of Canada, New England and New York. "Red Paint" in Maine, the "Algonkian" of New York, and similar cultures in this region contained ground slate, harpoons, and red ocher--traits which some archaeologists suggested could have come from Dorset (see deLaguna 1946, 1947; Spaulding 1946; Gjessing 1948). Ritchie (1951) (see also Hoffman 1952) took advantage of the new alchemy (Robert Stuckenrath, personal communication) of radiocarbon dating to reverse the temporal positions of Dorset (by cross-dating from the Western Arctic) and the New York archaic concluding that circumboreal contacts and cultural developments probably influenced both Dorset and Laurentian cultures (1951:50).

Elmer Harp, Jr., undertook an investigation of the Straits of Belle Isle region of Newfoundland in 1949 and 1950, excavating Dorset sites at Port au Choix (1951) as well as archaic or Beothuk sites. After an excellent summation of our knowledge of Dorset culture in 1951, Harp denied Dorset-

Laurentian cultural changes, pointing to the more important trait-linkages
with Alaska, at the same time suggesting the possibility of Dorset-Beothuk
contacts (1964a:165--written in 1951) and circumpolar drifts from an unnamed
and undiscovered ancient cultural stratum in the Old World (1964a:170).

In Greenland, one of the most important excavations of this period was
by an amateur, Hans Mosegaard, in 1948. He excavated at Sarqaq in Disko Bay,
West Greenland, and his collection was analyzed by Jorgen Meldgaard (1952).
The Sarqaq collection contained only 182 chipped and ground stone artifacts
whose discovery under controlled excavation techniques documented the existence of a "stone age" culture (see Solberg 1907 above). Meldgaard suggested
that this Palaeo-eskimo culture (following Steensby and Birket-Smith) was pre-
Thule and perhaps lasted to influence Inugsuk cultures (1952:230). Meldgaard
saw Sarqaq origins in Alaska with influences from Dorset. The importance of
another early cultural stratum in West Greenland was immediately appreciated,
and excavations were undertaken by Helge Larsen and Meldgaard in 1953 at
Sermermiut in Disko Bay (Larsen and Meldgaard 1958) and later by Mathiassen
in the same locale (Mathiassen 1958). The Sermermiut site is one of the rare
stratified sites in the Eastern Arctic where three occupations were separated
by discernible sterile layers. The earliest Sarqaq level was radiocarbon
dated at ca. 800 B.C. (subsequent dates place this occupation at ca. 1500 B.C.
--Fredskild 1967:39) while the Dorset layer is of the early decades A.D. A
classic Thule occupation tops the Sermermiut sequence.

These excavations demonstrated the existence of both Dorset and Sarqaq
sites but did not demonstrate any great affinity or continuity between Dorset,
Sarqaq or any later cultures. In West Greenland, there was little evidence of
any developmental sequence linking these cultures. Interpretations and hypotheses were made in terms of a number of separate migrations into Greenland--

a model which is still used today (see Gad 1970).

Count Eigil Knuth excavated in Northeast Greenland from 1948, at first discovering sites of Thule, or Arctic Whale Hunting culture (Knuth 1952:17) including a remarkably well-preserved umiak frame. Initially, Knuth lumped all of his "paleoeskimo" remains as remains of the Dorset culture. Subsequent excavations reported in 1954 and 1958 led to Knuth's establishment of the Independence culture whose closest affinities were with the Dorset culture and its possible antecedents in Alaska. Knuth suggested that the Independence culture might represent the cultural stratum ancestral to subsequent Eskimo cultures in Greenland (1954:378). His subsequent excavations in 1955 led to his distinction between a later more Dorset-like phase called Independence II (dated by Tauber at ca. 600 B.C.--Knuth 1958:570) and the earlier more exotic Independence I dated to the then remarkable age of ca. 1900 B.C. (1958:570). Because of the lack of evidence for slate grinding or lamps, Knuth characterized Independence II as Pre-Dorset (1958:573--it is now generally accepted as a regional variant of Dorset).

In 1954 and 1958, Collins published summary papers on Arctic archaeology and on the Dorset "problem" as seen from Southampton Island. His earlier paper was the first to use the term "Pre-Dorset" referring to the Sarqaq and Independence cultures as intermediate (both culturally and temporally) between Denbigh and Dorset (1954:304). His second paper paid tribute to Diamond Jenness for a "feat of scientific induction unequaled in the history of Arctic archaeology" (1958:557) in isolating Dorset from Thule in 1925. Solberg's 1907 attempt to substantiate a "stone age" culture in West Greenland might also rank with that of Jenness, given the state of archaeology and archaeologists at that time (see Collins 1953a) (you might wish to query contemporary archaeologists on their reactions to Richard S. MacNeish's

22

hypotheses, speculations, and interpretations in several areas of archaeological interest).

It is important to note that Knuth and Larsen and Meldgaard considered ecological factors in interpreting their finds. The relative elevation of the Independence sites was considered to be an indication of age as the sites were fossilized as beaches. The abundance of driftwood and lack of bone artifacts in certain periods were interpreted as evidence for warmer climatic conditions in northern Greenland. Stratigraphic evidence of renewed peat growth at Sermermiut was considered to indicate a more moist climate, even though the specific meteorological variable could not be determined.

Stranded by transportation problems on an intended trip to Cornwallis Island, Henry Collins, of the Smithsonian Institution, conducted excavations in 1948 at the Crystal II site on Baffin Island at Frobisher Bay. He excavated Thule houses reported by Charles Francis Hall 83 years before. Collins observed a Dorset component separated from the overlying Thule component by a buried sod line and developed a preliminary typology of Dorset harpoon types (which led to the use of Dorset harpoon types as "horizon markers"--Collins 1950:20). Collins felt that this Thule occupation was representative of the oldest manifestation of eastern Thule.

In 1949, Collins began excavations at Resolute on Cornwallis Island, excavating Thule houses (Collins 1951). A few Dorset artifacts were found in 1950 when Collins was assisted by William Taylor who returned in 1951 to look for evidence of Dorset occupations (Collins 1952). Taylor excavated in Middens in front of later houses, finding a deep Dorset stratum, raising hopes of finding Dorset houses. Collins and Taylor returned in 1953 to try to clarify the relationship between Dorset and Thule at Resolute (Collins 1955). Two of their Thule sites appeared to have been summer and winter

23

occupations of the same people, with the summer dwellings lacking whalebone roof supports and being located on a beach 44 feet lower in elevation, but only 280 yards distant, from the presumed winter occupation (Collins 1955: 22-23). This finding should caution those who assume a strict correlation between age and relative sea-level elevation.

In 1954, with National Geographic Society, Smithsonian Institution, and National Museum of Canada support, Collins excavated on Southampton and Coats Islands in Hudson Bay (assisted by Taylor and J. N. Emerson-- Collins 1956a). Their main goal was the excavation of a Dorset site discovered by a member of a geographical party in 1950. Tunermiut was the Aivilik Eskimo name for the locale at Native Point where the Sadlermiut Eskimo lived until they all died in the winter of 1902-03 leaving behind an extremely large number of house ruins and burials. A mile from the sea at an elevation of 85 feet above sea level, they found a Dorset midden whose artifacts suggested a previously unknown phase of Dorset (Collins 1956a:85). Naming this site T-1, Collins led a return party (with the addition of James V. Wright) in 1955 to continue research at T-1 and other sites, including sites on Walrus Island. Collins considered T-1 to be a proto-Dorset site (or early Dorset--Collins 1957a:23; 1956b) linking Pre-Dorset and Dorset. The T-1 radiocarbon dates in the seventh century B.C. substantiate this conclusion. The Walrus Island excavations confirmed the existence of a Dorset house seen by Thomas Manning's geographic party in 1936. A frequent artifact from T-1 was the "triangular microlith" which Meldgaard subsequently recognized as a "tip flute" at Igloolik (Meldgaard 1962) (being flakes driven longitudinally and unifacially from the tips of triangular end blades, giving the point a sharp edged ridged cross-section) and which are most prevalent in Newfoundland Dorset (Harp 1964), leading Meldgaard to infer a south to north movement

24

for this and associated traits found in early Dorset (i.e., the smell of the forest--Meldgaard 1962:95).

In 1953, J. Louis Giddings was investigating the tree line region of Manitoba taking tree ring samples and finding scanty archaeological sites in the thick forest (1967:282). It is coincidence in the extreme that the discoverer of the Denbigh Flint Complex in Alaska travelled two thousand miles to the timberline in Manitoba to acquire a collection of flint artifacts that were more like the Denbigh Flint Complex (see below) than any other known culture of Eastern North America. The collection from the Thyazzi site (Giddings 1956) on North Knife River documented another connection between east and west in the Arctic and set off renewed interest in an Alaskan culture that might be intermediate between Denbigh and Pre-Dorset or Dorset.

Jorgen Meldgaard excavated on a remarkable series of raised beaches in the Igloolik region of central Canada in 1954 and 1957 with joint Danish-American support (Meldgaard 1960a, 1960b, 1962). Here the horizontal and vertical raised-beach seriation contained remains of three cultural periods--Thule, Dorset and Pre-Dorset. Meldgaard emphasized the distinction between Pre-Dorset and Dorset at Igloolik and demonstrated a major break in artifact typologies, although housing styles were relatively unchanged. Meldgaard pointed out that attempts to derive Dorset from Pre-Dorset were not in accord with his data from Igloolik and he suggested that "The basic courses of the Dorset culture, however, must be searched far to the south" (1960a:593) specifically suggesting ". . .a possible source about 1000 B.C. somewhere in the triangle between the Great Lakes, James Bay, and Newfoundland?" (1962:95). Meldgaard also commented perceptively on the fruitlessness of the search for a single origin of Eskimo culture (1960b:65) as archaeological research continued to complicate the quest for "Eskimo" origins.

Father Guy Mary-Rousseliere worked at Alarnerk with Meldgaard in 1954 and conducted a preliminary survey in the Baker Lake region on the Thelon River in the central barren grounds in 1955. Several of his Baker Lake sites were subsequently excavated by Harp and Robert McKennan in 1958 during their archaeological reconnaissance along the lakes of the Thelon River. Harp (1958, 1959, 1961a) distinguished 5 occupations of the region: 1-Early Indian (?) interior adapted hunters--ca. 3000 B.C.; 2-Pre-Dorset; 3-Archaic Indian hunters; 4-Thule Eskimos; and 5-Caribou Eskimo. He found no indication of any Dorset occupation of the interior. Harp suggested that artifacts of the Pre-Dorset period evidenced contact and diffusion between the interior Indians and the coastal-tundra adapted Pre-Dorset peoples (1961a:70).

Harp also excavated on the Coronation Gulf littoral in 1955, finding evidence of the microlithic Arctic Small-Tool tradition and typologically separating out a larger flake-biface industry from the Kamut Lake site (1958: 233) which Harp felt were typologically related to cultures considered much earlier in the south. He did suggest that the "Arctic should not be propped too heavily on typologies that were developed primarily for the analysis of ancient complexes far to the south" (1958:242). In the light of Noble's and McGhee's subsequent work in this region (see below), his warning may soon be vindicated, even though his specific typological separation of the Kamut Lake sites may not be supported.

As a part of the National Museum of Canada participation in the 1958 International Geophysical Year programs of explorations, Moreau Maxwell conducted excavations on Ellesmere Island which had been hypothesized as the major route for any migrations to Greenland. Maxwell found slight evidence of a Dorset occupation with most of the discovered sites from Thule and Thule-derived Eskimo occupations. He found no evidence to indicate that the eastern

26

region of Lake Hazen and Conybeare Fiord had been important way-stations on any migrations in this region (1960a:88). No Pre-Dorset sites were discovered, although Maxwell felt subsequently that some of the higher structures which he had interpreted as more recent meat caches might be evidence of a Pre-Dorset occupation (personal communication 1966).

Maxwell (1960b) marshalled available evidence of changing ecological conditions in the Eastern Arctic, concluding that pre- and proto-Dorset peoples moved through the warmer phases of the waning climatic optimum, travelling by boat (1960b:10-11). He also pointed out correlations of the distribution of cultures with present January mean isotherms suggesting that with reductions of annual or seasonal temperatures ". . .there was a retrenchment of Eskimo settlements and a notable diminution of culture contact across the Arctic" (1960b:9; see Dekin 1969, 1972b, for an elaboration of his hypothesis). Maxwell also pointed out that these factors would account for the recent isolation of the Polar Eskimos and he suggested that the lack of Pre-Dorset remains in the interior of Ellesmere Island was because the migrants held to the warmer shores of Baffin Bay where the steep coast prohibited their extended settlement (1960b:13).

William Taylor, of the National Museum of Canada, excavated several sites of the islands and south shores of the Hudson Straits in 1957, 1958 (with Charles Martijn), and 1959. At the Imaha site (meaning "maybe" in local Eskimo), Taylor discovered the first human skeletal material from a presumed Dorset context. The individual was morphologically Eskimo (Laughlin and Taylor 1960). In 1958 at the western end of the Hudson Straits, Taylor found one human mandible on Sugluk Island and another on Mansel Island in Hudson Bay (Oschinsky 1960, 1964), both in Dorset cultural contexts. The morphology of the mandible suggests that these too were Eskimo, but a number

27

of the diagnostic traits of Eskimo mandibles are also shared by some
northern Indians. This skeletal material represented the then closest connection of Dorset culture to anything conceptually Eskimo (see Harp below).

At Ivugivik, Taylor excavated three small Pre-Dorset sites containing
an early occupation of the Pre-Dorset culture somewhere intermediate in time
between the very early Independence I and the late Sarqaq (Taylor 1962).
Taylor's investigations at the Pre-Dorset Arnapik site on Mansel Island and
at the Dorset Tyara site on Sugluk Island led to his conclusion that Dorset
developed rather directly from Pre-Dorset in the Eastern Canadian Arctic with
only superficial influences, if any, from any contemporary cultures outside
of this area (1965, 1968). He was specifically careful to deny evidence of
cultural influences and smells of the forest (placing himself in direct oppo-
sition to Meldgaard's hope for boreal origins of Dorset--[compare Taylor 1962
to Meldgaard 1962]).

In southwestern Alaska, Ales Hrdlicka, of the Smithsonian Institution,
conducted excavations in the 1930's on Kodiak Island and the Aleutians
(assisted at various times by William Laughlin and Robert Heizer) as a part
of his continued interest in the skeletal remains of Bering Strait populations (Hrdlicka 1933, 1935, 1937, 1944). His analyses of the Uyak site on
Kodiak Island indicated two cultural periods--Koniag and Pre-Koniag (1944)--
which seemed to relate to Kachemak Bay III of deLaguna. Unfortunately,
Hrdlicka's poor provenience data for both archaeological and skeletal material
has sabotaged much of their usefulness (Bank 1953:40; deLaguna 1956:260).
Heizer has published descriptive analyses of some of this material (1949,
1952, 1956) salvaging these by-products of Hrdlicka's search for skeletons,
but he admitted the fruitlessness of elaborate speculations and comparisons
without adequate provenience data (1956:10-11).

In 1945, Helge Larsen salvaged a large midden on Amaknak Island (site D) which had been reported by Alvin Cahn, a naval officer, to the Chicago Natural History Museum. Larsen corroborated the higher frequency of chipped stone and art work in the lower levels of the midden. Quimby (1945a) analyzed the art work on Cahn's earlier collection suggesting two distinct periods of Aleutian art, the earlier related to Dorset and the later related to Punuk. Quimby considered this site to contain ". . .links in the chain of evidence which some day will unmistakably tie Dorset to the ancient Eskimo culture of western Alaska" (1945a:79). He also reported on the harpoons from Cahn's collection and on his pottery which was the first reported from the Aleutians. A later reexamination of this "pottery" by Allen McCartney (1970) indicated that the vessel fragments were carved volcanic rock and reaffirmed the absence of pre-historic pottery from the Aleutian Islands (McCartney 1970:105-107). Quimby also pointed out that the sadiron stone lamp was a horizon marker in the North Pacific region dated to the eleventh century A.D. (dated by Japanese coins--1946b) and was found in several late sites in the Aleutians.

Archaeological research in the Aleutians must all be referred to the continued research results of William Laughlin starting in 1938 when he worked with Ales Hrdlicka for the Smithsonian Institution, and collected lamellar flakes, polyhedral cores and chipped tools from blowouts on Anangula Island (Laughlin 1951) as well as artifacts from the Chaluka midden on Umnak Island (Laughlin, Marsh and Leach 1952). Laughlin has continued his investigations with support from various universities and foundations to the present day. His archaeological studies were most complete at Chaluka near Nikolski on Umnak Island where three thousand years of occupation have erected an extensive midden (excavated in 1948, 1949, 1950 and 1952).

29

Laughlin interprets this site as containing ancestral Aleuts, suggesting that the Aleuts were firmly established in the Aleutians by the second millenium B.C. His studies of the physical anthropology of Aleutian populations corroborated Hrdlicka's dual division of Aleut and pre-Aleut. Laughlin preferred the terms Neo-Aleut and Paleo-Aleut, respectively. He saw a general cultural continuity throughout this physical change which may have taken place by 1000 A.D. in the eastern Aleutians, with a Paleo-Aleut refugium in the western Aleutians lasting much later. Laughlin and Marsh (1956) saw some lithic identity between the lower layers at Chaluka and the earlier Anangula site, suggesting that the core and blade technique lasted until 1500 to 1600 years ago (Laughlin and Marsh 1954:38) although subsequent excavations at both sites have not demonstrated this continuity (personal communication, Allen McCartney 1970; see McCartney 1971).

In 1948 Helge Larsen, accompanied by Erik Holtved, was sponsored by the U. S. Office of Naval Research and the Danish Expedition Fund on excavations and aerial survey in the Bristol Bay--Kuskokwim region of southwestern Alaska. A site on Chagvan Bay contained an Ipiutak-like flint assemblage but with gravel tempered pottery. Similarities with Kachemak Bay II indicated a guess-date at about A.D. 1000 (Larsen 1950:183). The Platinum Village site produced an Ipiutak-like assemblage without pottery but with oval stone lamps and bow drills (subsequently dated to the fifth century A.D.). Larsen noted the extreme inadequacy of our knowledge of this region and pointed out the "striking difference between later cultures with ground slate implements and rather crude pottery and earlier cultures with chipped stone implements and finer pottery or without pottery" (1950:186). He suggested that we tighten our definitions of Paleo-Eskimo and New-Eskimo so that "A Paleo-Eskimo culture would thus be a culture in which chipped flint implements are preferably used,

and a Neo-Eskimo culture one in which ground slate implements are predominant"
(1950:186). I believe these broad distinctions have lost any utility they
once possessed.

Theodore Bank collaborated with Laughlin in 1948 and then undertook a
series of Aleutian excavations for the University of Michigan in 1949, 1950
and 1952 with Albert Spaulding excavating a site at Krugloi Point on Agattu
Island (in 1949). Spaulding uncovered a unique culture with a distinctive set
of chipped stone tools and an absence of toggle harpoons, composite fish-
hooks, polished stone lamps, slate grinding or pottery. The radiocarbon date
of ca. 500 B.C., the Paleo-Aleut nature of the skeletal material, and the im-
poverished nature of the bone artifacts led Spaulding to suggest that this
site is a refugium of some of the earliest Aleuts, although Spaulding could
make no definitive statement of Krugloi Point cultural affinities (Spaulding
1962:42-44). Allen McCartney has recently reviewed several collections from
the Near Islands (including Krugloi Point). He suggested that they form a
"cultural phase whose particular stylistic development took place in relative
isolation from the remaining Aleutian populations" (1971:92) and that they
form a distinctive phase no ". . .less complex or inferior to other regional
phases or similar periods" (1971:106).

Excavating on Unalaska Island at the Amaknak-D site in 1950 and 1951
(following Cahn and Larsen--see above), Bank concluded that ". . .despite the
diversity and numerous changes of types of artifacts throughout the occupation,
there is no level at which several changes of types occur simultaneously in a
number of different artifacts" (Bank 1953:45), thus duplicating the preliminary conclusions of Laughlin regarding the continuum of culture change at
Chaluka on Umnak Island and of Spaulding at Agattu.

Bank suggested a mechanism for the presumed distinction between Paleo-

Aleut and Neo-Aleut. The Paleo-Aleut were a linearly expanded population with relative isolation in the western Aleutians and more frequent genetic and cultural mixing in the eastern Aleutians and the near-Alaskan mainland. His argument was weakened by his suggestion that "Local strife, geographic isolation and severe climate created temporary barriers to culture spread, and, conversely, warfare and slave capture between certain groups who became traditional enemies serve to mix genes. Thus small eddies became established in the main current of cultural diffusion, which of course worked in both directions, and tended to break up Aleutian culture into geographic entities, each of which developed along slightly divergent lines" (Bank 1953:48). Thus some sites show many minor cultural changes but no abrupt cultural changes occur throughout the Aleutians. I doubt that this mechanism as expressed could simultaneously account for a major change in physical type and a continuum of minor cultural changes. It may be that the warm period around A.D. 1,000 in the Arctic resulted in greater movements of people in southwestern Alaska greatly increasing gene flow and minor cultural changes, yet not causing major adaptive changes in this region. One might speak of a homogenization of breeding populations at this time producing a very generalized physical type. It may be that Bank's hypotheses merit greater attention and testing and that they are at least as attractive as Laughlin's movements of people without culture.

Our knowledge of the relatively recent occupants of the southern Alaskan coast and the Alaska Peninsula was increased by archaeological surveys by Wendell Oswalt in 1954 (1955) and by Wilbur Davis in the Katmai National Monument (Davis 1954). Davis and James Leach excavated village sites at Kukak and Kaguyak on the coast and a deep deposit at Naknek Lake on the Brooks River in the interior. Frederica deLaguna directed archaeological

32

work (beginning in 1949) leading to the study of the proto-historic Tlingit occupations in Yakutat Bay, Alaska. Catherine McClellan and deLaguna collected ethnographic data while Francis Riddell, Donald McGeein, Kenneth Lane and Arthur Freed were principally responsible for the archaeological work (deLaguna et al. 1964) which salvaged a great deal of ethnographic data tied in to local historic and protohistoric sites. DeLaguna's conclusions regarding the ethnographic identification of the proto-historic sites and of their relationships with other areas in southern Alaska "have been hampered . . .by the fact that so little is known about the archaeology of the northern and central Northwest Coast" (1964:207). Because we do not understand the near-historic archaeology of this region, it is no wonder that our understanding of the much longer and more complex prehistoric period is so often confused and incomplete.

In 1952, James VanStone surveyed Nunivak Island discovering 19 sites most of which were quite recent with pottery dominating most of the assemblages (VanStone 1954). VanStone observed that the archaeological data fit well with the culture as observed by Nelson in 1887 and with that of Oswalt at Hooper Bay indicating rather extensive late prehistoric contact of Nunivak populations with the mainland (VanStone 1957:112).

Between 1948 and 1952, Wendell Oswalt collected tree ring data from western Alaska and dated some recent Eskimo houses at Squirrel River (1949). His 1950 excavations at Hooper Bay Village kindled his interest in early Alaskan pottery and he published several papers working toward a synthesis of the last two thousand years of pottery technology (1952a, 1952b, 1953 and 1955). He suggested an Aleutian path from the Asiatic source of the recent situla shaped pot and of line-dot decorations, even though sites in the Aleutians contained none of these traits (Oswalt 1952a:27; see below, Chard

1964; McCartney 1970).

One of the most significant excavations in Arctic archaeology was undertaken at Point Hope in 1939 (continued in 1940 and in 1941 with Harry Shapiro and a crew supplied by the Civilian Conservation Corps). Helge Larsen and Froelich Rainey, assisted by J. Louis Giddings, excavated at Jabbertown and at the point itself, but the more spectacular finds were at the site they named Ipiutak, which differed drastically from any "Eskimo" site previously known. Evidence for whale hunting, slate and blades, lamps and pottery was absent. New forms of chipped flint dominated the assemblage (Collins 1940) and iron was used for engraving tools.

The Ipiutak skeletal material included skulls with carved ivory and jet eyes and was studied by George Debetz (1959) who noted that the population was racially Eskimo but were somewhat different from the typologically advanced Eskimo population represented at the Old Bering Sea culture site at Uellen on the Chukchee Peninsula and at the Birnirk-related sites at Point Barrow (Debetz 1959:61).

Larsen and Rainey (1948) suggested that many of what were considered Eskimo cultures could be lumped into several complexes. The first and most recent they called the Arctic Whale Hunting complex which consisted of the cultural phases Okvik, Old Bering Sea, Birnirk, Punuk, Thule and Inugsuk (1948:39). The second, and earlier, complex they called the Ipiutak complex which included Near Ipiutak, Ipiutak, Dorset, and Kachemak Bay I, as well as Weyer's Port Moller site (Larsen and Rainey 1948:156). This distinction seems to parallel earlier attempts to speak of Paleo-Eskimo and Neo-Eskimo stages of Eskimo culture which was made more explicit, but not necessarily more useful, by Larsen in 1950 (1950:186) (see Larsen 1961:8 and above). They also considered the Ipiutak culture to have its origins in western Siberia with the later Eskimos as the sole "survivors of an ancient circumpolar Arctic hunting culture" (1948:161), albeit an undiscovered and unnamed one.

Larsen and Rainey also grappled with the problem of what is "Eskimo", disagreeing with Birket-Smith's contention that the outstanding characteristic of Eskimos is their ability to live divorced from the forest with a rather unique adaptation to the sea (1929:pt.2:222). "A prerequisite to the formulation of a definition of Eskimo culture is that the bearers of that culture are Eskimo in physical type or, even better, speak an Eskimo language. Then we must extend its boundaries to include all variations of Eskimo culture. This cannot be done until we are positive that we have discovered all the variants, and of that we cannot be certain until all the Eskimo territory has been thoroughly investigated archaeologically" (Larsen and Rainey 1948: 150), thus leaving the "Eskimo question" as boggled as before (see below regarding the concept Eskimo). Larsen and Rainey also supported the evidence for a Thule movement from East to West bringing back from Canada cultural traits such as the use of the snow house, semi-lunar lamps, sledge shoes, and harness-trace buckles.

The Near Ipiutak burials, which Larsen and Rainey suspected were later in time than Ipiutak (1948:168) contained whaling harpoons and a more precisely executed chipped flint industry. One potsherd (similar to those later found in the Norton levels at Cape Denbigh) and a limestone lamp were also found in these graves (1948:164). Larsen and Rainey interpret the Ipiutak site as a summer occupation of the coast by seasonal migrants who wintered in the interior (148:146; Larsen 1953:598). Ties with the interior are indicated by the presence at Ipiutak of open fireplaces (which require wood), a caribou hunting complex (many arrowheads and antler artifacts), willow branch bedding, and birch bark vessels (1948:146-147). Winged "objects" and harpoon types

35

indicated ties with the Okvik-Thule continuum, but these were scanty. Here again, from one of the better reported sites in the Arctic, we cannot determine whether trait absences indicate seasonal behavioral variations, major adaptive differences in their culture, sampling error, or the vagaries inherent in negative evidence. The interpretation of minor trait correspondences is also difficult, particularly with the "winged objects," the potsherd and stone lamp from Ipiutak and Near Ipiutak (see Larsen 1954 and Collins 1954 for two interpretations of the relationship of Ipiutak to Old Bering Sea) (Larsen later suggested that Near Ipiutak was the equivalent of Gidding's Norton culture at Cape Denbigh--1961:10).

J. Louis Giddings from 1939 to 1964 was one of the most productive of Arctic archaeologists. His early interest in tree rings, dendrochronology, and Arctic sea currents (1940, 1942, 1943, 1944, 1948) led to an extremely profitable association with Froelich Rainey at the University of Alaska and the 1939 excavations at Point Hope. From that time on his major interests were in Arctic archaeology. In 1948, 1949, 1950 and 1952 Giddings excavated at Cape Denbigh on North Sound in a stratified site called Iyatayet, and at Nukleet (with Wendell Oswalt in 1949) and at Madjujuinuk. Iyatayet contained a Nukleet level with recent Eskimo remains over a level of Ipiutak-related culture called Norton containing stone lamps and pottery (like Near-Ipiutak) (pottery reported by James Griffin in 1953). Under Norton was a thin convoluted deposit containing what Giddings called the Denbigh Flint Complex, after its most distinctive lithic technology. Because of the absence of non-lithic remains and the presence of diagonally fine-flaked end blades and one "fluted point", Giddings considered the Denbigh finds to relate to "Early Man" in the Arctic (1950, 1951) estimating its age at a minimum of 6000 years. The presence of lamellar flaking (blades and micro-blades) and many burins

36

was unlike any complex reported in the New World, and perhaps was related to the Eurasian Mesolithic (Giddings 1951:201). The word Eskimo appears twice in Gidding's 1951 article on the Denbigh Flint Complex, once in a context that reinforces the interpretation that Giddings was thinking of much earlier adaptations: "Permanently frozen deposits in Alaska should soon begin to give us a fuller picture of the culture that enabled man to establish himself on both sides of Bering Strait before the elaboration of specialized Eskimo culture" (1951:202). Subsequent geological work (Hopkins and Giddings 1953) and radiocarbon dating suggest a more recent date of ca. 2000-3000 B.C. for the Iyatayet occupation of the Denbigh Flint Complex (Ralph and Ackerman 1961). Archaeologists have subsequently discovered a great number of sites which seemed related to Denbigh (as did Giddings in Manitoba in 1953--see above).

In 1950, Giddings, Larsen and Rainey coordinated their endeavors with financial support from the Wenner-Gren Foundation. Rainey surveyed the Bering Sea coast while Giddings continued his work at Iyatayet and Larsen excavated a thousand year old Ipiutak variant at Deering on Kotzebue Sound. The large rectangular house contained many wooden artifacts, kayak parts, and birch bark but no pottery or lamps and only one slate blade (Larsen 1953:605). Larsen and Philip Spaulding in 1950 also excavated caves along Trail Creek on Seward Peninsula south of Deering (reported to them by David Hopkins in 1948 and explored by Larsen and Charles Lucier in 1949). In poorly defined strati-fied deposits, Larsen found evidence of cultures ranging in time from A.D. 1750 (using the horizon marker of an Ambler Island arrowhead type--see Giddings 1952) through Ipiutak-like occupations, so-called Trail Creek Points related to Choris, to small antler arrowheads related to Denbigh and antler shafts with grooves for microblade side blades thought to precede Denbigh

37

(Larsen 1962). Early radiocarbon dates indicated that the deposits were at least 6000 years old (see below).

In 1952 (a) Giddings summarized his research on recent Eskimo occupations along the Kobuk River within the forest zone, suggesting a distinctive Eskimo culture which he called Arctic Woodland, dated back to A.D. 1200 using his dendrochronological series. He raised the archaeological problem: how do we differentiate archaeologically between Eskimos and Athabascans if they have the same exploitative adaptation and technology?

While decrying the fact that our archaeological knowledge of Athabascan-speaking peoples was practically nil (1952a:114) Giddings suggested "that the Arctic Woodland culture appears to be more than a phenomenon resulting from the meeting of two distinct forms of culture. It is, rather, the predictable combination of sea-river-and-forest-hunting wherever it is possible for a single ethnic group to practice these together under the special conditions of the Arctic. It is a material culture that will be practiced by whatever linguistics group happens to live in the particular environment, a culture that will outlive the physical appearance, the speech, and many of the social practices of its participants" (1952a:118). Giddings assumed that Arctic Woodland was the "phenomenon of a special sort of environment" and suggested that we look for it "in other areas where the environment is similar," perhaps in Southwestern Alaska or near the Anadyr river in Siberia (1952a:118). On a very general level we cannot deny that cultural parallels may result from similar adaptations to similar ecosystems, but we also cannot deny the importance of the historical factors which influenced the technological and adaptive specifics of the Arctic Woodland Culture. This concept has not proved as useful or as widely applicable as Giddings hoped.

After a brief excursion to Northern Manitoba where Giddings collected Denbigh-like flints at the Thyazzi site (see above; Giddings 1956) in 1953, Giddings, Robert Ackerman, and Melvin Richler surveyed the region around the Choris peninsula in 1956. The peninsula consisted of 8 parallel strand lines all at about the same height above the sea. On the fourth and fifth ridge were artifacts of the Northern culture. Three large (ca. 40' x 24') oval house pits were found on the oldest ridge. These proved to belong to a new culture which Giddings named Choris. Feather tempered pottery was abundant, a stone lamp was found, as were slate scraped into straight edged women's knives, a few burins, diagonally flaked points like those from Trail Creek, drilled prong harpoons, and toggle harpoons (Giddings 1957). This unique combination of traits in an unusual house form was thought by Giddings to date between 1500 and 500 B.C. (1960:127). In excavating at Choris, Giddings was impressed by the chronological possibilities of beach ridges, and in 1958 he began a search for long series of beach ridges in the Kotzebue Sound region. At Cape Espenberg, he found recent, Ipiutak, Norton and Choris cultures and, on the innermost beaches, artifacts of the Denbigh Flint Complex. These finds and similar ones at Cape Prince of Wales corroborated the potential of "beach-ridge-chronology" but the most extensive series found were those at Cape Krusenstern. There were about a hundred ridges capped with sod and gravel (stabilizing the ridges and the sites) revealing a relative chronology unsurpassed in previous Arctic archaeology. During four seasons from 1958 to 1961 Giddings (assisted at various times by Hans-Georg Bandi, William Simmons, Douglas Anderson, and Helge Larsen) defined the following sequence of cultures: Western Thule; Birnirk; Ipiutak; Choris-Trail Creek; Old Whaling; and Denbigh Flint Complex (Giddings 1961, 1966). In addition, he found a Battle Rock phase apparently intermediate between

Denbigh and Ipiutak and, on the mainland "Palisades" behind the beaches, two phases of culture (Palisades I and II) reminiscent of early cultures of the interior. Palisades I consisted of a rather crude flake industry while Palisades II contained side notched projectile points similar to those found in the Yukon and Alaskan interiors. This series allowed Giddings to summarize his views on Alaskan Eskimo archaeology in 1960 and 1961 suggesting that the Bering Strait region was a center of circumpolar ideas and not merely a junction of people merely passing thought (1960:121), thus arguing against those who continuously seemed to seek asiatic origins for anything archaeologically new in Alaska. Giddings emphasized continuities of culture in coastal Alaska while only hinting at well-formed traditions. In 1961 he looked at the data more synchronously, defining nine horizons from Kachemak to Birnirk. Here we have an example of his synthesizing insight as well as of the limits of his data and interpretive desire: "If whaling was successful more than 3,000 years ago at Cape Krusenstern, but not again until A.D. 1000, might this not be a sign of identity of whale migrations, and of open whaling lanes, rather than simply of human food preferences or cultural bias? The relationship of cultural change to environment is slowly clearing up, but we still can be thankful with Rasmussen that the more we know of Eskimos the more fresh problems appear on the threshold" (Giddings 1961:171). Giddings was consumed by fresh problems and chronologies, and he excelled at this combination, barraging the discipline with preliminary reports. During this period from 1935 to 1960 he was the most productive of Arctic archaeologists, yet he produced only two major monographs documenting his extensive data and applying it to archaeological problems (1952a, 1964).

One of the early landmarks in the archaeology of interior Alaska was Nels Nelson's 1937 report on artifacts from the campus of the University of

Alaska. Alaskan archaeology and the Campus Site in particular have benefitted
from the beneficence of Charles Bunnell, president of the University of
Alaska, who supervised the Campus Site excavations in 1934 and 1935, and who
nurtured archaeology at the University of Alaska. Nelson illustrated small
polyhedral cores (later called tongue shaped, wedge shaped or boat shaped)
and blades derived from them pointing out that similar cores, blades and end
scrapers have been found in Mongolia, and areas of the Americas including
the Aleutians and Greenland (illustrated by Solberg as part of the Greenland
Stone Age). Nelson suggested that the artifacts ". . .appear to suggest de-
finite cultural relations between Alaska and Mongolia" (Nelson 1937:267).

Frederica deLaguna turned her attention toward the interior in 1935
surveying the middle and lower Yukon Valley with the intent of finding evidence of early man and, secondarily, to define the relationship of the prehistoric Indians to the Eskimo (deLaguna 1936:7,8). No sites that could be
related to early man were found but a number of Indian and Eskimo sites were
discovered and their distribution indicated that, in the recent past, no
sharp frontier existed between the Indian and Eskimo cultures on the Yukon
(1936:10) (Zagoskin noted mixed Eskimo and Indian settlements on the
Kuskokwin--Oswalt 1962:3). The party also discovered a fine feather-
tempered pottery at the mouth of the Tanana River increasing the known distribution of presumed Athabascan pottery.

Froelich Rainey surveyed the Tanana River and the Yukon river adjacent
to their junction in 1936 and 1937. Sponsored by the University of Alaska,
he excavated the Dixthada site, near the present Mansfield Village, which
spanned prehistoric and historic Athabascan occupations. He also described
further excavations at the Campus site relating some of the artifacts at
Campus to those found rarely in the lower levels at Dixthada, hinting at

41

possible connections between the Campus site and Athabascan (Rainey 1940: 304). He later specified that Dixthada had at least two components of which one was microlithic (1953:46). Rainey also summarized recent archaeological finds made by amateurs in the frozen deposits of central Alaska, pointing out that the evidence was inconclusive and enigmatic.

In 1949, Charlene LeFebre excavated primarily historic sites near Telida on the Kuskokwim, relating them to excavations by Rainey in central Alaska. Several microliths were discovered, apparently in a recent Athabascan context (LeFebre 1956:270-271) (see Rainey 1940 at Dixthada and see Cook and McKennan 1970).

In 1941, the University of New Mexico sponsored Frank Hibben in a survey to the north of Cook Inlet, the lower Yukon around Koyukon, and the near vicinity of Fairbanks, looking for evidence of early man in areas believed unglaciated during the late Wisconsin. In his reconnaissance he found several Yuma-like points (similar to those from the Clovis site) in the Fairbanks muck (thought to be frozen loess deposits) and under the muck at Chinitna Bay. The last sentence in his article hinted at doubts concerning the age of some of these finds: "It has also been suggested that even modern Eskimo points are remarkably Yuma-like in their characteristics" (1943:259).

Raymond Thompson and a field party of the U. S. Geological Survey travelled down the Utukok River north of the Brooks Range discovering 17 sites, including one yielding a fluted point. All of these sites were surface finds, yet Thompson believed the fluted point to be of great age (1948: 63).

Ivar Skarland and Louis Giddings summarized archaeological finds during the war years in central Alaska when formal research was sharply curtailed (1948). Some of the illustrated finds were made in the mucks around

42

Fairbanks as well as additional finds from the Campus site. All of the lithic materials reported were not related to historic Athabascan and may be considered of Pleistocene Age (1948:119).

The quest for early man in Alaska spurred Ralph Solecki of the Smithsonian Institution to accompany a U. S. Geological Survey party down the Kukpowruk and Kokolik Rivers in Northwest Alaska in 1949 (Solecki 1950a). Many sites were found—several related to the Denbigh Flint Complex and others related to the prehistoric and historic Nunamiut Eskimo (1950b:67). In 1950, two other U.S.G.S. parties discovered 70 additional sites north of the Brooks Range. Of special interest are finds of Milton Lachenbruch and Robert Hackman. Lachenbruch discovered fluted points and polyhedral cores on the Kugururok River off the upper Noatak River. All of these were surface finds and Solecki (1951:56) mentioned that some of the artifacts cannot be distinguished from the prehistoric Eskimo flints found by Solecki in 1949.

At Anaktuvuk Pass in the Brooks Range, Robert Hackman discovered a site related to the Denbigh Flint complex near Natvakruak Lake and the artifacts were described by Solecki (1951; Solecki and Hackman 1951). William Irving excavated Denbigh materials near Anaktuvuk Pass the same summer, following information supplied by Eskimo informants (Irving 1951). He returned in 1951 excavating at the Imaigenik site and other sites and blowouts that seemed to trace a typological continuum from Denbigh to other paleo-Eskimo cultures in the Western and Eastern Arctic (Irving 1953:71-72). In his discussion of the cultural affinities of these finds, Irving used a rather flexible heuristic definition of the concept "Eskimo": "In using the term Eskimo somewhat promiscuously, I have intended to indicate a whole group of American Arctic and sub-Arctic cultures that can be most readily classed together on the basis of their language. In no sense do I mean to suggest

43

a unity of origin by this use of the word. It is just a convenient way to refer to a large group of people with many traits in common who tend to restrict themselves to the northerly sea-coasts and treeless regions" (Irving 1953:72).

Irving (1955) compared burins and blade cores from Alaska and the Yukon, distinguishing between Denbigh-like burins and polyhedral cores and flake burins and tongue shaped cores found at the Campus site and at Pointed Mountain and Fort Liard in the Yukon. He suggested the other side of the Bering Strait as the area where these two distinct industries may have been more closely affiliated (1955:382).

In 1953, Irving conducted a salvage survey of the Susitna Valley for the National Park Service. In discussing the predominantly historic and proto-historic Athabascan sites found, he related several artifacts to what he proposed as the "Arctic-Small-Tool tradition" (1957:47), and formalized his earlier distinction between coastal-tundra Denbigh-like burin-blade-core industries and boreal Campus-Fort Liard burin-blade-core industries (Irving 1955). Here on the Susitna was the only find of the Denbigh-Arctic-Small-Tool tradition in a forested region which also contained sites of this boreal culture (on the Tyone River). Irving suggested that the A.S.T.t. and the Campus-Fort Liard complexes (formalized as the Northwest Microblade tradition by MacNeish) had diverged from an unknown common ancestor (1957:47) thus linking two widespread and ancient lithic industries to a common heritage (as did MacNeish 1954:252).

In 1957, two archaeological locales on the Denali Highway were brought to the attention of the University of Alaska. These blowouts contained lithic material apparently related to similar artifacts found by Irving (1957) on Tyone River and the Northwest Microblade tradition. The side-notched end

44

blades illustrated by Skarland and Charles Keim (1958:84) are similar to those declared as boreal by Irving, but the sparseness of the collection made positive Northwest Microblade identification premature.

John Campbell conducted extensive and important excavations in the vicinity of Anaktuvuk Pass in the Brooks Range from 1956-1959, and discovered and described 28 sites and 6 archaeological complexes (1962). Because his sequence is one of the few known and published from Alaska and because it has been the object of much discussion, it will be necessary to treat it in some detail. Campbell has separated three complexes from one creek terrace making the separation on typological and, apparently, distributional criteria. The Kogruk complex from this Kayuk site was considered to be the earliest at Anaktuvuk and consisted of a relatively crude flake industry comprised principally of "tools of the moment" (Campbell 1962:41). Campbell considered Kogruk to have a Mousterian quality and he anticipated rather direct connections with Asia and even Europe. In 1957, with L. Pospisil, Campbell expanded his excavations at this site, identifying the Kayuk complex, whose lithic industry was characterized by "finely executed parallel oblique flaking" (Campbell 1959:98) on projectile points and blades and a low frequency of microblades. The projectile points were described as Angostura-like, reminiscent of the high plains. Campbell saw similarities with several lithic industries in the Arctic and was "presently inclined to consider the Kayuk complex as belonging somewhere in time (and cultural affinity?) between the Denbigh Flint complex and Ipiutak" (Campbell 1959:104) even though he suspected that the sample might contain a purer Ipiutak admixture (1959:104). Later, Campbell typologically separated an Ipiutak component from this site, and considered the remainder of the artifacts (after separating out Kogruk and Ipiutak) to represent a 5,000 to 7,000 year old

45

plano complex (1962b:44) (see Alexander 1969, below, for an alternate interpretation of the Kayuk site and its affinities).

In 1959, Campbell discovered the Tuktu site on a kame terrace in
Anaktuvuk Pass. The assemblage contained side notched projective points
similar to those found at Palisades II on Cape Krusenstern and to other
sites belonging to the Northwest Microblade tradition (MacNeish 1959a, 1960).
Relative dating placed it after Ipiutak, and Campbell hunched it at 3,000-
4,000 years old, calling it a part of a northern notched point tradition
(Campbell 1961:75) (a recent radiocarbon date of 4560 ± 55 B.C. has been
obtained--SI-114).

The Denbigh Flint complex was represented at Anaktuvuk by the
Natvakruak complex from two sites originally discovered by Hackman and described by Solecki (1951). Campbell believed Natvakruak to be 4,000 to 6,000
years old, thus older than Tuktu and the Northwest Microblade Tradition
(Campbell 1962:44-46) (see Solecki and Hackman 1951; Irving 1951, 1953).

An Anaktuvuk Ipiutak component, isolated typologically from the Kayuk
complex, two little-known Kavik and Toyuk complexes (see Campbell and Morlan
below for Kavik affinities), and 35 sites of historic and proto-historic
Nunamiut Eskimo sites complete the roster of former Anaktuvuk tenants.
Campbell saw these occupations not as related "traditionally" or "genetically"
but as representative of culture change characterized by successive intrusive
cultural replacement (1962:54). Rather than seeing the Brooks Range and
Anaktuvuk Pass as a refuge or marginal cultural area, he saw it as one of
the ". . .most favorable human habitation areas in either of the Americas
for most of the total length of time that man has occupied the western hemis-
phere" (1962:53) and suggested that its occupants represent the mainstream of
western Arctic cultural development. More recent work indicates that

climatic changes may have altered the attractiveness of Anaktuvuk to man (Porter 1964, 1966; Alexander 1969:109).

On the Yukon coast, the Mackenzie Valley Expedition of 1938, sponsored by the American Philosophical Society and the University of New Mexico under the direction of Wesley Bliss made archaeological collections of graves and associated artifacts west of the Mackenzie delta. Douglas Osborne described the collections in 1952 concluding that many of the artifacts were western Thule forms dating between ca. 1850 and 1910 (Osborne 1952:39). This reconnaissance is of interest because it is one of the few undertaken along this stretch of Arctic coast and one which demonstrates the apparent continuity between Thule and modern Eskimo in this region.

Richard S. MacNeish, expanding his Yukon investigations, investigated sites on the Firth River and the Arctic coast in 1954, 1955, and 1956. His huge Engigstciak site, 16 miles from the present coast, is one of the most extensively vertically stratified sites in the Arctic, although the soil processes have made stratigraphic interpretation and cultural separation difficult. In spite of these problems, MacNeish defined 9 sequential cultures (MacNeish 1956, 1959b, 1962). The British Mountain flake industry was the earliest at Engigstciak and MacNeish tentatively correlated it with Campbell's Kogruk complex at Anaktuvuk and some Asian paleolithic sites. Giddings (1961:159) considered his Palisades I at Cape Krusenstern to be related to British Mountain, but MacNeish did not consider the relation to be a strong one (MacNeish 1963:99). As there were only 200 artifacts representing British Mountain, we must be careful not to place too great an emphasis on the absence of presumed diagnostic tool types.

MacNeish's next phase is called Flint Creek which he initially related to the late paleolithic in the trans-Baikal of Asia, suggesting Flint Creek

47

as partially ancestral to the Northwest Microblade tradition (1959b:48).
Later, he recognized correspondences between it and Campbell's Kayuk complex,
other sites in the Yukon, and early sites in British Columbia, suggesting
that all of these were part of the Cordilleran tradition (1962:25).

The Arctic Small-Tool tradition was represented by the next phase
called New Mountain. This was one of the best represented cultures at
Engigstciak and it is significant that caribou and buffalo bones were frequent, although four seal flippers were found, indicating a basic tundra
adaptation (no information has been presented on the seasonality of occupation) with some access to sea mammal resources (MacNeish 1959:48). MacNeish
noted that Asiatic affinities were strong, "In fact the main difference between the early Neolithic of Siberia and these New Mountain-like remains are
that those in Siberia have pottery, usually net impressed, which as yet has
not been found in the New World Arctic" (MacNeish 1959:48).

The Firth River phase seemed to be a development out of New Mountain,
with the principal addition of fabric impressed and cord marked pottery (with
punctates) as well as a larger antler and bone industry (MacNeish 1962:22;
1959:50). The next phase was Buckland Hills which seemed to continue this
developmental sequence from New Mountain and was distinguished principally
by the addition of dentate stamping and the increase of drilling tools (1959:
50). The Joe Creek phase followed, and contained chipped and ground burins,
ground slate and linear decorated pottery, although check stamping and dentate decorations continued. The projectile points are a continuation of
those from Buckland Hills. MacNeish saw the closest similarities with
Giddings Choris horizon on the Bering Coast.

MacNeish guardedly suggested that the above cultural sequence was pre-
Eskimo and that the three final phases were related to Eskimo horizons of

48

Alaska (1959:52). His Cliff phase was related to Norton and Near Ipiutak, Whitefish Station related possibly to Birnirk (?), and the Herschel Island phase related to typical Thule (with Saint Lawrence Plain pottery and typical Thule harpoon types) (1959:52; 1962:23).

MacNeish concurred with Giddings's statements on the steady flow of people and ideas back and forth across the Bering Straits over a long period of time which varied because of ecological and cultural (adaptational ?) limitations (1959b; 1959a:53).

In interpreting the relationship among archaeologically known cultures in the Arctic, we must keep in mind the arch-nemesis of archaeological sampling error and the vagaries of negative evidence. MacNeish's entire pre-Eskimo sample (6 phases) from Engigstciak and the Firth River area totals about 2,000 stone and bone artifacts and about 5,000 to 6,000 potsherds (approximated from MacNeish 1959b). Because of behavioral differences in human occupations at different seasons and of the relative scarcity of some artifacts presumed to be analytically significant (lamps, harpoons, etc.), the small size of many Arctic archaeological samples can produce analytical differences between cultures and complexes which are artifacts of the data, its procurement and analysis and are not representative of actual behavioral differences between these cultures. If we combine this problem with the problem of archaeological "lumpers" and "splitters" (see Dumond 1974b), the "splitters" have the edge, hence the archaeological picture painted by many Arctic archaeologists is tremendously complex (and often idiosyncratic). Thus, the number of different "cultures" roaming the Arctic is very large. Again, much of this comes as a result of data gathering and data gatherers, who are often reluctant to "lump" and synthesize (Gad 1970:xii). MacNeish is a notable exception, and his syntheses and speculative hypotheses (1959a,

49

1959b, 1962, 1963, 1964) demonstrate his excellent command of Arctic and
Subarctic data and his ability to make splinters into boards, albeit rough
ones.

By 1960, when Diamond Jenness chaired a symposium on Arctic archaeology (collected and edited by John Campbell, 1962), our knowledge of Arctic
culture history has increased tremendously. The study of pre-Dorset culture
(only 12 years old) was creating great interest and potential as connecting
the rather dangling chronology of the Eastern Arctic to the Western sequences.
The interrelationships among Dorset, Thule and other occupants of the
Eastern Arctic were on the verge of being clarified. There was general
agreement of the cultural (and linguistic) continuity from Arctic Small Tool
tradition to modern Eskimo. Stratified sequences in Alaska and the Yukon had
given us a general picture of coastal chronology, with the Alaskan interior
and the Aleutians still unclear. Because of the important summations of this
1960 symposium and another edited by Frederick Hadleigh-West (1963), it is
useful to consider 1960 as beginning the present modern period of Arctic
archaeology.

V.   Archaeologists and Anthropologists (?)

Since 1960, publication of research results has not kept pace with the rate of discovery. In the following discussion, information not specifically cited to the investigator comes from the excellent "Current Research: Arctic" reports in American Antiquity, compiled by John Campbell and Robert McGhee. Unfortunately, many of the finds of the last fifteen years are reported only here.

In the Eastern Arctic since 1960, several surveys and continued exca- vations have increased our knowledge of Dorset and Pre-Dorset cultures and of their distribution. One of the most important series of excavations has been that of Moreau Maxwell near Lake Harbour on the south coast of Baffin Island. Graham Cooch, of the Canadian Wildlife Service, collected a small collection of proto- and developed Dorset from Juet Island in 1957 which made its way to the National Museum of Canada in 1959. Maxwell conducted explora- tory excavations on Juet Island and adjacent coasts in 1960. Five early sites were excavated, all of which were early in the Dorset period (Maxwell 1962:21) and which demonstrated a continuum of development from Pre-Dorset to Dorset as Taylor had suggested (Taylor 1959:18; Maxwell 1962:36). The ab- sence of any break in this continuum was seen as greatly significant. "Elements which contribute to the in situ development of Dorset culture seem to have differential rates of diffusion to the Eastern Arctic and perhaps different courses of diffusion" (Maxwell 1962:40). It was to test these pre- liminary conclusions (based on only 473 artifacts from 8 sites) and to docu- ment the coalescence of traits which led to Dorset that Maxwell continued his research in this area. These studies have established a 3,000 year continuum of Pre-Dorset--Dorset cultural development with the several components of the Closure site dating as early as 2500 B.C. During this long period, minor

51

stylistic changes occurred in several aspects of the technology, but in
general "there was such a closed cultural system that after the initial migration, nothing appears in material culture that could not have been derived
from within the system" (Maxwell 1967:10). The earliest components of this
continuum have yielded graphite lamp fragments, ground slate adze and projectile point fragments, ground burin-like tools, and chipped and polished
burins previously thought to appear in Dorset sites much later than the
2500 B.C. radiocarbon date. Pumice from the Closure site is related to a
pumice horizon noted by Weston Blake, who believes it to date about 5000
B.P. (Blake 1970). Maxwell has suggested that Meldgaard's smell of the
forest may be the result of the development of a specialized wood-working kit
in southern Baffin Island and vicinity which then spread to other areas of
the Eastern Arctic causing the rather abrupt change to Dorset that other
investigators have noted (Maxwell 1967, 1973a). Albert Dekin in several
papers (1969, 1970, 1972b, 1974, 1975) has suggested that climatic changes
in the Eastern Arctic have contributed to cultural drift and isolation by
altering local ecological conditions forcing, facilitating, or forbidding
population (and cultural) movements. He has pointed out that what were
generally warmer climatic periods were marked by widespread cultural homo-
geneity in the Eastern Arctic and that colder periods saw the development of
various locally-stamped phases of the eastern extensions of the Arctic-Small-
Tool tradition. Continued work by Maxwell and his students in this area
should allow us to establish a base line with which to study variations in
the phylogeny of Dorset culture.

Surveys were conducted by Gordon Lowther on Devon Island in 1960 and
1961 (Lowther 1962) and by William Irving on the barren grounds west of
Hudson Bay (in 1960, 1963 and 1964--Campbell 1964). Irving discovered the

52

Twin Lakes Pre-Dorset site near Churchill in 1960 which was later tested by
William Mayer-Oakes in 1964 and excavated by Ronald Nash in 1965. The site,
now some 15 miles from Hudson Bay, is thought to have been 1000 B.C. and
500 B.C. (Nash 1969a:55,89). Nash also excavated at the Thyazzi Site (reported by Giddings in 1956a), expanded the previously reported sample to include microblades and estimated its age at 1500 B.C. (Nash 1969:51). Nash
examined the Sea Horse Gulley site across the Churchill River from Churchill
in 1967 and 1968. Several large tools were found which Nash suggested were
obtained from boreal occupations or were a result of artifactual response
to the availability of wood (Nash 1969a:110). David Meyer has recently (1970)
worked on the site and has obtained a radiocarbon date of 950 $\pm$ 100 B.C. (S-
521) which is somewhat older than anticipated, but which fits rather well
with the estimated age of the Thyazzi site (Ronald Nash, personal communication 1970). Nash (in 1968) also found a small Dorset component at Sea Horse
Gulley and its radiocarbon date of ca. 100 B.C. made it the southwesternmost
Dorset site found to date (Nash 1969a:154; 1972). The large tool complex
(adzes, gouges, picks and scrapers) characteristic of the Pre-Dorset component of Sea Horse Gulley are not found in the Dorset component. Nash (1969b)
suggested that the large tool complex marked a regional Pre-Dorset variant
(whose extent was then unknown) but that such regionalism did not seem to
characterize Dorset.

Nash also undertook a four year study (1967-70) of the transitional
forest region of Northern Manitoba and adjacent Keewatin finding few remains
of Eskimo or Arctic cultures, but finding many sites relating to late prehistoric and historic Indian occupations. Nash felt that these sites might
represent a Chipewyan occupation, but the lack of cultural continuity from
the prehistoric to historic period has precluded conclusive proof of this

53

ethnic identification (1970).

Father Guy Mary-Rousseliere tested Thule, Dorset and Pre-Dorset sites
in the vicinity of Pelly Bay, west of Igloolik, in 1956 and 1960 (Mary-
Rousseliere 1964). In following years he excavated at Button Point, Bylot
Island, where Mathiassen excavated for the Fifth Thule Expedition (see 1976).
Rousseliere also discovered Pre-Dorset sites near Pond Inlet, Baffin Island
in 1965 (1965).

Elmer Harp returned to the Straits of Belle Isle in 1961, 1962, and
1963 excavating at Port Au Choix -2 and at Dorset and Archaic sites on the
Labrador coast. His Archaic sites date to 3500 B.C. (1963, personal communication) and his Port au Choix -2, occupied between A.D. 200 and 600, was interpreted as a summer settlement, representing only a part of the yearly
round (1964:4). Harp has also found human skeletal remains in an unmistakable
Dorset context (excavated in House 12, PC-2 in 1963) and he has obtained
others from local informants. Those found in a Dorset context were interpreted as being related to Eskimo populations and were distinct from those
considered by Harp to be late (?) Archaic (Harp and Hughes 1968). Harp concluded that these two populations coexisted in Newfoundland for ca. 500 years
with no apparent evidence for "biological or cultural contact or hybridiza-
tion" (Harp and Hughes 1968:46). Dorset sites in Newfoundland were also
found by Donald MacLeod at Twillingate and Helen Devereux (Linnamae 1975) at
Cape Ray in extreme southern Newfoundland--both are Arctic cultures found as
far south as 47°N. Lat. (Taylor 1968; Campbell 1967).

Archaeological research in 1969 and 1970 by James Tuck in the vicinity
of Saglek Bay in northern Labrador revealed extensive Pre-Dorset and Dorset
sites. One deeply stratified site contained a "Maritime Archaic" stratum
overlain by a Pre-Dorset occupation (Tuck 1963, 1976)--possibly, this region

may soon document an Eastern Sub-Arctic source for Pre-Dorset and Dorset ground slate (see Ritchie 1969).

William Fitzhugh excavated Dorset and Indian sites on Hamilton Inlet and Lake Melville in Eastern Labrador in 1968 and 1969. Arctic cultures included recent Eskimos and a Dorset occupation from ca. 800 B.C. to ca. 200 B.C. (Fitzhugh 1970a, 1970:373). Fitzhugh saw little evidence for acculturation between Dorset and contemporaneous Indian groups of the interior, reinforcing Harp's 1968 conclusions from Port au Choix. Both of the Arctic occupations of Groswater Bay occurred during colder climatic periods (800 B.C.-- 200 B.C. and ca. A.D. 1600) (Dekin 1969, 1970; Fitzhugh 1970b:582,670) which included southern shifts of Arctic fauna which forced, or allowed, this southern movement of arctic-adapted cultures. It may be that Harp's Newfoundland Dorset (A.D. 100-600) was also a part of this southern spread of Dorset which was then cut off from northern relatives by the Indian occupation of the Labrador coast ca. A.D. 1 (Fitzhugh 1970b:376).

Fitzhugh also reported a Pre-Dorset site at Thalia Point near Nain, Labrador, which was radiocarbon dated to ca. 1700 B.C. (Fitzhugh 1970b:674). He suggested that "Pre-Dorset here resembles Greenland Sarqaq more than it does Canadian Pre-Dorset" (1970b:391) but his illustrations indicate that the Thalia material would fit rather well in the Pre-Dorset--Dorset sequence from Lake Harbour. Just as southern Greenland was not occupied by man until the cooler climatic episode beginning ca. 1500 B.C., it seems that the southern coasts of Labrador and western Quebec were not occupied by Arctic peoples until this same cool period (the dating of this climatic change by ca. 1500 B.C. is tentative but may be compatible with the Thalia Point Pre-Dorset date of 1710±140 B.C.--GSC-1264).

In 1962, James VanStone, James Anderson and Charles Merbs published an account of an archaeological and osteological collection from Somerset Island and Boothia Peninsula. The collection was obtained from a manager of the Hudson's Bay Company between 1939 and 1949 and contained a good representation of Netsilik Eskimo culture and a very homogeneous osteological sample, all with only general provenience data (VanStone, Anderson, and Merbs 1962). Their analysis documents the development of modern Netsilik culture from a Thule base.

In 1964, 1965, and 1966, Thomas Lee reexcavated and reevaluated Taylor's previous work in Northern Ungava, suggesting a Norse origin for what were previously interpreted as Dorset remains (Lee 1967).

Bernard Saladin d'Anglure discovered Dorset sites with associated petroglyphs near Wakeham Bay on Hudson Straits (in 1961, 1965, and 1966--Taylor 1968:106) which were reconnoitered again in 1968 by George Barre (Campbell 1970:244).

Excavations by Patrick Plumet in 1969 at a Pre-Dorset site near Great Whale River on a raised Hudson Bay strand line now inland from the coast have provided a radiocarbon date of ca. 1300 B.C. (personal communication 1970). Elmer Harp has done archaeological survey north of Great Whale River in 1967 finding Dorset and more recent sites in connection with his aerial photo-interpretation project. Noting that Harp test excavated where there were surface indications (personal communication 1968), the discovery of Plumet's Great Whale River Pre-Dorset site may lead to the further elucidation of Pre-Dorset and Dorset cultures.

Jorgen Meldgaard continued his archaeological work near Igloolik in 1965 accompanied by Bent Fredskild (paleobotanist). Meldgaard's preliminary analysis of the "Transitional Period" of Dorset (1100-700 B.C.) indicated that the influx of ground slate artifacts was rapid and well marked in his

Igloolik sequence (Campbell 1966:898) pointing again to the abruptness of the Pre-Dorset--Dorset transition in the Igloolik region. Hopefully, a more complete report of these important excavations will be forthcoming.

Archaeological survey and excavation in northwest Hudson Bay was initiated by Charles Merbs in 1967 and 1968 with the goal of recovering adequate samples of skeletal material of known age (Merbs 1969a:46). Allen McCartney continued excavations at Silumiut in 1969 attempting to define a regional variant of seventeenth century Thule culture (Archaeology Division 1969:3). His research indicated that the cultural adaptation by the Thule culture to a colder ecosystem lacking whales was more rapid than had been thought previously (personal communication 1970).

Merbs analyzed the orientation patterns of more than three hundred Thule Eskimo skeletons buried and aligned in stone structures. His preliminary analysis indicated that each body was oriented according to the position of the sun at sunrise on the day of the burial with adult males, adolescent and old women usually buried head to sunrise and adult females and adolescent and old males usually oriented in the opposite direction (1969b:2,8). Merbs suggested that orientation to survive may have related to maleness "not in terms of actual sex, but in terms of active hunting prowess" (1969:8) and that orientation in the opposite direction may have been related to "females in terms of actively caring for a child as opposed to being able to bear children or having borne children" (1969:9). Merbs noted that this distinction paralleled the ethnographic distinction among Hudson Bay Eskimos between the "Land of the Day People" and the "Narrow Land Under the Sea", the former lying toward sunrise and the latter toward darkness. The researches of Merbs, McCartney, and George Wenzel (in 1970) are some of the most significant developments in Thule research since the 1920's and mark a revival of

Thule anthropology.

In Greenland, excavations continued to increase our knowledge of the Sarqaq culture. Jorgen Meldgaard in 1960 and Hans Berg with Louis Giddings in 1963 excavated Sarqaq sites near Godthaab (Harp 1961; Campbell 1964) and Robert Peterson excavated Sarqaq remains near Ikamiut in 1963.

Eigil Knuth continued his significant excavations of Independence sites in Northeast Greenland in 1960, 1963 and 1964 (Campbell 1965) and in Ellesmere Island in 1965. In 1966 he returned to Northeast Greenland and completed excavations of the first interior-adapted sites of Independence I (Taylor 1968:104; Knuth 1967). Knuth's important Independence I sites date about 2500 B.C. and contain principally musk ox bone with no caribou and rarely seal (there is one phalange of domesticated dog) (Knuth 1967:30,32, 63). Knuth reiterated the uniqueness of the Independence cultures, suggesting that they represent followers of the "Musk Ox Way" who lived in northern Greenland and adjacent Ellesmere Island during a warmer and driftwoodier period than at present (1967:21).

William Taylor excavated Thule materials from Bathurst Island and Somerset Island in 1961, and in 1963 he inaugurated what proved to be a profitable series of National Museum of Canada excavations in the Western Arctic by surveying between Cape Parry and Cambridge Bay on Victoria Island (1964a). The Pre-Dorset Buchanan site on Ekalluk River contained large quartzite bifaces and scrapers (1964a:54-55) thought by Taylor to be a part of the Pre-Dorset technology at Buchanan and not representative of Archaic Indian contamination. He suggested that they were added to the Pre-Dorset industry by stimulus diffusion (Taylor 1967:221,228). Taylor returned to this area in 1965 (with Robert McGhee, Peter Ramsden and Richard Inglis) and obtained radiocarbon samples for this site which bracketed 1000 B.C. (Taylor

1967:228).

In 1966, Robert McGhee returned to Victoria Island, surveying along the Kuuk River and Kuujuua River finding scanty Pre-Dorset sites at their mouths and early Dorset finds which relate rather directly to those found at Ekalluk River in the previous year (Taylor 1968:106).

McGhee conducted excavations in 1968 near Bloody Falls on the Coppermine River. His Pre-Dorset component at Bloody Falls contained a small amount of ground slate, copper pins, and dated at ca. 1350 B.C. (McGhee 1970: 58). McGhee considered the affinities of this site to lie with those from Ekalluk River (Taylor 1964a, 1967), rather than with Harp's Dismal-2 sites to the south (McGhee 1970:58-59; Harp 1958). "The Bloody Falls assemblage shows no trace of the quartzite biface industry characteristic of Victoria and Banks Island Pre-Dorset assemblages of the late second millenium B.C. (Taylor 1967), suggesting that this industry did not diffuse southwesterly as far as the lower Coppermine valley" (McGhee 1970:59). Nash has reported similar bifaces at the Twin Lakes Pre-Dorset site in Manitoba, guess-dated between 1000-500 B.C. and the Sea Horse Gulley Dorset site guess-dated at 500 B.C. (Nash 1969:82-83,103-105).

William Noble has discovered large bifaces on sites which he feels are Arctic-Small-Tool tradition but not Pre-Dorset (Wright 1970:244) on Great Slave Lake guess-dated between 1500-1200 B.C. (his Tundra Complex) in the middle of a long sequence of Northern Plano and Taltheli Shale cultures (Wright 1969; Noble 1969). Noble's McKinley River phase, which he dates at ca. 1000 B.C., represents a result of late Archaic-Small-Tool tradition and late Northern Plano tradition acculturation and is a syncretism with correspondences to Taylor's Victoria Island sites (Noble 1969). It seems likely that the spread of large bifaces in late small-tool cultures was the result

59

of a late northern plano stimulus and might be expected to have moved in a
northerly direction ca. 1000 B.C., rather than in a southwestern direction as
McGhee suggested (see above). Perhaps the quartzite bifaces from Melville
Island obtained by Henock (1964) and described by Taylor (1964b) represent
the northward extension of this movement, although the dates of between A.D.
200 and 800 imply a much later spread (Taylor 1964b:126).

McGhee's 1968 survey also found some rather remarkable archaic or
northern plano artifacts in the Sandwillow site on Bloody Falls which were
similar to southern artifacts believed to be as old as 6000 years. Parallels
were suggested with MacNeish's Taltheilei complex on Great Slave Lake and
with other presumably old barren grounds sites of Harp (Harp 1958, 1961;
McGhee 1970:60). McGhee's radiocarbon date on caribou bones, teeth, and
antler (occasionally found to be anomalous) was ca. A.D. 160. McGhee's apparent confusion over whether to opt for an early or late position for the
Sandwillow site may be alleviated or confounded as soon as Noble's analysis
of his Great Slave Lake sequence is complete. In a preliminary statement,
Noble suggested a guess-date for MacNeish's Taltheilei complex as between
700 and 900 B.C. (Noble 1969). It should be obvious that we cannot arbitrarily
separate the Arctic from the Subarctic in the barren grounds, partly because
the ecological zones have shifted (see Irving 1968:51) and partly because
the tree line may never have prevented cross-cultural contacts. Any further
discussion of relationships between the Arctic-Small-Tool tradition or Dorset
peoples and Archaic or Northern Plano peoples awaits Noble's publication.

The Lapointe site at Bloody Falls contained lanceolate points similar
to those found elsewhere in the central Arctic (see MacNeish 1964; Harp 1958,
1961; Irving 1968) as well as a ground slate point (McGhee 1970:61). A
radiocarbon date of A.D. 570 is now considered intrusive and two dates on

caribou bone, one ca. 1000 B.C., raise the possibility of connections with Alaskan Choris (Robert McGhee, personal communication 1970). It seems that the cultural dynamics of the central Arctic are rather complex and that the region has been a center for acculturation of eastern Arctic, western Arctic, and Archaic cultures. As the cultural history and climatic history of this area become better known, I hope we may reach a better understanding of the changing relationship between man and nature.

McGhee excavated in the vicinity of Tuktoyaktuk in the Mackenzie delta in 1969, upstream from recent Mackenzie whaling peoples. "At Point Atkinson the party located the first Arctic Small Tool Tradition site to be found in the Mackenzie Delta area" (Archaeology Division 1969:3).

Don Dumond and the University of Oregon conducted excavations on the Alaska Peninsula between 1960 and 1968 assisted at various times by Wilbur Davis, Harvey Rice, Michael Nowak and Mark McLaughlin. Dumond excavated small-tool, Norton-related, and Western Thule sites in the Naknek drainage (Dumond 1964) indicating that the cultural affinities of the Alaska Peninsula through time were generally with the Bering Strait region and that this cultural tradition (small-tool--Norton--Thule) did not generally extend south of the peninsula. Only after A.D. 1000 did northern (Eskimo) cultures exert much influence beyond the Alaska Peninsula (Dumond, personal communication 1970) as demonstrated by the southern spread of Thule-like pottery, the near identity of cultures across the Alaska Peninsula and by the inferred change in Pacific Eskimo language believed to date ca. A.D. 1200 (Dumond 1964:42). Prior to this time, cultures south of the peninsula were more closely related to Aleut than Eskimo, both linguistically and culturally, suggesting that Eskimo and Aleut had a long period of separate development in southwest Alaska. This has led Dumond to suggest that any cultural heritage common to

both Eskimo and Aleut cultural traditions should date about 4000 B.C.
(Dumond 1965:1250). Discoveries relevant to this hypothesis were made on the
south coast of the peninsula at the stratified Takli site on Takli Island.
The lower Takli Alder phase dates ca. 4000-3000 B.C. and contained stemmed
and stemless projectile points with polished adze and gouge blades (G. Clark
1968; Dumond 1969, personal communication 1969). Dumond saw this phase as
possibly representing a culture "ancestral to the known prehistoric culture
of all the Aleutian Islands, and [suggested] that they represent a population
of ancestral Aleuts" (Dumond 1969:1111). Dumond documented specific artifact
similarities with the Krugloi Point site on Agattu Island and Ocean Bay I on
Kodiak Island (Dumond 1970:103). The temporal and spacial distance between
these sites makes it difficult to define the exact nature of their relationships. Allen McCartney suggested that these affinities "result from conver-
gent forms which are genetically unrelated. . ." (McCartney n.d.:40). He saw
Dumond's evidence as insufficient ". . .to see the Alder phase as specifically
representative of an early pan-Aleutian horizon from which more recent influence has been felt only at the far western tip of the chain" (n.d.:40).
However, McCartney also felt that "the cultural differences between the populations of the Near Islands and the other central and eastern islands is the
greatest throughout all the archipelago" (n.d.:8) and so the idea of a
generic relationship between the Near Island phase (McCartney n.d.) and the
earlier Takli Alder phase seems a reasonable explanation both for the uniqueness of the Near Island culture and for the similarities mentioned by Dumond.
The archaeological stratum that Dumond hypothesized may prove to fill the requirements for a similar stratum (or continuum) suggested by Chard (1960) to
explain widespread ethnographic similarities among the now-distinctive cultures of the North Pacific region.

The next phase at the Takli site is the Takli Birch phase, dated between 2200 and 800 B.C. which was an outgrowth of the earlier phase. The technology was dominated by ground slate (Dumond 1969:1111), possibly originating from the south (Dumond 1968). Dumond noted no evidence for contacts across the Alaska Peninsula with the contemporaneous small-tool tradition. There was evidence of increasing contact across the peninsula in the early Christian era when a Norton-like culture moved to the south coast and evidence of cultural identity across the peninsula after A.D. 1000 (see above, Dumond 1969:1111,1114). It is important to note that this increased northern influence (Thule) in the Alaska Peninsula coincided with the date given for the widespread North Pacific occurrence of the sadiron lamp (Quimby 1946a) and with the date generally given for the presumed shift from Paleo-Aleut to Neo-Aleut, raising the possibility of population movements altering breeding patterns and adding to the gene pool of the Eastern Aleutians. Perhaps roundheadedness is a result of these cultural and genetic processes?

William Laughlin and his students at the University of Wisconsin continued their active investigations in the Eastern Aleutians: Sosuke Sugihara and William Workman excavating Weyer's site at Port Moller in 1960 (Workman 1966a); William McHugh excavating the saataq site on Sitkalidak Island in 1961 (Campbell 1962c) and various sites on Kodiak Island (McHugh 1962); Laughlin at Chaluka in 1961 and 1962 (with Christy Turner) and at Anangula in 1962; Glenda and Carter Dennison at the two-component Ashishik site on Umnak in 1963; Allen McCartney at Anangula in 1963; Donald Clark and William Workman on Kodiak Island and Chirikof Island in 1963 and on Kodiak and Afognak Islands in 1964 (D. Clark 1966a, 1966b, 1970); Laughlin and Jean Aigner at Chaluka and Anangula in 1968; and Laughlin and Robert Slack and Richard Sense on Amchitka Island in 1968 (Campbell 1970:240).

63

This intensive activity has produced a number of site reports and a volume on Aleutian-Koniag Prehistory in _Arctic Anthropology_ (Laughlin and Reeder 1966), which now carries the bulk of research reports on Aleutian archaeology. Unfortunately, we have never received a synthesis of Aleutian prehistory or an anthropological monograph on the Chaluka site and its cultural affinities. The published preliminary reports on Chaluka seem stratigraphically incompatible due to the incompleteness of the excavation, the complexity of the strata, and the lack of abrupt cultural change and corresponding artifactual horizon markers throughout the midden (compare Aigner 1966:57,68 with Dennison 1966:85,86,110-112).

The Anangula unifacial core and blade site, dating to at least ca. 6000 B.C. (Laughlin 1963), has been excavated during several seasons. Alan McCartney and Christy Turner (1966) have described the stratigraphy in some detail and Laughlin and Jean Aigner have made a preliminary analysis of the lithic industry, setting up an excellent system for the precise descriptive analysis of chipped stone. In his "Introduction" to "Aleutian Studies" in the volume on Aleutian Kodiak prehistory, ecology, and anthropology, Laughlin commented on the general intent of their analysis at Anangula and on its general cultural relationships.

"Comparisons between Anangula and other sites in Asia and Alaska are not discussed here because we wish to finish the analysis before undertaking comparisons and because our major concern lies with understanding the history of this area. There is no single site in Alaska that bears important similarities common to all industries that strike blades from cores. More similarities are found with Asiatic sites in Japan and in Siberia.

"Many of the traits showing probable continuity with Chaluka also distinguish this industry from those of the Alaska mainland. The decline in

64

frequency of lamellar tools in Chaluka from lower to upper levels, the abraders, rubbing stone with ochre, stone dish and sinkers are among those things indicating a patent continuity with Chaluka" (1966:23). Laughlin went on to suggest the probability that the Anangula people were ancestors of later Aleuts (see McCartney 1974) and that they are dealing with an 8000 year record of Aleut evolution, both physical and cultural (Laughlin 1966:24). I think it is unfortunate that the cultural affinities of these two important sites (Anangula and Chaluka) have been left so long for others to speculate, even though the sites have been in the process of excavation for over twenty years.

Donald Clark saw the latest Konyag phases on Kodiak Island as receiving different influences from the Northwest Coast and from the Bering Sea cultures (1966a:173) and judged the present state of our knowledge inadequate to make further analyses or syntheses, suggesting that we need much more data from this rather cosmopolitan region (1966a:175).

Workman's Chirikof Island sites correlate well with Clark's Konyag phase (Clark 1966), with Ackerman's Chagvan Bluff phase in Bristol Bay (Ackerman 1964), with the Norton culture, with Clark's Ocean Bay I and II assemblages on Kodiak Island (Clark 1966) and with Chaluka (Workman 1969). However, the preliminary nature of his reconnaissance limits the hypotheses that could be made from this data (Workman 1966a:191).

Workman and Sosuke Sugihara excavated the Hot Springs site at Port Moller, which Weyer had excavated in 1928. Workman suggested the closest affinities of this site were with the Eastern Aleutians and not with deLaguna's Kachemak Bay III period in Cook Inlet as she had suggested in 1934 (deLaguna 1934:218; Workman 1966b:145). He suggested that "membership in a common diffusion sphere and possible common ancestry in the remote past will adequately

65

explain the similarities in inventory between the Port Moller material and that from Kodiak Island and Cook Inlet. . ." (1966b:145).

Allen McCartney recently reviewed Aleut influences at Port Moller, suggesting that ". . .the cultural similarities between the eastern Aleutians and Port Moller were perhaps greater on the earliest time horizon but that prehistoric Aleut influences as far east as Port Moller were minimal during the Christian era" (1969:3). McCartney did not see the Port Moller material as Aleut, suggesting that the difference in artifact sequences leads to the conclusion ". . .that the prehistoric Aleut boundary, however irregular or wide, was further west of Port Moller rather than to the east of that bay" (1969:12).

Workman's comments on suggested field work emphasize the tremendous cultural complexity of this region through time and it seems that much work establishing chronologies and contemporaneous horizons remains to be done before we can attack more sophisticated anthropological problems in this region. There is a desperate need for complete publication of the data from the southwest Alaskan and Aleutian sites so that previous preliminary reports and syntheses may be evaluated.

Archaeological salvage work in 1960 in the Kenai Peninsula was conducted by the University of Alaska under the direction of Frederick Hadleigh-West with fieldwork by Frederick Kent and Carl Peterson (Kent et al. 1964:101) This pipeline survey revealed a number of protohistoric and historic sites, the most important of which were off the proposed right of way. Three important problems encountered in the survey were "The large number of storage pits, the thinness of the floor layer in house pits, and the small amount of artifacts in the northwest Kenai area" (Kent et al. 1964:126).

An extensive archaeological salvage and protective program was begun

66

on Amchitka Island in the Western Aleutians in 1968 under contract to the U.S. Atomic Energy Commission. In 1969, Archaeological Research, Inc. conducted excavations at six sites dating from 600 B.C. to the present. They noted that ". . .the lower levels of the several midden sites possess an assemblage as elaborate as the upper levels. In fact, with respect to vertical distribution, the tremendous number of stylistically complex artifacts show no major changes within the cultural inventory during the more than 2500 years of Amchitka's human settlement" (Archaeological Research, Inc. 1970: 348). They also noted a complex of traits which form a late Aleut horizon ca. A.D. 1000 which they relate to Laughlin's Neo-Aleut on the Eastern Aleutians. "If this model [a neo-Aleut population influx from the east] reflects the historical reality of Aleutian prehistory, then the Amchitka finds indicate that the westward "neo-Aleut" movement was peculiarly rapid, indeed they would seem to have established themselves on Amchitka earlier than on Umnak, and in some way have bypassed the eastern islands" (1970:349). Because of the presence of sadiron lamps (presumed to have an Asian origin), we should not eliminate prematurely the possibility of much greater historical complexity ca. A.D. 1000 in the North Pacific region (see Archaeological Research, Inc. 1970:351). This 1970 report on excavations made in 1969 is a big example of prompt complete reporting which is sorely needed in Arctic archaeology.

Sam-Joe and Joan Townsend surveyed and excavated late prehistoric and historic Tanaina sites in the Iliamma Lake area of the Alaska Peninsula in 1960 and 1962. Sam-Joe returned in 1964 and Joan excavated in 1966 (with James VanStone), 1967, and 1968. At Pedro Bay the later component of the Pedro Bay Site (ca. 1750) and the Russian Point Site (ca 1800-1850) consisted of semi-subterranean house pits with some meal and glass beads, boulder-chip

67

serapens and bayonet grooved ground slate projectile points (Joan Townsend, personal communication 1970) (Townsend and Townsend 1961). The Kijik site was excavated in 1966 and represents a historic Tanaina occupation from ca. 1838 to ca. 1900 (VanStone and Townsend 1970). Excavations in 1967 at the Pedro Bay site allowed the separation of an early component dated at ca. 2370 B.C. and ca. 2580 B.C. This component is similar to Dumond and Gerald Clark's Takli Island series and to Ocean Bay II on Kodiak Island. Specific similarities are in the ground slate industry and the flaked points, knives, and serapens (Joan Townsend, personal communication 1970).

Several archaeological surveys were conducted along the Alaskan coast with the intent of planning future excavations or assessing the potential of known sites following the devastating Alaskan earthquake of 1964 along the Kenai Peninsula (Hans-Georg Bandi on Saint Lawrence Island in 1965, H. Morris Morgan in 1964 along the Kenai Peninsula, and Edward Hosley in 1967 at Point Hope).

Recent Eskimo and Athabascan sites were discovered by VanStone in 1964, 1965 and 1967 along the Nushagak and other rivers, by Albert Spaulding in 1966 along Cook Inlet and the Susitna River, by Hosley along Kachemak Bay in 1967 and by Wendell Oswalt and VanStone in 1963 at Crow Village on the lower Kuskokwim (Oswalt and VanStone 1967).

Frederick Hadleigh-West excavated on southern Seward Peninsula in 1961 at a large Norton-related village and at a cave on the Sinuk River containing Ipiutak and possibly Denbigh related artifacts. Alan Bryan surveyed in the Pribilof Islands looking for evidence of early man, but finding possible Pre-Aleut sites. Bruce Lutz worked around Norton Sound in association with Douglas Anderson. His excavations at Unalakleet revealed Denbigh sites and a long time span of Norton Development (1969, 1972, 1973b).

68

Robert Ackerman excavated in Glacier Bay National Monument in 1963, 1964, and 1965 finding historic (Tlingit) sites (Ackerman 1964, 1965, 1968). A small early component of the Ground Hog Bay-2 site was radiocarbon dated at ca. 8000 B.C. (Ackerman 1968:66). Ackerman saw possible relationships with Arctic Small Tool or Northwest Microblade traditions, but the small sample and preliminary nature of the reconnaissance precluded any elaborate interpretations (1974, 1975).

In 1962, 1966, and 1967 Ackerman excavated sites at Chagvan Bay, Security Cove, Nanvak Bay, and Cape Newenham. His excavations covered a cultural _continuum_ lasting from Norton to recent Eskimo, with sites at Chagvan and Nanvak Bays showing the continuous occupation of this region during this time period. A significant site at Security Cove contained patinated side notched points similar to Palisades II and Tyone River (etc.) dating to about 3000 B.C. and lasting until a pre-Norton (small tool?) occupation.

Chester Chard and Barbara Merbs suggested that the late Alaskan pottery horizon known as "situla pottery," whose Asiatic origin had been accepted for some time (deLaguna 1947; Oswalt 1952a, 1953), came as a result of a direct transmission by sea, thus accounting for the hiatus between the similar Okhotsk maritime culture pottery and that found in the Yukon Valley and the Bering Coast between the Yukon and Kuskokwim Rivers (Chard and Merbs 1964:12-14). Admitting the speculative nature of this hypothesis, they closed their article with an apt quote from deLaguna: ". . .while sober caution must be valued, let us realize that always to keep within the bounds of the bounds of the surely provable, always to cling to the indisputable, never to run the risk of error, is to renounce the hope of gaining that insight which may perhaps be won only through the hazards of imaginative speculation" (1949:647).

Larsen published a final report on the 1949-50 Trail Creek excavations in 1968 indicating that the earliest men had visited and eaten there ca. 11,000 B.C. but left no artifacts--only butchered bone. The next occupants used microblade side blades thought to relate to the Northwest Microblade tradition, although this is a tenuous conclusion. The sequence of occupations then continues to Denbigh, Trail Creek-Choris, Norton-Near Ipiutak, Ipiutak, Western Thule, late prehistoric and historic Eskimos (Larsen 1968: 76)--an illustrious list of tenants from two caves containing only 243 artifacts with often disturbed stratigraphy (Larsen 1968:65).

Giddings and Larsen continued their work around Kotzebue Sound in 1961 excavating Western Thule, Ipiutak and Old Whaling Culture occupations on Cape Krusenstern. Campbell (1962) noted that the excavations confirmed that Ipiutak changed locally to Birnirk, thus linking ancestors of Eskimos further back in time. Later in the summer, the party split, with Douglas Anderson going up the Noatak, Larsen excavating Near Ipiutak at Point Hope (subsequently called Norton by Larsen--1961:10), and Giddings travelling up the Kobuk River to Onion Portage where he had tested house pits in 1941 finding several microblades and cores. He tested beneath the floor of his previously excavated house 1, finding evidence of several older cultures--enough to justify further work.

Dennis Stanford and Mary Rushton excavated several stratified sites in the vicinity of Point Barrow in 1968. The Walakpa site contained 15 houses, two of which had stratified living floors revealing a cultural sequence at the site of Modern Eskimo, Utkiavik (pre-contact Eskimo), Western Thule, Eastern Thule, Walakpa (defined by a single harpoon head type), Birnirk and Denbigh (like?) (Stanford 1971, 1972; Campbell 1970:242). This is the first Arctic coastal site with good vertical separation and a long stratified

70

sequence of Eskimo occupations.

Almost every investigator of Alaska's interior encountered recent Eskimo or Indian sites. Until relatively recently, few archaeologists have considered the discovery and investigation of such sites a research objective. Annette McFayden in 1961 studied late precontact and early historic sites near Allakaket on the Koyukuk River. Donald and Annette McFayden Clark returned in 1968 to continue her study of recent sites. On Norutak Lake they found tongue shaped cores, microblades and rough flaked tools in four distinct complexes. "The Clarks report that with the exception of the most recent, none of these components appear to closely resemble previously reported complexes" (Campbell 1970:240). The archaeological skies become hazy. Donald Clark returned to the Koyukuk in 1969 finding chipping stations related to other "Clovis" finds in northern Alaska (Clark 1974d; Archaeology Division 1969:3).

Edward Hosley in 1962 tested recent Athabascan sites on the upper Kuskokwim at Minchumina, assisted by Robert McKennan. Hosley returned in 1967, excavating ca. A.D. 1300 Athabascan sites (Denetasiro tradition) as well as earlier sites related to the Campus site and similar to finds of the Northwest Microblade tradition.

Edwin Hall conducted extensive surveys in the Brooks range, its foothills, and the northern coastal plain concentrating on very late prehistoric/ early historic Eskimo sites. He surveyed the Noatak River in 1962, 1963 (with Richard Morlan) and in 1964. In 1965 he surveyed around Howard Pass, excavating the sixteenth century A.D. Kranikrak Creek site. Hall's analysis of the Kangiguksuk site on the middle Noatak River is a model study of a single occupation single house site (1966, 1971). The permanently frozen deposit was related to recent Eskimos and was dated dendrochronologically to

71

1578 A.D.   Hall's analysis of technological micro and macro patterns and of

the faunal remains are the most complete of any comparable site report from

the north--an example to be emulated.

In 1967, Hall surveyed part of the western Brooks Range and its foot-

hills between the Itkillik River, the Kukpowruk River and the Noatak River.

Most of the sites were prehistoric/historic villages, but several small-tool

tradition sites were found as well as a site on Walker Lake containing

notched and lanceolate points reminiscent of Campbell's Tuktu and Naiyuk com-

plexes at Anaktuvuk Pass (Hall n.d.:5-6; Campbell 1961, 1963). Campbell

separated these complexes typologically from the same general locale at

Anaktuvuk Pass, but the association of artifacts from both complexes in sites

at Walker Lake and at Healy Lake (see Cook and McKennan 1968) suggests that

they may form one complex (see Alexander 1969:Fig. 2).

Five of the late prehistoric sites surveyed in 1967 had been heavily

disturbed by vandalism and "pot-hunting" to the extent that some may have

lost their scientific value. "Unfortunately, violations of the Antiquity

laws have become common on both the coast and in the interior of northern

Alaska" (n.d.:8).

In 1968 and 1970, Hall returned to Tukuto Lake on the Arctic Slope on

the headwaters of a tributary of the Colville River. Extensive excavations

of houses, pits, hearths, middens, and a karrigi wielded several tons of

animal bones and nearly ten thousand artifacts most of which resulted from

late prehistoric/early Eskimo occupations probably between 1800 and 1850

(Hall n.d.:12-14). A small-tool component and an unidentified component con-

sisting of primarily unifacial flint artifacts were also found, but are not

yet described in print. The Tukuto Lake site contained a wide variety of

house types, which, because of the brevity of their occupation, suggests

72

seasonal, social, or cultural diversity. Hall's research may help to clarify the relationship between Eskimo and Athabascan speaking peoples in northern Alaska during the protohistoric/historic periods (Hall 1969) and may shed some light on the relationship between recent climatic changes and Arctic peoples and cultures.

Campbell returned to Anaktuvuk Pass in 1961 expanding his sample of the earlier assemblages. In 1967, he excavated at the Kavik site which he now believes to be very recent Indian (1968). Campbell returned with Charles Amsden in 1968 to excavate and locate Nunamiut sites in the vicinity of Anaktuvuk Pass. Edwin Hall revisited the STT-Historic Eskimo site on Natukmuk Lake reported by Campbell pointing out that recent pot hunting has almost destroyed it (n.d.:3).

Ivar Skarland in 1961 surveyed along the Susitna River and the Denali Highway. Along the Teklanika River, he found assemblages similar to the Campus site, and the Northwest Microblade tradition. In 1962, Skarland excavated pre- or proto-historic Athabaskan camps in the vicinity of Fort Yukon. Skarland's 1963 excavations at the Ratekin Site on the Susitna River found many side and corner points related to Tuktu, Palisades II, Kobuk River Complex and Security Cove.

William Irving surveyed and excavated in the Howard Pass region on Itivlik Lake. His punyik Point site was the first inland site of the Arctic-Small-Tool tradition to be extensively excavated. The faunal remains were predominantly caribou and the artifacts mostly chipped stone (Irving 1962: 77). Irving had intended to return to Punyik Point in 1962 (Irving 1964) but problems of river travel limited his archaeological work to the Noatak and Amsak Rivers and Desperation Lakes where he found several complexes like Kogruk, one with side notched points, and one related to Denbigh.

73

Herbert Alexander surveyed the Chandler Valley in Anaktuvuk Pass in 1962, finding many tent rings. He returned in 1966 to the Atigun Valley, finding many recent Eskimo sites and sites related to Denbigh. In 1967 (with Robert Stuckenrath) his finds were more extensive including an early flake (Kogruk-like?) complex, sites related to Tuktu and Palisades II, some related to Denbigh, one site with Birnirk-like artifacts and many recent Eskimo camps (Alexander 1969b).

Alexander reviewed Campbell's Anaktuvuk Pass sequence, in conjunction with these finds, concluding that Campbell had split complexes which would more realistically be lumped together on the basis of his sites and analysis of site settings. In particular, Alexander lumped Kogruk, Kayuk and Anaktuvuk Ipiutak into a Kayuk complex which followed the ASTT Itivlik complex. He also lumped Naiyuk, Tuktu and Toyuk into the earlier Tuktu complex (Alexander 1969b:66). He established the integrity of these lumpings by the analysis of site locations.

Ralph Solecki, with Bert Salwen and Jerome Jacobson, surveyed in the Shubelik-Sadlerochit Mountains in the northeastern Brooks Range finding four Arctic small-tool sites and an extensive flake-tool site related to British Mountain and to the Kogruk complexes (reported in 1973-see below).

Gordon Lowther and Edwin Wilmsen excavated at MacNeish's Engigstciak site in 1961 and 1962, finding small numbers of flakes and chips of the British Mountain component. Wilmsen subsequently suggested that the Arctic flake tradition came from Central Siberia arriving between 21,000 and 11,000 B.C. spreading through a tundra-foothill region subsequently developing what we recognize as Paleo-Indian culture in the New World (Wilmsen 1964:341,343).

Wilmsen is less sanguine about the British Mountain materials feeling that they are a specialized part of a larger technological system and do not

constitute a true complex by themselves. Technically they could be of late
pleistocene age but he feels that the dating of the British Mountain materials
is still open to question (personal communication October 1970) (see Gordon
1970a).

Another flake-tool industry was discovered north of the Brooks Range
on May Lake in 1964 by Karl Schlesier and Lyle James. The Sedna Creek complex contains many artifacts fashioned on flakes or blades struck from prepared cores (pebble, turtleback, and discoidal) (Schlesier 1967:211).
Schlesier returned in 1967 excavating more flakes and flake tools which he
related to British Mountain, Kogruk and Katakturuk River Lookout in Alaska
and to the Siberian Upper Paleolithic. Unfortunately, all the presumed artifacts are from relatively recent stream deposits with no associated charcoal
or faunal remains (1967:210). Schlesier considered Sedna Creek to be the
fourth site of the British Mountain tradition considering this tradition a
valid cultural unit: "Despite the questions concerning the British Mountain
tradition, its existence can neither be overlooked nor wished away"
(Schlesier 1967:218; 1971).

Gordon's analysis of flake "tools" at Trout Lake (1970a) suggests
that these flake industries are best seen as partial inventories of more recent technological systems and casts doubt on the existence of a flake-tool
tradition in the Arctic.

In 1965 Robert Humphrey surveyed the Utukok River finding sites related to southern Plano complexes and to the Campus site. He revisited the
site of the fluted point find reported by Thompson in 1948. Humphrey returned
in 1966 finding several fluted points and blanks in situ at several surface
sites on Driftwood Creek. The Driftwood Creek complex contained well made
fluted points and burins in ". . .a blade tool assemblage resembling the

Aurignacian industry of the Old World more closely than they do any other
American collection" (1966:588). Humphrey saw the southern Clovis finds as
descendents of the Driftwood Creek complex which he saw as a way-station of
the developing Paleo-Indian culture en route from Asia, supporting the
arguments of C. Vance Haynes and John Witthoft. To reconcile these data
and interpretations with Wilmsen's (see above) would require more than one
migration into Alaska--a possibility foreseen by Müller-Beck (1966). A
radio-carbon date on mammoth tusk loosely associated with the Driftwood Creek
complex was greater than 13,000 B.C., as reported by Humphrey at the 1967
meeting of the American Anthropological Association, where he reiterated the
antiquity of Driftwood Creek and its ancestral relationship to the Llano
Complex. Presently, the opportunities for speculation on early man in Alaska
are unsurpassed by any other archaeological problem in the Americas.

Frederick Hadleigh-West and Hans-Georg Bandi excavated near Donnelly
Dome, Twelve Mile Bluff and Minto Flats in 1963. The Donnelly Ridge site was
an early core-blade-burin complex. The extensive Tangle Lakes sites contained side notched points related to the Tuktu. Hadleigh-West continued
his excavations to Minto Flats and Dixthada also surveying in the Tangle
Lakes region. He returned to Tangle Lakes in 1966, 1967, and 1968 to excavate sites containing side notched points associated with "wedge shaped cores".
The assemblage resembled those assigned to the Northwest Microblade tradition,
but Hadleigh-West denied any strength to this connection, lumping several
sites, including the Donnelly Ridge site, into the Denali complex. He saw
this early core-blade-burin complex as typologically and culturally distinct
from Tuktu, Pointed Mountain, and the Northwest Microblade tradition. On
examining Alaskan sites, Hadleigh-West reduced the Northwest Microblade
tradition concept to a group of non-Arctic-Small-Tool tradition sites

containing microblades (1967:374) emphasizing the differences between the
excavated industries, especially in cores and burins. Furthermore, he and
Bandi believed that the presumed diagnostic side notched point found in the
Campus assemblage was intrusive (1967:371) (this idea is perhaps reinforced
by Hosley's 1967 paper at the meetings of the Society for American Archaeology when he stated his belief that the Campus site had several components).
Hadleigh-West's statement "Evidence of certain intrusions may be seen at all
sites except Donnelly Ridge" (1967:377) raises severe questions of interpretive and sampling error. His plea for greater precision in describing and
comparing artifacts such as cores should be well-taken, but this would only
be possible if more elaborate publication is made of all results and data.
The Denali complex was guess-dated at greater than 10,000 years. The issues
that it has raised are important.

Robert McKennan and John Cook conducted excavations on and near Healy
Lake in the Tanana drainage in 1966, 1967, 1969, and 1970. Data from the
Garden and Village stratified sites has clarified the chronology of central
Alaska. The earliest finds, called the Chindadn complex, were dated at ca.
9000 B.C. and McKennan and Cook saw vague similarities with the Akmak levels
at Onion Portage, but they saw no other parallels in North America (1970a:5).
Above this complex was a rather sparse, ill-defined "transitional" phase
dated ca. 7000 B.C. followed by a local manifestation of the "Tuktu phase of
the Athapaskan tradition" (1970a:2)--MacNeish's Northwest Microblade and
Denetasiro ?   This complex should date ca. 4500 B.C. from the Tuktu date at
Anaktuvuk Pass. It is important to note that the next complex at Healy Lake
is the Denali phase of the Denali Complex as isolated by Hadleigh-West (1967--
see above). Because of its stratigraphic position overlying Tuktu and because
of comparisons with other dated sites, they suggest that the Denali phase

should date in the first millenium B.C. (compare this with Hadleigh-West's guess date of 10,000 years--see above). Cook and McKennan's statement of the probable authenticity of microblades at Dixthada and their temporal assessment of the Denali complex makes their following statement an understatement: ". . .it appears that the core and microblade technology is much more recent than has been heretofore believed" (1970b:2). Above these levels were some microblades and then the remains of the Healy Lake band of Athapaskans. In one series of excavations, they have increased the age of dated interior Alaskan sites back to 9000 B.C. and pushed the Denali complex ahead 6,000 years. McKennan and Cook feel that the Tuktu complex represents the founders of the Athapaskan tradition, thus giving Athapaskan speaders a 6,500 year antiquity in Alaska (1970b).

From the summer of 1961 on, Arctic archaeologists have treated the Onion Portage excavations like the Superbowl, eagerly anticipating any news or changes in the players. The first extensive excavations in 1961 revealed a sequence of cultures going back to Denbigh, or earlier times, in good stratigraphic order. Several of the cultures were without known coastal or inland parallels. The main results of the early stages of excavation were principally chronological and sequential, although the geographic position of Onion Portage between the Arctic coast and the interior boreal forest provided a unique opportunity ". . .to determine further what possible surges of influence could have taken place between the interior and the coast" (Giddings 1962:19). This site presented the first good evidence for interaction between the interior and the coast, or between Indians and Eskimos. In 1963, Giddings worked in Greenland, and then returned to Onion Portage to dig deeper, but once more they were unable to excavate to sterile deposits. By this time, they had discovered 28 distinct cultural layers going back to cultures related to Palisades II, which he was guess-dating at ca. 7000 B.C. (Giddings 1965:196), although current dating would be several thousand years more recent. "The evidence thus far amassed from Kotzebue Sound and the Kobuk strongly indicates that an inland influence dominated the cultural cast of peoples both of the Kobuk River and the coast from the end of the Wisconsin period to the time when microblades appeared on the coast" (1965:203).

Giddings reiterated Collins's (1953,1960) belief that microblade cultures represent an extension of the European Mesolithic which later was represented in cultures that evolved into recent Eskimo. "Throughout all this time and earlier, the language spoken in the far inland forests appears to have been Indian. Who knows that it might not have been Athapaskan?" (1965:203). Giddings's party returned to Onion Portage in 1964 while Douglas Anderson surveyed on the Noatak and associated rivers finding sites related to Tuktu and Palisades II as well as Denbigh sites. Giddings was killed in the Fall of 1964, in the middle of an exemplary career. His last scientific paper was published in 1966 corroborating the beach ridge cultural sequence at Cape Krusenstern with the excavated stratigraphy at Onion Portage.

Giddings's work at Onion Portage was continued by Douglas Anderson and Ruth Giddings under the general supervision of Froelich Rainey. Excavations in 1965, 1966, 1967, and 1968 elaborated the technological inventories of the cultures previously discovered, and extended the record of human occupation to the 6000 B.C. Akmak phase (possibly related to the early components at Healy Lake--see above and Cook and McKennan 1970a:5). Anderson published a preliminary report on the site in 1968 (1968a) and has read several papers at scientific meetings, but statements of the cultural implications of the long sequence of occupations at Onion Portage have only been preliminary and sketchy. Hopefully the future will see the establishment of the chronological and general cultural affinities of these cultures represented at Onion Portage so that we may use these data to approach some anthropological problems.

VI. Recent Developments

The years since 1970 have seen intensive activity in some regions and a reduction of research in others. In part, this is a result of the shift in sources of funding which saw more research being conducted in support of cultural resource management decisions as a result of oil and natural gas development in the Arctic. Arctic researchers who responded to these needs found themselves too busy doing this work to pursue some of the research projects which had dominated their interest up to that time. Other shifts were a result of the general fluctuations of research interests characteristic of Arctic researchers.

In the Eastern Arctic, Greenland has seen a reduction in research and publication in recent times, in part because of the backlog in research results awaiting analysis. Very little field research has been reported, and the pace of archaeological work in Greenland has seemingly slackened. Petersen (1975) reported results of analyses relating environmental changes to the internal structures and artifact distributions of Greenlandic longhouses as part of a festschrift issue of _Folk_ honoring Helge Larsen. The volume contains other significant articles which span the Arctic from Greenland to the Aleutians, including a selected bibliography of Larsen's numerous and important writings.

The Queen Elizabeth Islands have been the subject of expanded exploration for mineral deposits, with the resulting archaeological survey producing significant results. When McGhee began this field work in 1972, the prevailing understanding of the culture history of this region would have suggested that a pattern of broad changes intermediate between Independence I and Pre-Dorset would characterize the early occupations, forming a cline

81

between well-known sequences in northern Greenland and Igloolik. However, instead of such a cline, McGhee's researches suggested an early distinctive occupation by Independence I followed by a population movement of Pre-Dorset people with distinctive technology, settlement pattern, etc. (McGhee 1973, 1974b, 1975a and 1976). While recognizing the common Arctic Small Tool tradition heritage of these occupations, McGhee reinterpreted the co-occurrence of Independence I traits and Pre-Dorset "elements" in the low Arctic as evidence of multiple occupation of the same site, thus mixing of components rather than a combination of behaviors by the same people (1974b:130). McGhee's interpretations are consistent with his stated theoretical approach of historic particularism (1976:39) as expressed in his normative approach to the study of behavioral variation. From these studies and perspectives, he suggested the existence of a previously undefined and undiscovered culture in Alaska from which spread Independence I, Proto-Denbigh and Pre-Dorset cultures, as well as all other Arctic Small Tool tradition variants (1974b; cf. Harp 1964a:170). However, the prediction of presently unknown cultures is as risky as the prediction of presently unknown "cultures" of "early man", and we must be cautioned regarding what is essentially a reliance on the interpretation of negative evidence to understand what is known of a region's culture history (Koch 1968). Similar differences in theoretical perspective among Arctic researchers may be responsible for the seemingly different and incompatible interpretations included in "Eastern Arctic Prehistory: Paleoeskimo Problems" (Maxwell 1976a) and other discussions of attempts to define systematic causation in the processes of cultural adaptation to environmental change in the Eastern Arctic (cf.: Dekin 1975, etc., Arundale 1976a,

1976b; Fitzhugh 1976a, 1976b; Nash 1976; McGhee 1972a, 1974c) (for further discussion of similar matters, see Dekin 1975:Ch.1, Ch.8). To summarize, McGhee's work in this area was an important contribution because it partially filled the crease between two well-known regions and because it resulted in a re-thinking of our understandings of Arctic archaeology in general and a revitalization of concern with the conceptual setting and cultures as units of analysis.

Research continued on the south coast of Baffin Island in the Lake Harbour Region, where Arundale devised a model of cultural and environmental change, relating the adaptive changes in settlement location (and faunal contents) to changes in location of the sea ice/fast ice boundary and changes in atmospheric circulation (Arundale 1976a, 1976b). Her research refined previous models of the relationship between environmental and cultural change, and suggested alternate mechanisms linking these changes (cf. Dekin 1975).

Moreau Maxwell contributed to our conceptual understandings of Eastern Arctic prehistory in general, by organizing and chairing a seminar on Pre-Dorset--Dorset problems at the School of American Research in Santa Fe in 1973. This unusual opportunity for scholars to share data and ideas on a variety of topics of relevance resulted in the publication of a memoir of the Society for American Archaeology (No. 31--Maxwell 1976a), whose contents reflect the diversity of interpretations in this area. One of Maxwell's contributions was the result of his extensive efforts to examine and to depict at the same scale the diversity of artifacts from the Eastern Arctic (1975, 1976b). As a result of his empirical studies, the study of cultural

83

processes of change was placed on a firmer foundation and variations in
cultural diversity through space and time were readily apparent. Maxwell
cautioned those who were willing to assume that variations among archaeological collections were due to differences in cultural adaptations,
suggesting that they may as well reflect differences in the scheduling of
activities by people of similar or identical cultural systems (1976b:78).
The need for explicit sampling strategies of archaeological data representative of the entire seasonal round of a cultural system was readily
apparent, if we are to make meaningful conclusions regarding processes of
cultural change from these data (cf. Dekin 1975:Ch.4).

Dekin prepared a methodological assessment of Pre-Dorset archaeology
as part of the development of an explicit approach to modeling human
behavior using archaeological data (1975). Portions of this research were
presented in the above mentioned seminar in 1973, as explicit attempts to
model the internal structure of Pre-Dorset structures and artifact distributions (1976a). Models of the artifact/rock distributions from the Closure
site were derived and the significance of the distributions assessed with
nonparametric statistics. While these particular models may not apply elsewhere, this research marks the first time that the significance of such
archaeological models had been tested statistically, providing an empirical
evaluation. The model suggests activity areas in an oval "tent" structure,
with the presence of what may be an analogue to the historic sleeping
platform.

Dekin also prepared a model of the Arctic Small Tool horizon,
describing it as a migration from a generally common source across the
Eastern Arctic, with increasing stylistic diversity resulting from the

84

dispersal processes. This was seen as explaining part of the increased artifact diversity across this distribution, in a manner analogous to the declining commonality of information sharing which would accompany such a migration across such a vast area. Again, this model was evaluated statistically and its test implications were found to be suggestive and significant (1976b). This interpretation runs counter to that suggested by McGhee (1976) and McGhee and Tuck (1973, 1975, 1976) which relies on separate migrations from distinct "parent cultures" in the Western Arctic to explain the observable diversity in the Eastern Arctic at early times. Reconciliation among such competing ideas must await more representative data obtained in a rigorous and replicable manner and more explicit methods of hypothesis testing (Dekin 1975:Ch.9).

Schledermann conducted an extensive survey of Cumberland Sound, Baffin Island, emphasizing the extensive Thule remains in this region, and building upon his earlier researches in Northern Labrador (1971a). Perhaps the major contribution beyond the extensive data obtained and described was his discussion of the adaptive response of Thule culture to the changing environmental conditions of the period (1976a). Schledermann saw the snow house as a Dorset trait whose utilization in conjunction with the fall structure, the quarmat, was the result of changes in the distribution and mobility of fauna during the period AD 1200–1550 in the high Arctic. These innovations spread to Greenland and Labrador during the worsening climatic episode which followed. "The use of communal dwellings is seen at least partially as a response to climatically worsening conditions affecting general game availability" (Schledermann 1976b:45).

85

Father Rousseliere (Mary-Rousseliere 1968, 1976) continued his field
work in northern Baffin Island, with particular emphasis on the Button
Point sites threatened by continued erosion and native "bone mining".
Masks and other wooden artifacts discovered there have provided a new
dimension to our knowledge of Dorset artifacts (Taylor 1972b, 1975) as well
as an appreciation of the continuing destruction of archaeological data
from this region. The region is characterized by relatively little uplift
in the last 2000 years, which has led to few well marked raised beaches,
upon which the "linear" settlement pattern of Independence I peoples may
be dependent (1976:53). While a complete sample of the region has not been
completed, he considers the region to be a relatively marginal area, when
compared with Foxe Basin cultural developments.

> Indeed one of the conclusions that can be drawn from the Nunguvik
> material--reinforced by similar earlier finds at Button Point--is
> that the Dorset people possessed watercraft probably much like the
> Eskimo kayak, and perhaps also the umiak...(1976:54).

These data also corroborate the continuity which demonstrates the Pre-
Dorset--Dorset continuum from the Foxe Basin/Lake Harbour region, particularly the continuity of distribution of burins, angular soapstone
vessels, slate blades and stemmed end-blades (1976:54). Rousseliere's
research and interpretations are tempered by his deep understanding of
historic and contemporary cultural processes, which serve him well in his
discussions of the human behaviors which result in known movements of
artifacts and ideas (1976:53-57).

McCartney continued his researches in the Hudson Bay region, with
particular emphasis on the Thule occupations (1970a, 1972a). His
subsequent research was part of the Thule Archaeology Conservation

Project, sponsored by the Archaeological Survey of Canada and the Department of Indian and Northern Affairs. This project represents a responsible reaction of the Canadian Government and interested archaeologists to the problem of native mining of archaeological sites for the preserved bone resources which they contain. The research of Schledermann, Mary-Rousseliere and others has also been tempered by the imminent threat to the integrity of archaeological sites which these native carving needs represent. With continued cooperation among all interested parties, perhaps the potential conflict among contemporary social values and past cultural values may be reconciled.

These interests culminated in a McCartney organized symposium "Thule Eskimo Culture: An Archaeological Retrospective" for the 1977 Tenth Annual Meeting of the Canadian Archaeological Association. The number, diversity and quality of papers presented is suggestive of the maturity of the discipline and of the diversity of methods and analyses which are appropriate for Thule data.

The archaeology of Northern Ungava was elucidated by the continuing work of Plumet (1974, 1976) and colleagues (Gosselin et al. 1974; Pierard 1975; Hartweg and Plumet 1974). These papers report on the meticulous work and technical innovations (use of stereo pair photographs of houses and excavations, for example) in Ungava Bay and at Poste de la Baleine (Great Whale River) and Richmond Gulf on Hudson Bay. The majority of these studies are published in Paleo-Quebec. The emphasis in these volumes is apparently on the publication and dissemination of well collected and depicted information on the archaeological sites themselves and on their

87

contents (e.g., Hartweg and Plumet 1974 on human skeletal material, and
Pierard 1975 on faunal remains). The cooperation of Plumet and Elmer Harp,
Jr. on the exchange of information regarding concurrent explorations in
this region serves as a good example of the mutually supportive results
which occur too rarely in a discipline where politics, territoriality and
vested interest may prevail (Gosselin et al. 1974). Plumet's excavations
on Pre-Dorset structures at Great Whale suggested that there was considerable diversity of activities conducted within them (with resulting
differences among houses presumably occupied by the same people). This
further evidence of adaptive variation within a single "culture" is an
important contribution to the study of such behaviors and opens up new
avenues of research regarding the cultural processes which may account for
the behavioral diversity of the archaeological record. The study of the
structure of artifacts and features distributions within houses is another
hallmark in Quebec research and one which holds considerable promise (Plumet
1976:Fig. 11). It is particularly important to note that Plumet interprets
the juxtaposition of Pre-Dorset houses with central passages with round or
rectangular houses lacking central passages at BAL.1 as evidence for several
different seasons of occupation by the same people (Plumet 1976:210).
Moreover, the organizational structure of activity areas within these
structures is essentially bilateral (cf. Dekin 1975, 1976a) with or without
a central hearth feature. Presumably, further research will attempt to
relate these variations in space and time to the paleoecology of the region
(Gosselin et al. 1974; Plumet 1974).

Barre published the results of his Wakeham Bay reconnaissance (Barre
1970), concluding that there was continuity of settlement pattern (in

particular with regard to those criteria for which a habitation site was chosen) from Dorset and Thule periods to the present (Barre 1970:104). He also made management recommendations prioritizing discovered sites on the basis of their potential to contribute data towards the solution of research problems in this region.

Harp continued his investigations of the Hudson Bay area, expanding his field surveys to include the Belcher Islands in 1974 and 1975. Harp continued to use this field research to test technical approaches to field photography, with particular emphasis on remote sensing using aerial photography (1974, 1975b). His findings of a late Dorset amulet of non-North American copper raised again the complexity of cultural relations in the second millenium AD among Norse, Thule and Dorset (1975a) and did little to simplify our understandings of this period. Harp's contribution to the School of American Research advanced seminar was an analysis of population trends at settlements in Newfoundland and Hudson Bay. This represents one of the few attempts to reconstruct population trends during the prehistoric period in the Eastern Arctic and to compare settlement characteristics in two separate districts. In general, the Port au Choix houses were more numerous, had greater artifact densities (possibly because they were more winter occupations) and were culturally conservative. Harp suggests that winter houses were occupied by at least two-family groups and that in both areas settlements of "small clusters of households were the prevailing social expression throughout centuries of time" (1976:136).

Fitzhugh continued his researches along the Labrador coast, expanding his consideration of environmental studies (e.g., 1972) and extending them to more general studies of maritime adaptations (1975a,b,c). His substantive contributions on the Dorset and Pre-Dorset occupations were summarized (1976a) at the School of American Research Seminar in Santa Fe (1973) and his core-pulsation model of population dynamics represents further attempts at modeling of the complex interrelations between environmental changes and human adaptations in "marginal" areas where population extinctions and withdrawals are more common than in the core areas of Hudson Bay, Foxe Basin and Hudson Straits. The Smithsonian has provided extensive programmatic support of ancillary research in this area, with further refinement of environmental changes by Jordan (1974, 1975) and technical applications to faunal dating by Spiess (1976). These researches extended into cooperative studies (with the Institute of Arctic and Alpine Research of the University of Colorado) of lake sediments, pleistocene geomorphological features and pollen accumulation studies in the interior and coastal regions of Labrador, most of which have yet to be published. This line of research holds great promise for correlating environmental episodes and for increasing our understanding of cultural processes through increasingly complicated and sophisticated behavioral models.

This general sequence of cultures from Maritime Archaic and Pre-Dorset through Dorset (but without more recent Indians) was also found by Tuck at Saglek Bay in northern Labrador (Tuck 1975b, 1976b), confirming the far northward extension of coastal archaic peoples. While the broad picture of cultural change in this region was clearing, the specific micro-adjustments in settlement pattern and subsistence remained cloudy, as small samples and incomplete settlement systems hampered attempts at interpretation. Recognizing the deterrent which these problems presented, Tuck preferred to retain an inductive approach to the study of culture history (1975:144,199). He reiterated the complexity of models of relations between environmental changes and cultural changes (his pollen analyses demonstrated the apparent impact of settlement at the micro-scale) and suggested that one of the more pressing interpretive problems was that of the apparent demise of Dorset culture, which remained ". . .perhaps the most perplexing problem in Canadian prehistory" (1975:198).

Robert McGhee and James Tuck initiated a collaboration on the archaeology of Newfoundland, with special emphasis on the Indian occupations along the Straits of Belle Isle (1975) and the remarkable maritime archaic occupation. Their discussions of radiocarbon dating at the School of American Research Seminar in Santa Fe (1973) led to a considerable re-evaluation of problems inherent in radiocarbon dating in the Arctic (cf. Campbell 1966a) and to cautions against the uncritical acceptance of radiocarbon dates (1976). Their revised cultural chronology using those dates presumed to be the most reliable with conversions to calendar years has produced a more systematic approach to the interpretation of such dates and a more normative statement of the duration of cultural periods across the Eastern Arctic.

Tuck's investigations of Eskimo and Indian occupations of Labrador has produced considerable empirical evidence of an area once poorly known. The remarkable series of burial sites at Port au Choix, Newfoundland (first reported in any detail by Harp and Hughes--1968) reported and analyzed in detail in the increasingly significant publications by the Memorial University of Newfoundland (Tuck 1976a) has allowed comparison across the coasts of the Straits of Belle Isle and led to the establishment of an intensive and extensive Maritime Archaic Tradition throughout Maine and the Maritime Provinces (see researches by Sanger, Harp, Fitzhugh, MacLeod, et al.). This tradition is seen as having

91

great time depth in the maritimes (from the fifth through the second millenium, BC--Tuck 1976a:112), being distinct but perhaps ancestrally related to the Shield Archaic and the Laurentian Archaic. The assemblage from the Beaches Site in Bonavista Bay (Newfoundland) suggests that the relationship between the Maritime Archaic and the Shield Archaic may be very strong (Carignan n.d., 1975; Tuck 1976a:114) and that there is a combination of both clinal and adaptive differences within the northeastern Archaic during this period (Carignan 1976a:143).

> If the ground stone elements were subtracted from this assemblage...
> we would be left with a complex superficially similar to the Shield
> Archaic. Therefore, the relationship between these two traditions
> warrants a closer look (Tuck 1976a:114).

Researches by Helen Devereaux and Urve Linnamae at White Bay and Port Aux Basques focused on the Dorset occupation of Newfoundland, although Indian sites were encountered (Linnamae 1975:8). The Pope's Point site was investigated (but not yet published) as it was the only known inland Dorset site from Newfoundland (cf. Lee 1967:35). Linnamae presents a detailed analysis of Dorset assemblages, including an interesting discussion of differences and similarities between her complete population of microblades and a sample as measured and categorized by McGhee (1970b). While McGhee's sample was not systematically drawn and may have been subject to introduced bias, it coincided rather closely with that of the population excavated, with the exception that variable variation was generally less. This appeared to be the result of selective bias (Linnamae 1975: 194) and may be used to provide some idea of the nature and extent of observer bias in non-systematic sample selection.

Archaeological surveys and excavations were continued in the District of Keewatin by Bryan Gordon, James Wright and Urve Linnamae. Linnamae's survey

92

of Rankin Inlet confirmed the extensive prehistoric occupation of this area, ranging from Pre-Dorset to historic sites. Excavations were conducted on a late Thule-Transitional site containing tents or snow houses which may yield important information on the origins of historic Eskimo populations in that area and on recent adaptive changes. Wright continued his research on Lake Athabasca (1975), in the Dubawnt River area and at the Aberdeen Site, leading to the refinement and definition of The Shield Archaic (Wright 1972a, 1972b). Several sites indicated that the area had been continually occupied since late Paleo-Indian times by populations subsisting on caribou and occupying sites advantageous for this pursuit (1972a:75). These people appeared to have abandoned this area at approximately 1000 B.C., possibly because cooling conditions forced the

> tree-line too far south to permit the Shield Archaic bands to make their seasonal visits to the Aberdeen site. Certainly the distribution of prehistoric remains in the barrens that can be attributed to Indian cultures indicate that these seasonal caribou hunters retreated to the Tiaga or forest proper before the onslaught of winter (1972a:78-79).

The following period is reflective of Pre-Dorset movements southward into the barrens. Inasmuch as Wright's monograph on the Shield Archaic is a major statement of ideas which developed over a period of at least a decade of research and discussion, the hypotheses which he suggests warrant closer attention.

> The Shield Archaic evolved from a late Paleo-Indian (Plano tradition) cultural base in the eastern Northwest Territories and probably the western portions of the Boreal Forest-Canadian Shield.

> Plant and animal reoccupation of land freed by the retreating Laurentide ice permitted northwestern Plano-Shield Archaic hunters to expand, particularly in the easterly direction.

> Cultural continuities between the Shield Archaic and subsequent developments in the Boreal Forest-Canadian Shield permit the speculation that the Shield Archaic people probably spoke an Algonkian language.

The Shield Archaic populations of the Keewatin District abandoned the area some time about 1000 B.C.

The relationship between the Shield Archaic and adjacent contemporaneous populations appears to have been both relatively limited and insignificant in terms of cultural innovation. (Wright 1972b:85-88).

While syntheses of the prehistory of any area are always large targets for criticism, Wright's tapestry is sufficiently conservative in its treatment of the many sparse data on which it is based to have a lasting potential. Perhaps one of the more controversial hypotheses is with regard to the relation between the Shield Archaic and the later Pre-Dorset occupation, where others have seen significant contact and exchange of ideas and culture traits (cf. Noble 1971:110).

Wright's excavation at the Grant Lake site and his publication of detailed artifact provenience data from the site are a major hallmark in the depiction of archaeological data from the central barrens (1976: Figure 3, etc.) (his Figure 9 also provides an excellent visual summary of areas surveyed north of 58°). Wright's preliminary analysis of these Agate Basin artifact distributions (using quadrants of circles fitted to the field data) revealed several patterns of interest regarding the differential distribution of scrapers, projectile points and other artifacts, although Wright did not pursue these analytically (1976:10,22). However, these results do indicate that activity areas may be determined within tent structures (see Dekin 1975, 1976a; Plumet 1976) and suggest that the analysis of detailed provenience data may be fruitful across a broad spectrum of Arctic cultures, from Agate Basin to historic Eskimos. These data also support Wright's earlier hypothesis regarding the Agate Basin-like origins of the Shield Archaic and Gordon's interpretations of the relations among caribou herds and bands of human hunters (see below).

Bryan Gordon continued his interest in the barrens with investigations in the Baker Lake and Back River regions, following up on Wright's work on the Dubawnt River. Gordon's major contribution, in addition to the extensive excavated data, is his demonstration that the structure of Arctic Small Tool variation among assemblages is concordant with that of the historic structure of barren ground caribou bands, thus his "discrete band/discrete herd" hypothesis, wherein the tendency for human hunters to pursue discrete herds leads to stylistic distinction in their artifacts. His extensive analysis and depiction of the data in varied and informative media (e.g., Figures 8-19) is a technical contribution. While his hypothesis is somewhat dependent on areas of investigation and methodology, it is certainly innovative and suggestive that its testing should be conducted in the areas between the herds/bands to evaluate their discreteness through time (compare Gordon 1975:Figures 17 and 18 with Wright 1976; Figure 10) (Gordon 1975:296-297). Gordon's accumulation of historic and ethnohistoric evidence for such man-animal relations substantiates the time depth of this pattern (Gordon 1975, 1976:267).

The Migod site reflects ca. 8000 years of barrenground prehistory in a stratified context, as follows: Northern Plano Agate Basin; Shield Archaic; Pre-Dorset; Talteilei Athapascans; and historic Chipewyan until they were displaced by Caribou Inuit. Such sites provide the distinct continuity of occupation in support of other analyses and are thus vital to the establishment of meaningful patterns of space-time relations. They are all too few. Additionally, perhaps the greatest contribution of this excavation and interpretation is in Gordon's demonstration of the dynamic interdependence among the "fluctuations of cultures, caribou and climate at Migod site for the past 8000 years" (Gordon 1976:273).

Pursuing an interest in the archaeology of ecotones, Ron Nash conducted

an archaeological survey of portions of the transitional forest region west of

Hudson Bay, with annual field work from 1965 through 1971 (Nash 1975). Nash

considered the general sequence of occupations to span the Paleo-Indian, Early

Archaic (possibly Shield Archaic) and Late Archaic periods with considerable

evidence to indicate ancestors of historic Chipewyan by approximately 500 AD

(Nash 1975:175-6). Interestingly enough, these researches revealed no ceramics

and no rock paintings, both of which are characteristic of various historic

(and late prehistoric) Algonquian speaking groups to the south. Nash

concluded:

> If we take a broad look at the course of cultural development in
> this region we can recognize, in spite of large gaps in the
> archaeological sequence, that cultural evolution has been minimal.
> Congruent with this observation is the general continuity indicated
> in Wright's derivation of the Shield Archaic culture from a late
> plano base. The economic strategy and probably the settlement
> patterns underwent few changes from Paleo-Indian times onward and
> the eventual definition of the practically unknown Early Archaic
> cultures will probably not alter this idea. Similarly, I would
> suggest little change in the community pattern at least in the
> past 2000 years. . . . At present, the most significant changes
> seem to be an increase in population around 500 A.D. and a possible
> increase in functional specialization among sites (Nash 1975:177-178).

Nash contrasted these circumstances with those characteristic of the Eskimo

occupations of the Hudson Bay coast of Manitoba (as described elsewhere) relating

them to his ideas of cultural systems as Tightly Constrained Systems (Nash 1976)

(cf. Maxwell 1967:10).

> The Eskimo cultures are initially more complex and remain so. . .
> Over 3500 years, these cultures changed so that we can recognize
> Pre-Dorset, Dorset and Thule cultures and these reorganizations
> and shifts are much more pronounced and rapid than changes
> occurring in the interior cultures... Thus unlike the interior
> forest cultures, we have relatively complex cultures manifesting
> significant changes, but like the interior cultures, there is no
> evolution into a higher order of complexity (Nash 1975:178).

Nash's analyses represent one of the few attempts to infer general systemic models of these occupations, going beyond the more simple statement that these lands have always been occupied by "archaic" peoples in a simple and satisfying adaptation (cf. Nash 1975:179).

The high central Arctic has received considerable attention with regard to mineral and energy exploration, but relatively little has been published and most of the information is not yet available. Muller-Beck collaborated with Taylor on further investigations of his Banks and Victoria Islands Dorset and Pre-Dorset data (Muller-Beck et al. 1971), focusing on a descriptive analysis of structures and faunal materials (Derry 1974), but the complete analytic potential of these materials is not yet realized.

Robert McGhee summarized the available data on Copper Eskimo Prehistory, extending it backwards to the Thule culture, based on excavations at the Memorana site on Victoria Island and Bloody Falls (McGhee 1972b). Continuities through time were demonstrated for the Kuujjua River sites on western Victoria Island and the Kunana site on Prince William Sound (Victoria Island). McGhee made good use of linguistic and historic information to demonstrate the essential similarity among historic peoples in this region (a similarity also characteristic of the Thule period) and hypothesized that the "Thule period population of the area between Cape Parry and Queen Maud Gulf formed a distinct 'tribe'" (1972b:57). McGhee evaluated the culture changes in these populations between the Thule period and the Historic period, wherein the

> most significant change, the decline and eventual cessation of whaling, seems to have been well under way during the Thule period while most other elements of Thule culture in the region remained similar to those of whale-hunting Thule peoples in the eastern and western Arctic. A second significant change, that from small coastal winter settlements to large temporary winter settlements on the sea ice, seems to have occurred during the Intermediate interval, after which the situation reverted to that of the preceding period (McGhee 1972b:118).

This latter change seemed to involve a reduction of caribou hunting and a greater reliance on coastal sealing, which McGhee viewed as an adaptive response to the changed climatic conditions of the Neo-Boreal episode. He concluded that "most of the major cultural changes which have occurred over the past 1000 years in the Copper Eskimo area are consistent with continuous adaptation to changing environmental conditions" (1972b:125).

In related research, McGhee combined ethnohistoric and archaeological information to reconstruct the history and culture of the Mackenzie Delta Kittegaryumiut, based in part on excavations along the East Channel of the Mackenzie Delta. The unusually large population of the Kittegaryumiut was apparently the result of their distinctive "beluga hunting adaptation which saw the estuary of East Channel used as a trap for the white whales" (1974a:91) for several centuries, until the channel may have filled to the point where this pursuit was no longer possible or attractive. General affinities with western Alaska Eskimo populations may have been the result of trade with interior North Alaskan peoples, but the remote history of these people appears to be more complex than such a simple explanation for most of these similarities would suggest (1974a:93). McGhee concluded with a plea for study of the history of this delta region using living informants before the data are lost forever.

Bryan Gordon summarized Mackenzie Delta archaeology through 1972, reiterating the results of MacNeish, McGhee and himself. Data are sparse prior to ca. 0 A.D., with no assemblages dated prior to ca. 3500 B.C. (1974a:75). Based on scanty data from blowouts on terraces of the Blow River, Gordon identifies the Mackenzie Blade complex, estimating its age at greater than 3500 B.C. (that is, prior to the British Mountain Complex of that date—Gordon 1970a). Both of these complexes appear restricted to the mountain front of the Eastern Brooks Range, but Gordon believes that their range may be more extensive and that they may represent evidences that "northern Indians bearing a material culture, of which the British Mountain tool kit represents a portion, actively intercepted migrating barren ground caribou herds along the northern mountain front" (1974a:82).

The Whirl Lake site was occupied by Mackenzie Flats Kutchin Indians during the eighteenth century A.D. as a fishing camp, whose contents and structure appear to reflect accurately the historic accounts of Athapascans in this area (Gordon and Savage 1974:185). The lower levels of this site contain stone tools and blades similar to those from the Franklin Tanks site on Great Bear Lake described by MacNeish (1953) and possibly dated to ca. 1500 B.C. (Gordon and Savage 1974:187). As in other regions, the archaeology of the coastal areas is better known than that of the interior, and many of the significant empirical contributions of recent years have helped to alleviate this disparity.

Richard Morlan investigated the later prehistoric and historic occupations in the northern Yukon, with limited excavations at the Cadzow Lake site (Morlan 1972a) and NbVk-1 site in Old Crow Flats (1972b). These two sites are historic Kutchin camps, both of which were occupied in the 1930s, allowing Morlan the extensive use of ethnohistoric and interview data for interpreting the remains. NbVk-1 reflects the 1930's crash of muskrat populations in the Old Crow Flats, being occupied as a fish camp (with remnants of the fish trap still visible in the adjacent stream) during the mid to late summer (1972b:38). The Cadzow Lake site was occupied at least three times for the interception of spring migrations of caribou (1972a:67), probably in 1933, ca. 1880 and ca. 1850 (1972a:73). Through this time span, the data suggest an increasing significance of fur bearing animals and the final occupation demonstrated a "generally more diversified economic base which included greater use of avian resources and foodstuffs of Euro-Canadian origin" (1972a:67). This report on the Cadzow site is noteworthy for Morlan's artifact plots and attempts to use cumulative frequency graphs and horizontal artifact profiles in the analysis of the horizontal and vertical artifact distributions, both within and among the distinct soil layers.

Much of the later prehistory of this region must be related to Morlan's massive description and analysis of the large stratified Klo-kut site, whose layers revealed occupations spanning the last 1000-1500 years. While Morlan was reluctant to "re-write" the later prehistory of the Yukon, his extensive comparative studies allowed the formulation of a rather comprehensive set of hypotheses regarding the prehistory of this period. Their widely synthetic quality makes them worthy of relatively extensive consideration.

> 1. By 1000 years ago the entire south flank of the Brooks Range was occupied by groups of people engaged, at least seasonally, in the exploitation of the northern reaches of the boreal forest in Alaska and the Yukon. . . .The principal technological hallmarks of human adaptation to these conditions include a well developed bone industry on which much of the land hunting weaponry and fishing technology are based. . . .Technologically it is feasible in such a context to find local industries which lack techniques of bifacial stone knapping, because the major implement category for which such techniques are used can consist of bone and antler examples. . . (Morlan 1973a:512).

Morlan interprets the dearth of such bifacial tools at Klo-kut to indicate their absence from the cultural inventory (rather than seasonal variation or sampling error), marking a major difference between the western and eastern Brooks Range occupations in the early centuries A.D. (1973a:513).

> 2. This broadly shared technological complex characterized both prehistoric Eskimo cultures (on the Kobuk) and prehistoric Kutchin cultures (east of the Kobuk as far as the middle Porcupine). This fact led to considerable confusion concerning the identity of the bearers of the Arctic Woodland Culture when that concept was first defined (1973a:513).

3. For some reason, which I cannot yet specify, the particular forms of bifacial stone points which developed in Ekseavik spread eastward as far as the middle Porcupine around 600 years ago. Indeed many of the traits shared across this broad zone became even more specifically similar from one end of it to the other. . . .The introduction to the middle Porcupine of bifacial stone working techniques was associated with very few other changes. The major one was a reduction in the use of birch bark, and if climatic variables are partially responsible for the bark decline they might also be invoked as partial explanations of the diffusion of bifacial techniques during the Ekseavik time period (1973a:513-514).

4. Sometime during the last 500 years the historic Brooks Range distribution of Kutchin, Koyukon, and Eskimo took shape (1973a:514).

"Regardless of this recent phase of prehistory, however, I think it likely that the southern Brooks Range should be regarded as an ecological and technological unit throughout much of the period since A.D. 500, and this unity is responsible for the similarities between prehistoric Kutchin technology, as revealed at Klo-kut, and that of the later prehistoric Eskimo of the Kobuk River" (1973a:514-515).

Following his research at Klo-kut, its scientific potential was severely impacted by construction of a road through the site, leading to an increased awareness of the dangers of poorly planned construction and to a heightened sense of responsibility of both the government and the scientific community for the sound management of cultural resources in the Yukon (see Morlan 1974a).

As part of a massive festschrift issue of Arctic Anthropology, in honor of Chester Chard on his retirement from active teaching at the University of Wisconsin, William Irving and Jacques Cinq-Mars summarized the archaeology of the Old Crow Flats region (1974). In general, this sequence is similar to that of neighboring areas of Alaska, with the exception of early Eskimo complexes which are not identified (1974:65). There appears a dichotomy between early sites found usually on "lookout" locations and later Kutchin sites found along

lakes and rivers, in conjunction with caribou surrounds. While recognizing the
potential for sampling error and differing archaeological survey strategies,
they suggested several hypotheses to account for this presumed shift in land-use
patterns: a change in major prey species, from bison to caribou; a change in
the topography of the Old Crow basin; or a cultural change resulting from
technological changes, such as the introduction of the caribou fence (1974:79).

Perhaps one of the major research contributions of widest potential
significance and controversy from this region was the discovery of artifacts
made on the bones of Pleistocene fauna found on the banks of the Old Crow
River (Irving and Harington 1970, 1973). These deposits, which had been known
for their abundance and variety of Pleistocene fossils, yielded a toothed
flesher made on a caribou tibia (colored like other fossils from extinct fauna
in the assemblage), as well as fragments indicative of human workmanship.
Radiocarbon dates ranged from ca. 14,000 radiocarbon years to ca. 41,000 radiocarbon years (on associated wood and bones), with dates on the artifacts themselves at between 25,000 and 29,000 radiocarbon years (the flesher was
sacrificed for dating--GX 1640: 27,7000 +3000 -2000--Irving and Harington
1973:336). Fractures on these artifacts seem to indicate that the bone was
fresh and not fossilized when worked.

However, all of these materials are secondary riverine deposits and no
in situ finds were made. Morphologically, the flesher is similar to similar
implements known historically from Athapaskan sites. Frozen bone retains its
mechanical properties suitable for workmanship, thus the artifact could have
been made much more recently than the age of the bone itself. While there is
little doubt as to the authenticity of the artifacts or of the age of the bones,
the issue of whether the age of death of the animals and the manufacture of the

implements are basically the same remains problematical, and we look longingly at the continued efforts to find in situ remains from the later Pleistocene within the Beringia refugium. This research is extremely significant, because it bears on our understanding of human adaptive potential during the Pleistocene and of processes of cultural change and human evolution (Irving and Harington 1973:340).

Moving up the Mackenzie, Canadian attention has increased as mineral and petroleum finds have led to extraction facilities development and to the construction of transportation facilities along a "Mackenzie corridor". Surveys of these areas by Millar, Gordon and Cinq-Mars (Cinq-Mars 1973, 1974) contributed to our general knowledge of the area, but the full impact of their extensive surveys on our knowledge and understanding has not yet been felt, except in a preliminary fashion (see Irving and Cinq-Mars 1974:65).

William Noble surveyed the central District of Mackenzie north of Great Slave Lake and east of Great Bear Lake from 1966 to 1969 building on MacNeish's pioneering work of 1949 (see above). Noble categorized his sites into nineteen archaeological complexes, creating three new traditions and establishing a regional culture history based on scattered radiocarbon dates, beach ridge chronologies, etc. While the integrity of some of these categories is now subject to some rethinking (due to problems of component mixing in surface sites--Clark 1975a:55), the overall pattern is useful to structure the rather complex history of this area which shared the cultural developments of both the interior Mackenzie and the Arctic coast. Noble summarized his findings:

> Acasta Lake clearly places northern Plano Indians among the
> first occupants of the Canadian arctic and subarctic regions,
> rather than the often touted Eskimos. Too, the newly defined
> Canadian Tundra tradition sheds light on hitherto unknown
> migrations and developments of small tool peoples whose ethnic
> identity remains uncertain. With the Taltheilei Shale tradition,
> we have one of the most complete and continuous developmental
> sequences yet defined for any central northern Athapascan group
> (Noble 1971:116).

103

Clark surveyed the region north and west of Great Bear Lake in 1969, 1970, and 1972, finding numerous small surface sites ranging from Agate Basin-type artifacts through Arctic Small Tool tradition and early Archaic to the historic period. His summary of the current status of archaeology in the District of Mackenzie is an excellent statement of our current knowledge, building on the earlier work of MacNeish, Noble and Gordon.

> To recapitulate, prehistoric entities recognized in the central and interior Mackenzie District consist of (1) the Taltheilei Shale tradition which lasted from before the Christian era to contact; before that and of relatively short duration; (2) the Arctic Tool tradition (sic); (3) to a degree concurrent with ASTt but geographically separated to the west or southwest sites more or less relatable to the Northwest Microblade tradition; (4) other sites in the west and southwest spanning parts of the last 2000 years or more which for the present I would hesitate to place in any of the first three categories; and (5) yet earlier sites including Acasta Lake and some reported assemblages from Fisherman Lake (1975a:63).

Clark defined the "Colville-Horton Heavy Stone Complex" on the basis of a consistent association of heavy (large, thick bifaces and unifaces, often of quartzite) stone tools in geographically separate contexts, often including smaller tools not assignable to other components (Clark 1975a:89-90). However, he is understandably reluctant to create meaningless analytic units, thus he suggests that "the most we can say of the Heavy Stone complex is that it presents a target to be verified or rejected by further research" (1975a:92). A single radiocarbon date of ca. 1600 B.P. (NMC-714) suggested meaningful comparisons with Noble's Taltheilei, Windy Point and Waldron River complexes (Clark 1975a: 93) of the Taltheilei Shale tradition, believed ancestral to the Yellowknife Indians (Noble 1971:115).

In the southwest Yukon, William Workman and John Cook conducted research in the Aishihik River-Kluane Lake areas supported by the National Museum of Man.

The Basin Canyon site provides the earliest direct dating of human occupation
(ca. 7200 B.P.) and is apparently related to Plano-related occupations to the
east (Workman 1974b:94). While the site is extremely small (both spatially
and in terms of artifacts), the association of bison bone fragments at depth
in a stratified site and in association with a discrete radiocarbon dated
component is significant. While the Plano affinities are best documented,
Paleo-Indian materials from northern Alaska at the Putu site have similar
bilateral flaking and burination, yet apparently date at least a thousand
years earlier (Alexander 1974: Figures 3,4).

In related research, Workman combined evidence from linguistics,
hypsithermal climatic events and ethnohistory in support of his hypothesis
which, if correct, will be of significance to cultural processes and sequences
across a broad area of North America. He suggested:

> Sometime toward the middle of the First Millenium A.D., a cata-
> strophic rain of volcanic ash covered many thousand square
> miles east of the St. Elias Mountains, displacing at least
> several hundred individuals and causing adjustments in the
> range of a number of bands. Displaced peoples would most
> likely have moved north or south into occupied land at or
> near its carrying capacity. . . The "primary refugees",
> those affected directly by the ash fall, if successful in
> establishing themselves on the peripheries of the affected
> area, would have displaced in turn other groups of Athabaskan
> speech. . . . Eventually, at the southern periphery of the
> Athabaskan world, some groups would have been detached to
> the south into the domain of alien peoples. . . . It does
> not seem unreasonable that such small detached groups might
> be obliged to move a long distance before they found land
> in which they could settle. Such, in my opinion, is a very
> likely origin of both the Pacific and Apachean speakers of
> historic times (Workman 1974c:254-255).

While the specific mechanisms and the timing of these proposed processes may
vary, these ideas build on earlier suggestions and provide a clearly causal
explanation of widespread and significant population movements.

Morlan, as part of a reexamination of sites and complexes in the south-west Yukon, conducted excavations in 1973 at MacNeish's Gladstone site on Kluane Lake. While the analysis of these data is not yet complete, Morlan has provided spatial data and analyses of five artifact clusters, or concentrations. These represent some of the first efforts at statistical approaches to spatial structure in artifact distributions, using nearest neighbor analyses. While Morlan does not discuss the effects of domain borders on these statistics, he does suggest the existence of weight stones for skin tents and of significant clustering of different artifact types (Morlan 1974b). While nearest neighbor statistics may be of use in evaluating the randomness or nonrandomness of artifacts once clusters have been determined and delimited (so that the nearest neighbor statistic is evaluated within the defined cluster), recent work by Newell and Dekin (in preparation) suggests the inappropriateness of using this approach to define artifact clusters. Nevertheless, this research marks a significant development in the sophistication of artifact distribution analyses and should cause additional attention to be focused on within-site dimension of archaeological data (and a concomitant refinement in data gathering precision --Morlan 1974b:92).

Turning to Alaska, the years since 1970 have seen a real "boom" in archaeological research, not incidentally related to the boom in federal and industrial activity within the state during this time. The impact of these activities has been to triple (or more) the number of professional archaeologists active and resident in the state (a marked change from the "summers only" researches of non-residents which characterized earlier periods) and to stimulate the intellectual development of archaeological programs. The Alaska Anthropological Association was formed to facilitate and coordinate

these developments in 1974, sponsoring meetings with sessions summarizing
Arctic research contributions and addressing issues facing archaeologists
under increased cultural resource management programs and projects in Alaska.

Initial corridor surveys in advance of the trans-Alaska oil pipeline
were conducted by the University of Alaska and Alaska Methodist University,
following a transect of Alaska from Prudhoe Bay to Valdez. Initially, the
University of Alaska assumed responsibility for survey from Livengood north
to Prudhoe Bay, with Alaska Methodist responsible from Livengood to Valdez.
However, this arrangement was soon altered in 1970 and the line responsibilities
were divided at Hogan Hill, just south of the Alaska Range. These surveys were
essentially completed by the fall of 1971, with somewhat unexpected and uneven
results. More than two hundred archaeological sites were discovered in the
northern portion and only one in the shorter southern portion (Campbell
1973:7). This disparity apparently resulted from several factors, including
facilities siting differences, little road construction in the southern
section, and an environment which was physiographically homogeneous at the
micro-scale in much of the southern transect. William Workman directed these
southern efforts, with John Cook directing the northern portion. These
extensive efforts during the summers of 1970 and 1971 resulted in a preliminary report of surveys (Cook et al. 1970; Workman 1970; Hadleigh-West and
Workman 1970) and a final report on additional work and site excavations
(Cook 1971). While these reports contain extensive data on site locations
and on excavated sites, they were published in limited editions, are out of
print and are not widely available. While it is impossible to summarize all
of their contributions in limited space, their nature makes them worthy of
consideration at some length.

While some areas had extensive linear site distributions along rivers (Sagavanirktok River Valley on the North Slope; Jim River Valley north of Prospect Creek Camp), there were several areas of unusual concentrations of sites. From the North, these included the Atigun River Valley near Galbraith Lake (see Derry 1971; Bacon 1971; Corbin 1971; and Alexander 1974), the South Fork of the Koyukuk River south of Coldfoot Camp (Holmes 1971), the Bonanza Creek area south of Prospect Creek Camp (Holmes 1974), the Kanuti Valley south of Old Man Camp (Holmes 1974), and the Tolovana Valley near Livengood Camp (Boraas 1971). In all of these areas, sites were found on eminences rising above the valley floors, whether they be glacio-fluvial features (in the Atigun and Koyukuk Valleys) or bedrock outcrops and hills (especially Bonanza, Kanuti and Tolovana). Apparently, these raised features provided good views of the surrounding terrain, are impediments to the easy travel of caribou on their migrations through the Brooks Range, or offer the most suitable well-drained areas for human activities (camping, hunting or resting?).

With the construction of the pipeline, more research was conducted as right of way and facilities clearance, again by Workman and Cook, et al. These studies involved field survey and excavation in 1974 and 1975 (see Humphrey et al. 1975-76), including extensive pioneering winter survey work in the northern portions of the line. Results of these studies are not yet published, but they will shed extensive light on all presently known cultures in interior Alaska, from Paleo-Indian to historic Athabascan. The more significant results of these surveys and excavations will be discussed below.

The early nineteen-seventies also saw extensive field work in Alaska's
Parks and federal and state properties. The National Park Service's Cooperative Park Studies Unit, under the direction of Zorro Bradley, operated out
of the University of Alaska, Fairbanks, in close coordination with the
Department of Anthropology there. Field researches were sponsored in Mt.
McKinley National Park and on other federal properties whenever the particular expertise of the National Park Service in cultural resource studies
was requested. Perhaps the most extensive studies were conducted at the
request of and in conjunction with the Native Corporations established by the
Alaska Native Claims Settlement Act. Under Section 14(h) of this act, Native
Corporations were allowed to select lands for withdrawal if they were significant to their historic or prehistoric heritage. Through the University of
Alaska's Institute of Arctic Biology in Fairbanks, the Cooperative Park
Studies Unit coordinated these researches, which saw archaeologists and
historians working out of Fairbanks in all areas of native Alaska. While
these researches did not result in coordinated reports, they did prepare
inventories of historic and prehistoric sites and statements of local histories.

Within the last few years, much attention has been focused on the
resurgence of oil exploration within Naval Petroleum Reserve No. 4, which
occupies an extensive area between Point Barrow and the western Brooks Range.
Management of this reserve and of its resources was being shifted from the
military to civilian federal land managers (principally the Bureau of Land
Management). Under existing federal laws and regulations, concern for this
area's cultural resources has caused archaeological surveys to be conducted
in advance of further development of exploration facilities on the North Slope.
We can expect that any further development of federal land will involve some
consideration of its cultural resources in the planning stages.

The State of Alaska conducted an extensive series of surveys of its parks and highways as well as in areas to be affected by federally funded projects (Alaska Office of Statewide Cultural Programs 1975a,b,c,d,e,f,g). These studies are representative of the increase in concern for cultural properties and of the cooperation between state and federal agencies towards their protection.

Lest one get the impression that these major programs dominated the Alaskan research scene, the research effort across Alaska increased dramatically and much has been reported since 1970. The research seeds planted by Laughlin and others in the Aleutians have continued to flourish, dramatically increasing our knowledge of the area. Concern for the archaeological sites on Amchitka Island and the potential impact of the atomic explosion testing program there led to the excavation of a late prehistoric Aleut midden and house depressions in 1971 by John Cook and others from the University of Alaska. The site (49-RAT-32) apparently escaped the brunt of the "pot hunting" which occurred during the extensive military occupation during World War II (Cook, Dixon and Holmes 1972:6). The midden apparently extends to ca. 0 A.D. at ca. 1.3 meters with houses cut partially into the conglomerate bedrock (Cook, Dixon and Holmes 1972:18). Following this excavation, the Cannikin detonation occurred on 6 November 1971. This site was closely monitored for impact and attempts were made to shore-up the sidewalls left from the excavation. The detonation resulted in some slope slump into the sea and the collapse of excavation sidewalls (in spite of the shoring attempts). About ten percent of the site had been excavated by Cook and an additional five percent was apparently lost irretrievably as a result of the explosion (Merrit 1972:6). No other archaeological sites on the island were significantly impacted, although several other midden sites had cracks develop near the bluff edges (Merritt 1972:7).

Christy Turner continued his studies of Aleut occupations of the Eastern Aleutians, focusing on their ability to provide baseline data on rates and directions of human evolutionary changes (1974; see especially his Table 1, summarizing a chronology of Aleutian prehistoric studies). Turner's studies have dealt with Arctic dentition and dental changes (1965, 1967), as well as with archaeological studies (1970, 1972) from which his human biological studies are derived. Research in the Akun district suggested that the strait "has been a marine, geographic, and cultural bottleneck for many centuries. It has unquestionably served to guard the cultural and genetic integrity of all other Aleut communities. Indeed, this evidence of trade supports our view that Akun Island is the 'gateway to the Aleutians'" (Turner and Turney 1974:46). These researches reinforce the developing understanding that the Aleutians were occupied by Asiatic Aleuts more than eight thousand years ago, and that the eastern end of this distribution has a more complicated history as the results of adaptive shifts, population movements and Eskimo influences.

Allen McCartney contributed to these understandings with management-oriented excavations at Izembek National Wildlife Refuge (McCartney 1971b; 1974a; Yarborough 1974) and a coastal survey from the research vessel Aleutian Tern (McCartney 1974c). The latter was conducted largely from circumnavigation of the islands, with very little on-shore visits. Results were therefore limited to those areas where surface vegetation made coastal sites distinctive. While viewing all previous efforts at island survey as biased in a conservative direction (comparing results with those from the virtually completely surveyed Amchitka Island), finding only those large and highly visible sites, McCartney ventures to list those variables of site setting.

> To summarize, site locations are determined on various islands
> by coastal height, exposure, favorable beach conditions, breaker-
> surf patterns, availability of fish, marine mammals, birds, marine
> invertebrates, kelp and other resources, volcanic proximity and
> other factors (1974c:119).

Hopefully, a rigorous approach to these attributes will allow the valid pre-

diction of resource location, facilitating the management of what has proved

to be a productive natural laboratory for the study of human evolution,

adaptation, and culture process (see McCartney 1974c:120).

The Izembek excavations included a unique whalebone house dating ca.

1000 A.D. The data suggest a single occupation demonstrating an integrated

amalgam of traits showing influences both from the Aleutians to the west and

the eastern portion of the Alaska Peninsula, which McCartney views as trans-

itional (in the sense of culturally intermediate) to them both (1974a:69).

He sees a cultural continuum along the Alaska Peninsula during that time,

flying in the face of a presumed cultural discontinuity associated with

linguistic division between Aleut and Eskimo at ca. 1000 A.D. (Dumond 1964,

1965a, 1974c). McCartney's analyses raise the possibility of discordant

variation among various dimensions of culture in the latter part of the first

millenium A.D. along the Alaska Peninsula, suggesting further work in testing

these ideas for intervening areas which are poorly known (1974a:80,82).

Jean Aigner's excellent summation (to 1971) (Aigner 1974) of the

studies of Nikolski Bay and environs provides a substantive framework on

which to discuss recent contributions to our understanding of the evolution

of Aleut culture over the last eight thousand years (Laughlin 1975a). Black

has continued to focus his researches on the geological and environmental

processes to which ancient Aleuts adapted (1974a, b; 1975, 1976):

> The aleutian Islands are now, somewhat belatedly, recognized as
> having had in the Holocene the most equable climate, the best
> year-round food supply, and the least horizontal and vertical
> displacements of coastlines from sea-level fluctuations of all
> Beringia (1976:7).

Seemingly, the Aleutians may demonstrate a long and stable (Turner, Aigner

and Richards 1974; Laughlin 1975b:105) adaptation to only moderately changing

environmental conditions, occasionally influenced by acculturation pressures

from the Alaska Peninsula (cf. McCartney 1974b:158; Aigner, Fullem, Veltre

and Veltre 1976:88). Black concluded that "Of all Beringia the Aleutians

changed least in climate and food resources during the Holocene" (Black 1976:

33). The earliest occupants seemed to have been successful (Laughlin 1975a)

(by any measure, including population and cultural "richness").

> The kind of adaptational configuration represented by the Aleuts
> presupposes a good-sized population with a diversity of fabrica-
> tional and nutritional resources and a sophisticated material
> culture. I suggest that the initial critical mass consisted of
> more than a few villages with a high degree of economic security,
> and a developed transportation system with active trade indicated
> by the Cape Chagak obsidian in the Anangula lithic industry--rather
> than the more traditional model of New World immigrants composed
> of a few founding fathers precariously eking out a meager existence
> from a hostile environment. Aleut culture began with vigor and
> robusticity. It continued to reformulate new styles, technological
> changes, to expand geographically to the natural geographic limits
> of its ecosystem and to undergo demographic alteration, all the
> while evolving in its own direction (Aigner 1974:22).

Laughlin pointed out that "The open water adaptation was established at least

8700 years ago. The ice hunting adaptation, of walrus and seals, must have

been effected even earlier because these people immigrated south along the

coast to the Umnak area of the Aleutians" (1975b:107). Perhaps other core

and blade cultures from the Bering Coast will fill the antecedent needs for

adaptations from which Aleuts, Eskimos and Chukchis descended, following

Laughlin:

113

. . .I would reiterate the suggestion that the Aleuts represent
the terminal population in a series of coastal, marine adapted
populations that (lived) around the southern coast of the Bering
Sea, and that the Eskimos and Chukchi as well are derived from
these coastal Mongoloids. The American Indians, on the other
hand, were separated from the coastal Mongoloids by their
adaptation to the interior of the Bering Land Bridge and Alaska
(Laughlin 1975b:113).

With the realization that the stability of Aleut occupation and adapt-

ation presented unusual opportunities to study adaptive processes in a

controlled situation, more formal and sophisticated methods were applied to

both environmental and cultural data (see Turner, Richards, and Turner 1974;

Yesner 1973, 1975; Yesner and Aigner 1976), both at the microenvironmental

level and at the regional level (Yesner and Aigner 1976:102,110). The

importance of regularity and seasonal scheduling to the maintenance of Aleut

populations was demonstrated for the historic and prehistoric periods (Turner,

Richards, and Turner 1974). With the disruption of seasonal patterns of

subsistence, resulting from the Russian influence, the "large population of

16,000 could not maintain itself when there was interference with the summer

economic activities, especially on the western islands. As Veniaminof....

noted, the total Aleut population low of about 1,500 stabilized around 1822-

1829. It is possible that this is about the holding capacity of the Aleutians

when seasonal marine resources cannot be fully exploited" (Turner, Richards

and Turner 1974:22).

Many of these recent developments were reported at yet another landmark

symposium of the Society for American Archaeology in 1972, published in an

extensive series of papers in Arctic Anthropology (13:2) compiled and edited

by Jean Aigner (1976a). In addition to the summarizing effect of this volume,

and the description of previously unreported burial patterns in the Aleutians

(Aigner and Veltre 1976: Aigner, Veltre, Fullem and Veltre 1976), perhaps the
most significant dimension of the reports was the increased attention to study
of spatial distributions of artifacts and the attempt to define episodes of
occupation and activity areas (Aigner and Bieber 1976; Veltre and Aigner 1976;
Aigner and Fullem 1976). These several studies used several approaches to
these general problems, ranging from the exploratory use of factor analysis
to define tool-types with which to characterize "factory loci within the
village in terms of their activity-complexity and activity-specificity"
(Veltre and Aigner 1976:60) to a study of the processes of core manufacture
and use, and the spatial differentiation of these activities (Aigner and
Fullem 1976:71,73). In general, these studies are mutually supportive, and
demonstrate the utility of more sophisticated approaches to the analysis of
the within-site dimension of these data and hold hope for the further characterization of episodes and activities as processes of deposition.

Additionally, significant data from the Sandy Beach Bay Aleut village
site spanned the hiatus between the Anangula site and the Chaluka site (which
has loomed large in assessing the cultural continuity in this area--McCartney
1974b;158, etc.). Differences which were not clinal between the Anangula and
Chaluka assemblages were interpreted (tentatively) as indications of specialized
site-functions as "an ancient base village tactical unit" (Aigner, Fullem,
Veltre and Veltre 1976:88) dating ca. 4500 B.P.

Okada and Okada (1974) reported on the 1972 excavations at Port Moller,
on the Bering Sea side of the western end of the Alaska Peninsula. They
continued the previous investigations of Weyer (1930) and others (Workman 1966a)
at the Hot Springs village site. The midden area, clearly marked by thick and

high green grass, contains the hot springs and its outflow steam. There are about 300 house depressions and ca. 60,000 square meters of midden. While the variety within this site has not been clearly evaluated, there are marked differences in house size (some of which are 10mm long) and in presence or absence of associated shell midden. Two houses were excavated, with careful attention to artifact provenience, dating at ca. 1400 B.P. and 600 B.P., respectively (Okada and Okada 1974:123). These dates demonstrate that occupations extend from ca. 3000 B.C. to relatively recent in time, but precise statements of the cultural changes during this period await further work. The authors supported Workman's (1966a:145) inference of nearest cultural affinities with the Aleutians, rather than with the Alaskan mainland (1974:123).

The affinities of these and other coastal nineteenth century occupations were reassessed by Dumond, Conton and Shields (1975), using more rigorous methods and techniques of cluster analysis to assess relative similarities among collectio In general, one seriation which could be derived from this analysis was indicative of a ". . .linear relationship of the units that accords closely with the geograph position of the sites whence the collections were drawn" (Dumond, Conton and Shiel 1975:58), with Port Moller occupying an unusual position at the apex of this distribution. Like other attempts at distinguishing Eskimo and Aleut affinities by analysis of technology, the conclusions were somewhat ambivalent, indicating that present data suggest a cline (or clines), rather than a dichotomy along the Alaska Peninsula. They concluded that ". . .there is no reason to reject the historical literature suggesting that the westernmost Eskimo settlements were east of Port Moller" but that ". . .it is a mistake to expect to find that any material cultural boundary between Eskimos and Aleuts has ever been as sharp as the cleavage between their languages" (1975:58) (see also Dumond 1974c:4; Laughlin 1951b).

116

These conclusions were part of the debate regarding the location of a presumed Eskimo/Aleut boundary, placed west of Port Moller by McCartney (1969), but modified by his investigations at Izembek to suggest ". . .that the very notion of a boundary location anywhere on the Peninsula is questionable in any but the broadest terms" and that ". . .both regions display differences along their lengths and together form a continuum at least during the late prehistoric period" (McCartney 1974a:81).

These issues attracted great attention during recent scholarly meetings and discussions, calling into question the appropriateness of historic ethnic categories up-streamed into the prehistoric period. "The Aleut-Eskimo language stocks may in fact be divergent but can we detect such divergence archaeologically? I question that we can accurately derive material culture, physical type and language from one another" (McCartney 1974a:82). If Aleuts were descended from those early occupants of the Aleutians (see Laughlin and others), and if Small Tool bearers were ancestral Eskimos (see Dumond and others, especially for southwestern Alaska), then the significant change in cultural continuities before ca. 2000 B.C. in this region (which may prove to be a product of discontinuous data) leaves open questions of the cultural affinities of Kodiak Island and the south coast of the Alaska at that time. Whether there is a very early cultural continuum along the north Pacific rim (Dumond 1974c:4; Henn 1975), whether the proto-Koniag descended from early Aleutian populations (Dumond 1971a), or whether the proto-Koniag were descendents of some other people not related to either Eskimos or Aleuts (Clark 1974b:44,45) remains a subject of controversy, not yet resolved to anyone's apparent satisfaction. With Clark's recent evaluations of phylogenetic cultural and linguistic relations, based in part on McGhee's rethinking of Artic Small Tool relations (1974b) and Dumond's hypotheses on

Eskimo sources from the Alaska Peninsula (1972c), the way is cleared for a
complete examination of what we actually know about the culture history of this
region, and of the Arctic in general. Clark basically eliminates the Arctic Small
Tool tradition from a direct ancestral relationship to "Eskimo" development
as the original North American carrier of Eskimo adaptation and language (1976a:3)
seeking its origins at an earlier time and specific links in a chain whose base
lies in the Alaska Peninsula. Clark suggests that "There are two alternatives
for Aleut-Eskimo divergence: on the Land Bridge 11,000 years ago or on the
Alaska Peninsula 8000-9000 years ago" (1976a:10). While the picture of intervenin
developments is unclear, Clark suggests that a Pacific-Alaska Peninsula co-traditi
(comprising Takli Birch, Kachemak and Western Peninsula-Pacific traditions) develo
into Norton culture which subsequently moved northwards (Clark 1976a:19) as a
clearly identifiable "eskimo" culture. While the complexities surrounding the
origins and developments of Choris culture (and in particular, its affinities
with Denbigh and Norton) are presently insurmountable, Clark sees Norton as
developing largely independently from Choris, contributing to the influences
which apparently led to the breakdown of the efflorescence of Small Tool tradition
along the Bering coast (1976a:30-34). In short, Clark sees Eskimo origins reflect
in a major movement of people from the Alaska Peninsula northwards at about
3000 B.P. (1976a:33,34). "I visualize this movement as having drawn cultural
elements from the entire Pacific-Peninsula co-tradition discussed earlier,
although most of the people directly involved in a migration probably came from
the Alaska Peninsula rather than Kodiak Island or Cook Inlet. This spread of
ideas, lifeways, techniques, and people persisted over a number of centuries"
(1976a:34).

We must recognize the highly speculative nature of Clark's ideas on these
matters, as he does. However, it is characteristic of the state of the interpreti

art at this time (see Dumond 1974b) to have such dramatically different ideas
being put forth for scrutiny and further testing. I believe this to be a result
of the rather loose weave of culture history presently available, such that its
warp and weft provide numerous opportunities for the insertion of different
organizing threads. With the recognition of the increasingly complex picture
which emerges as data gaps are filled and of the rapidity with which cultural
migrations occur across vast distances (e.g., Thule, Arctic Small Tool horizon,
etc.), new configurations of culture history are being formed and considered as
alternates to "standard" interpretations. While Clark's ideas may not stand the
tests of time, discussion and new data, they are welcome as they prevent us from
mindlessly perpetuating old structures and they cause us to undertake critical
evaluations of the framework in which we attempt to insert rapidly increasing
amounts of new data.

Clark and Milan also summarized the results of their limited reconnaissances
on Kodiak Island of sites dating to the second millenium A.D. These sites
contributed to an appreciation of variety in site content of the Koniag phase
(with ceramic and aceramic facies). It is most important to note Clark's
assessment of recent and continuing impact on the integrity of these coastal
sites, resulting from construction of facilities and from chronic erosion
which follows the subsidence of 1964.

> Although only partial surveys of Kodiak and other areas on the Pacific
> Coast of Alaska have been undertaken following the subsidence of 1964,
> I would not hesitate to say that the ensuing erosion eventually will
> destroy up to 50 percent of the archaeological potential of the Kodiak
> Island group. The outer part of the Kenai Peninsula likewise is very
> seriously threatened (Clark and Milan 1974:120).

Hopefully, increased federal responsibility for its cultural resources will result
in further efforts to save and manage those important resources which remain.

Robert Ackerman continued his excavations at the GHB 2 site at Ground Hog
Bay on Icy Strait about 40 miles west of Juneau in 1971 and 1973, strenghthening

his earlier conclusions (1968a). Three stratigraphically distinctive occupations dating from ca. 150 to 10,000 years have been examined. The latest occupation is a late prehistoric· phase spanning ca. 900 to 150 B.P., with artifacts known ethnographically from the Northwest Coast. The earliest component is dated at 10,180 $\pm$ 800 B.P. (WSU-412), 9220 $\pm$ 80 B.P. (SI-2112), and 9130 $\pm$ 130 B.P. (I-6304) (Ackerman 1975b, 1974:3). "Our recovery from this early level is unfortunately meager, consisting of two obsidian bifacial fragments, a water rolled chert scraper, and three flakes" (1974:3). The bulk of the sample from GHB 2 is from the middle component, with dates from 8880 $\pm$ 125 B.P. (I-7057) to 4180 $\pm$ 65 B.P. (SI-2109) (1975b:3; 1974:3). "From this middle zone, we recovered microcores and blades, macrocores, flakes, choppers, scraping and cutting tools based on flakes, bifacial fragments and detritus" (1974:3). Perhaps the most distinctive (and the most studied) dimension of this collection is the microcore technology. Chord length (see Morlan 1970c) is apparently a key variab[le] with chert and obsidian microcores having a short chord length similar to those from Healy Lake and the Denali complex and the argillite/andesite cores having a longer chord length similar to those from the Lehman complex of British Columbia (1974:10). Ackerman describes these artifacts in some detail, concludin[g] in part that while these cores are comparable to those from Alaskan early sites, several stages in their preparation represent a Levallois-like technique (1975b). Experimental replication of these cores by Jeff Flennikan (Washington State University) confirms this inference, leading Ackerman to suggest that other northern collections may contain evidence of the Levallois technique being used as a step in biface production. Perhaps one of the more significant results of these studies is the indication that a microcore and blade industry has great time depth in the Western Arctic (to ca. 8000 B.P.) and that finely detailed analyses of attributes may be necessary if we are to use microcores and microblades in any system of cultural identification or as any indication of cultural affinity.

Moving northwestward to Bristol Bay, Washington State University's interest in this area continued and major studies followed the earlier work of Ackerman and others. While earlier publications covered the ethnohistory of this area (Ackerman 1970; Koch 1968), Richard Ross applied matrix analyses to the Norton components of the Chagvan Beach area north of Cape Newenham (ca. 500 B.C. to ca. A.D. 1000). These studies demonstrated the utility of matrix analysis to provide a linear arrangement of units (houses) which provided the basis (along with radiocarbon dates) of a chronological sequence spanning this time period. The dendrogram produced allowed division of this sequence into phases which related to cultural developments in southwestern Alaska. While Chagvan I is somewhat enigmatic, but pre-dates Norton, the Chagvan Beach II is representative of the Norton efflorescence (500 B.C. to A.D. 250), with similarities along the Bering Coast and the Alaska Peninsula.

> As a result of the examination of external relationships I see Chagvan Beach II as part of a cultural manifestation which is wide spread geographically and which occupies a niche in time around 2000 years ago. Utilizing standard practice of names, the whole complex would probably be referred to as Norton and/or variations thereof. There are strong relationships between assemblages at this time depth from Point Hope to the Alaskan [sic] Peninsula. Each of the assemblages have local characteristics thus none enough to suggest a very wide spread and persistent culture (Ross 1971:243-244).

Chagvan Beach III is apparently a continuation of Norton, but with other cultural influences (a situation which Ross believes is paralleled in the cultural sequence on the Brooks River of the Alaska Peninsula--Dumond 1969a).

It is difficult in the extreme to summarize the extensive research contributions of James VanStone along the Nushagak River. Following initial field work in the mid-nineteen sixties, VanStone concentrated his analytic

121

and publishing efforts on the ethnohistory and later prehistory of the
Nushagak River. His research, beginning with an ethnography/ethnohistory
(1967), is a classic example of anthropological scholarship and methodology.
Fieldiana Anthropology (publications of the Field Museum of Natural History
in Chicago) has carried the brunt of this work beginning with an annotated
ethnohistorical bibliography of the Nushagak (1968a), followed closely by
a series of site reports which combine archaeological research results
with ethnohistoric data (Tikchik, 1968b; Akulivikchuk, 1970a: Nushagak,
1972; and Kijik, with Joan Townsend, 1970). While the archaeological data
themselves were often disappointing because of their low frequency, the
bulk of the flesh of interpretation resulted from the ethnohistoric and
historic data which VanStone brought to bear. In general, trade goods
were a rare occurrence in the late nineteenth century sites along the river,
both Tanaina and Eskimo. Those that were found were of the sort which could
be used by "both white men and Eskimos. This is in contrast to many areas
of North America where certain artifacts were made specifically for trade
with Indians. It would appear that relatively few of this latter type of
trade goods were used in the Alaska trade (1970a:99). There was also a
striking continuity of artifact function through this period, in spite of
the introduction of new raw materials from which to make artifacts. "Like
Tikchik and Crow Village, the collection of artifacts from Akulivikchuk
indicates more than anything else, a basic continuity with emphasis on the
retention of traditional forms. The fact that the village was less than 100
miles from the most important center of contact intensity in all southwestern
Alaska, appears to have mattered very little indeed" (1970a:102).

Tikchik, Crow Village and Akulivikchuk exhibit all the characteristics of a riverine Eskimo configuration. One might expect that of the three, Akulivikchuk would show stronger ties with the coast, but this is not the case. We can be certain that the presence of the Nushagak post drew the residents of Akulivikchuk to Nushagak Bay at least once a year and that while they were there, they traded for coastal products. And yet, as at Crow Village and Tikchik, coastal subsistence techniques are not reflected in the recovered material culture from the site. This would seem to indicate that, unlike the Kobuk River Eskimos, those of the interior Nushagak villages did not actually take part to any great extent, aside perhaps from fishing, in the various coastal subsistence activities. They only traded with their coastal neighbors for the products of such activities (1970a:109).

VanStone's disappointment at the limited data available on material goods, both from archaeological and historical research, is exemplified as follows: "It is impossible to escape the conclusion, however, that whatever the reasons, both the ethnographic and archaeological collections reveal disappointingly little concerning the specifics of changing material culture at the settlement [Nushagak]. Without such information, it is virtually impossible to make meaningful comparisons with the upriver villages" (1972:84). However, VanStone's effective combination of historic, ethnographic and archaeologic research will remain a standard for future work in Alaska for a very long time.

In recent years, relatively little archaeological research has been conducted on the Bering Seas islands or adjacent coasts, and published information is scarce. In fact, most of the published work is based on research conducted during the late sixties. Bruce Lutz conducted an extensive analysis of lithic variation within Norton culture sites, focusing on his own researches at Ungalaqliq (1969, 1970, 1973b). His in-depth lithic typology is a contribution of explicit precision in artifact morphology, using statistical tests to demonstrate degrees of separation of morphological categories. This is one of the few explicit attempts at analyzing the within-culture among-site dimension of archaeological variety, using a typology developed explicitly for that purpose. One difference is in the attempt to resolve fine distinctions in technological variation, at the expense of breaking up categories which might be useful for other purposes at higher levels of abstraction (Lutz 1972).

John Bockstoce conducted excavations at Cape Nome, emphasizing the remains from the Norton and Birnirk periods (1973b). Bockstoce chose this area because of its intermediate character between the deeper waters of Bering Strait and the shallower (almost estuarian) waters of Norton Sound. "I thought, therefore, that excavation at Cape Nome might reveal changes through time in its residents' use of resources and changes in resource availability. It seemed likely that these changes, if they had occurred, might be related to climate" (1973a:794). Bockstoce was able to differentiate apparent subsistence changes during the Norton occupation using artifactual and site location information. Based in part on the presence of float hunting apparatus in Birnirk (absent in Norton) and on the distribution of known sites with regard to fishing vs. sea mammal subsistence possibilities, Bockstoce suggested that Norton sites were located where caribou, fish and sea mammals could be found (seasonally), with a requirement for caribou hunting and summer fishing (since summer sealing was not as effective). "Permanent coastal Birnirk settlement, on the other hand, was possible in many areas under the conditions that were intolerable to Norton settlement. Use of the float apparatus provided a food resource in spring and summer that could not be reliably exploited with Norton technology" (1973a:800). ". . .the superior technology of the Birnirk culture allowed its bearers to survive on one principal food resource, when other resources may have been minimal, a severity that the bearers of Norton culture, with a more limited technology, could not tolerate" (1973a:800). Bockstoce correlates the demise of Norton on the coast with an inferred climatic change ca. A.D. 300-400 (Dekin 1972b), suggesting that associated resource distribution changes (especially fish and caribou) led to adaptive changes in Bering Coast populations and a replacement of Norton by Birnirk at Cape Nome.

In 1972 natives of St. Lawrence Island discovered the naturally frozen body of an adult Eskimo woman which had eroded from a coastal archaeological site during a storm. The body was re-buried in frozen ground until the following year when Zorro Bradley, National Park Service anthropologist at the University of Alaska, Fairbanks, brought the body to Fairbanks for analysis. Muscle tissue was radiocarbon dated ca. 1600 years B.P., being correlated with the Old Bering Sea phase on St. Lawrence Island of the early centuries A.D. An autopsy was performed by Michael Zimmerman, who determined that the woman died when trapped by a landslide or earthquake and suffocated. She had suffered from coronary artery disease and anthracosis (from smoke and soot inhalation), demonstrating that air pollution is no recent phenomenon (Zimmerman and Smith 1975:835).

The body had extensive tattooing on the backs of both arms, hands and fingers, all of which was in Old Bering Sea style (Smith and Zimmerman 1975:436). In contrast to other evidence from Ipiutak pendants (VanStone and Lucier 1974), there were no marks on the chin or cheek. However, in both cases, the line and dot technique predominated. We are indeed privileged that all concerned with this find recognized the remarkable scientific opportunity which it provided and which has been so well realized by Zimmerman and Smith.

Dennis Stanford reported on finds near Point Barrow on Walakpa Bay (1971, 1972). While his major research dealt with the later Eskimo occupations leading up to Thule and modern Eskimo (1972), his paper in 1971 contained much information of significance to Arctic Small Tool and American Paleo-Arctic

125

traditions. The Kahurok Site was apparently a major cache of bifacially flaked cores, similar to those described by Anderson from the Akmak site (Anderson 1970b) (in point of fact, nearly half of the artifacts from this site were such cores). "Most probably it was a lithic station where occupants of the area cached cores which could be obtained and worked when the occasion demanded" (Stanford 1971:2). However, the remainder of the artifacts were somewhat equivocal in their affinities:

> As may be noted from the above artifact descriptions the Karhurok assemblage is quite similar to Akmak. It is also similar to the Driftwood Creek Complex for which large poly-hedral cores and lanceolate projectile points were described (Humphrey 1970). A relationship between Karhurok and the Chindadn complex of Healy Lake is not inconceivable (1971:5).

Stanford identified the Walakpa Phase of the Arctic Small Tool tradition, thought to be transitional between Denbigh and Choris, dating at 300-1400 B.C. (Stanford 1971:6). The Coffin Site is perhaps best described as Denbigh with ground slate and pottery, although the slate is extremely rare.

> In conclusion I submit that the ceramic Denbigh discoveries at the Walakpa and the Coffin Sites represent a transition between Denbigh and Choris. The hallmark of this cultural change would be the utilization of pottery and ground slate, with the underlying mechanism being the change to a colder climate (1971:13).

These data are beginning to fill in the variety inherent in developmental sequences and to suggest widespread cultural similarities during several "hey-days" of cultural distribution along the Bering Straits coast—American Paleo-Arctic, Late-Denbigh and Norton. With these gaps being filled in, we will be able to study contemporaneous variety, looking at the diversity within similar adaptations.

Douglas Anderson reported the results of surveys conducted in the sixties (1961, 1964, 1965 and 1966) of the Noatak River drainage in northwest Alaska (1972). In spite of the rather limited nature of the sites encountered

126

(many were "chipping stations" near local sources of chert, while others were "lookouts" where various flaking activities were conducted while observing the landscape for caribou—1972:66), Anderson suggested that they were representative of ". . .eight or nine different groups of assemblages, each from a different time period" (1972:66) ranging from American Paleo-Arctic to recent Eskimo. Several assemblages have microblade cores seemingly related to both the Campus site and the Denbigh Flint complex, which Anderson sees as representing "transitional American Paleo-Arctic and Arctic Small Tool components" (1972:66), which is obviously suggestive of a linear ancestral relationship between the two.

However, these results and those which follow from similar surveys demonstrate the necessity for a rethinking of methodology and data publication from the Arctic, as the difficulty in fitting the data structure encountered into a meaningful scheme of the prehistory of the region suggests that we need to evaluate first the integrity of the activity sets encountered (what some have come to call "behavioral episodes") and then build these blocks into meaningful analytic units at a higher order. This will be difficult, if not impossible, as long as we rely exclusively on a "guide-fossil" approach to these data. Thus clusters themselves deserve scrutiny as being the results of associated and integrated behaviors, and their character requires definition and publication, even if presumed diagnostics are lacking. Many of us have jumped rather quickly from artifacts to components of occupation, without evaluating the integrity of artifact clusters and comparing these units as remnants of behavioral episodes. With Anderson's data from the Noatak, it appears that they may represent many different (yet comparable) behavioral episodes of occupation, which are difficult for us to deal with comparatively because we

127

lack a frame of reference at this level of analysis (cf. Anderson 1968b:397).

Anderson's survey does point out that there is considerable difference in the degree to which the Noatak is affected by coastal cultural processes, as opposed to those of the interior, through time.

> During some periods there seems also to have been a cultural separation between the lower and the upper half of the Noatak drainage. Assemblages of the upper part (including the middle and upper zones) were closely affiliated with those from the Anaktuvuk Pass region and areas southeast of there, but unrelated to those nearer the Noatak river mouth or adjacent coast. . . . It is interesting that a cultural distinction between the western and eastern tundra areas has also been noted by Hall (1970[c]) for the late prehistoric times, and perhaps similar factors may prove to explain both cases.

> Another interesting point is that some periods represented by the archaeology of the coast are not represented in the interior. One of these is the time immediately prior to the occupation of the modern Eskimo. In this light Irving's observation that between about 500 A.D. and the middle of the present millenium there was "an interval of sparse activity" (Irving 1964:319) is born out by our survey. It may be that the factors that account for this are ecological, and that times of sparse human activity in the interior reflect periods of lower caribou population density (1972:100).

Anderson suggests further research to elucidate not only those reasons why people have lived here (or behaved) where they did, but why those changes characteristic of northwestern Alaska as a whole occurred (1972:100).

In 1968, Donald Clark, of the National Museum of Man, National Museums of Canada, surveyed sites on the height of land between the upper Kobuk River and the Koyukuk River around Norutak Lake (an area previously visited briefly by Giddings in 1963--Campbell 1964a). Seven sites were located within about a quarter mile square along the north shore of the lake, and while most of these contained relatively few artifacts, Site 4 (SeIg-4; Borden 1952a) contained evidence of several (mixed) components (1974a:11-12), albeit in convoluted horizons. The complicated associational data suggest that little can be ascertained regarding the site's internal structure of components, but that the presence of several cultural units may be demonstrated (especially in the near-surface horizons), including Denbigh, Norton and Kobuk Eskimo (1974a: 14-19).

In 1970, William Patton and Thomas Miller reported the location of a geological source of obsidian in the Koyukuk River Valley, southeast of the village of Hughes (Patton and Miller 1970). Donald Clark and Annette McFadyen Clark conducted field reconnaissance of this source, in conjunction with their continuing work on Koyukuk Athabascan archaeology and ethnography (see above). This source "consists of mid-Tertiary age perlitic ash beds in which the obsidian occurs as 'Apache tears' or small bombs. The ash beds have disintegrated wherever they are exposed... Obsidian pebbles also were found in the gravelly soil that mantles Batzatiga and they occur secondarily in stream and lakeshore gravels of the region" (Clark 1972a:3). Numerous sites were found in the vicinity of the source, with artifact scatters and clusters located on raised "flat spots, benches and knolls along the ridges. . . and [on] lake shores" (Clark 1972a:4). Once again, these data proved difficult to categorize, even for descriptive purposes, and the preliminary reporting of these artifacts is best seen as treating them in their entirety (Clark 1972a:15). The more significant finds included 16 fluted points of obsidian found in a cluster of related sites near the top of a small ridge (Clark and Clark 1975:31). These artifacts are described individually and the various hypotheses relating these Alaskan fluted complexes to those from the lower portions of North American were discussed, but no conclusions could be supported with these data (Clark and Clark 1975:35). The fact remains that these artifacts must be discussed as isolated entities not related to larger analytic groups or even more than loosely among themselves. It was apparently not possible to discuss their affinities with artifact clusters or with other artifacts found in the same

129

locations (for example, three sites also contained associated side-notched points), in part because of "Interference produced by excessive flake accumulations and a preponderance of ubiquitous broken semifinished bifaces [which] hinders our recognition of discrete cultural assemblages" (Clark and Clark 1975:33).

From a regional perspective, Clark was able to describe a sequence of occupations from the Koyukuk River, based largely on the presence of diagnostic artifacts whose sequence and significance were established elsewhere (Clark 1974d). These include: Paleo-Indian (fluted points); leafshaped, lanceolate and oblanceolate points; microblade and core industries; Tuktu complex; Hahanudan of Ipiutak influence; the Lake 324 complex; later prehistoric materials; and protohistoric and early historic houses (1974d:34-39). However, once again, we are faced with the difficulty that this is largely a listing of the presumed diagnostic artifacts found in this area. It is impossible to weave any larger comparative units from these data (a fact recognized by Clark when he titles his article "Filaments of Prehistory. . .", with the exception of historic houses and presumably homogeneous clusters, not yet fully described in print. Clark's own summation of the results of this pioneering work in the Koyukuk river valley are an appropriate statement:

> A preliminary periodization of Koyukuk prehistory has been presented in terms of eight units, spanning probably 10,000 and possibly as many as 14,000 years. With further work on the Koyukuk River several of these units will be redefined and new complexes will be added. Also, during some periods the upper, middle and lower parts of the Koyukuk system may have had regionally distinct prehistories. In terms of populations, the Koyukuk is seen as a dynamic area, and the numerous prehistoric culture units there may represent nearly as many distinct peoples. Some of these are significant, in a broader context, to the prehistory of the New World (Clark 1974d:42).

130

Several houses dating from the late nineteenth century were also excavated by the Clarks in 1968 (Clark and Clark 1974). These are of interest because their structure may be compared with both historic and ethnographic data of basically the same period. One house was excavated at each of three two-house settlements, representing a rather uniform "semi-subterranean four-center-post type" (Clark and Clark 1974:29), with entrance tunnel cut to floor depth or below. Artifact distribution structure was compared with activity structures of the historic period, reflecting well the seating of females to the rear of the houses, but not clearly showing distinctively male areas mid-way along each side (1974:36). In addition to demonstrating the contributions which ethnographic and historic data can make to archaeological interpretations, the Clarks make a strong plea for the inclusion of archaeological studies as major components of salvage ethnography work and ethnographic reconstruction from the perspective of the ethnographer.

As a by-product of geological research, eleven sites were located along ridge crests south and southeast of Utopia in the Koyukuk drainage.

> The artifacts described herein are treated on a site-by-site basis because consideration of them as a single collection suggests a cultural correspondence between sites which cannot be supported by available data. These surface collections must be treated as being mixed both temporally and culturally, especially in view of disturbances by frost action and lack of a stratigraphic framework, so that even contemporaneity of artifacts within each site is very questionable (Reger and Reger 1972:28).

With this caution, the data were rather completely described (complete with site and provenience) and the fragmentary points related to others with similar attributes found and described by Clark (above) and others. They explain the site locations as indicating "utilization of the sites as outlooks for spotting game. That all projectile points are broken and consist mainly of point bases

131

indicates the sites were stations where projectiles were re-tipped following breakage" (Reger and Reger 1972:34). Once again we are indebted to geological research for contributions to the archaeology of Alaska (cf., Patton and Miller 1970; Solecki 1950b; Thompson 1948).

The predominance of surface sites in interior Alaska has led to an increased search for stratigraphically distinctive occupations, recently revealed in the stratified Dry Creek site. Charles E. Holmes, then a graduate student at the University of Alaska, discovered archaeological deposits in stratified loess overlying outwash gravels on Dry Creek in the Nenana River Valley north of Mt. McKinley in 1973. Testing of this site by W. Roger Powers (University of Alaska, Fairbanks) in 1974 revealed four archaeological horizons separated by loess and sand (aeolian) radiocarbon dated to before 10,000 years B.P. The lower horizons contained faunal remains, some of which are now extinct. Powers excavated additional portions of this site in 1976, leading to a consolidation of two intermediate strata into one, thus demonstrating three occupations (Smith 1977:32). While relatively few data are presently available from these excavations, there appear to be specific artifact and chronological comparisons with the Chindadn, Denali and early Athabascan notched-point complexes represented at other sites in the Alaska interior. These occupations date from ca. 10,000 B.P., 9000 B.P. and 4000 B.P. (respectively) (Smith 1977:69). While the analysis of these materials is presently underway, preliminary work by Smith has demonstrated the unreliability of the present art of obsidian hydration dating and pointed the way for needed technical research in this area. The 1976 data indicate the potential for dividing the components into activity-specific flaking events, thus the Dry Creek site will be significant for the definition of sequential occupations of this area

132

and for the definition of discrete episodes within each occupation. When taken in conjunction with present and planned environmental and geological analyses, Dry Creek demonstrates considerable research potential towards an understanding of early ecological relationships in interior Alaska.

Extensive multi-disciplinary research stemming from the potential of the Dry Creek site has been conducted by the University of Alaska along the northern front of the Alaska range, but the results are not generally available. Survey in the Nenana Gorge resulted in the excavation of several sites by David Plaskett, supported by the Geist fund of the University of Alaska. Again, these results are unpublished, but the discovery of pottery at this location was unexpected and full results should provide useful information regarding the later prehistoric distributions of pottery in interior Alaska (Plaskett 1976). Of further note, these Nenana Gorge sites had been impacted by previous construction along the gorge, principally that of the Fairbanks-Anchorage highway and the Alaska Railroad, which cut directly through one of the sites, leading to its discovery.

One of the more significant contributions of recent research has been the substantiation of the Denali complex, first suggested by Hadleigh-West (1967b; see above), and now found throughout interior Alaska after 10,000 B.P. Hadleigh-West continued his investigations in the Alaska range, with extensive research in the Tangle Lakes region (1974, 1975) leading to its designation as a district on the National Register of Historic Places. Denali complex occupations in this area are associated with raised beaches and buried soils which contribute to the dating at between 10,000 and 8000 B.P. (Hadleight-West 1975:78-79), corroborated by other sites (Dry Creek, Campus, etc.) and by comparable complexes at Onion Portage (see above; Hadleigh-West 1975:79-80; Hosley and Mauger 1967; Mauger 1970).

133

However, the definition of the Denali complex as other than a series of associated traits awaits further work, given the complicated nature of the surface sites from which it has been defined (Hadleigh-West 1974:217, 219). Other complexes of artifacts from sites in the Tangle Lakes area are seen as workshops, specialized inventories, or full cultural complexes (Hadleigh-West 1974:220-221) of a very early time: ". . .in the long sequence of occupation now seen in the more than 150 sites thus far discovered in the Tangle Lakes, I take this to be the basal series and furthermore to represent the leavings of some of the earliest people in Alaska" (1974:221). Generally, these rather crude unifaces and flake tools were seen by Hadleigh-West to belong to a ". . .generalized, late Middle Paleolithic stone industry" with a provisional combination into the Amphitheater Mountain Complex (Hadleigh-West 1974:224-225), supporting Muller-Beck's ideas of New World migrations by technologically Middle Paleolithic peoples (Muller-Beck 1966). With the designation of this area as a nationally significant historic area, perhaps further research in support of cultural resource management decisions will elucidate these alternative interpretations and clarify the alternatives recognized by Hadleigh-West.

Further work in the Lake Minchumina area was conducted by Charles Holmes, of the University of Alaska, in 1972, following earlier work by Hosley along the upper Kuskokwim (1967: see above). The Minchumina site lies on land owned by the University of Alaska and was first discovered by Hosley and named the White's Roadhouse Site. A single radiocarbon date is ca. A.D. 800 from a well-defined hearth (with caribou and small mammal bones) (Holmes 1974a:100). The association of microblades, burins and lanceolate points at this date is in accord with the late prehistoric levels at Healy Lake and the pre-midden levels at Dixthada, but differences with the Birches sites on the

134

other end of Lake Minchumina (Hosley 1967) at a somewhat later date (ca. A.D. 1300) suggest a later immigration (Holmes 1974a:102). Holmes suggests that this area has the potential for revealing a long cultural sequence for this rather poorly known area of interior Alaska.

On the other side of the Alaska range, in the Matanuska valley, Glenn Bacon continued earlier investigations by Dixon and Johnson (1972) on Long Lake, where a series of localities are found on glacial and terrace features. Locality one is apparently representative of the Denali complex with wedge-shaped microblade cores, bifaces, and microblades, etc. (Bacon 1975). Bacon suggests that these relate to the later phases of the Denali complex, including the Minchumina finds (above) and those from the upper levels of the Village site at Healy Lake. As such, they represent the southernmost finds related to Denali and are suggestive of a rather long and widespread tradition. With further work in this area, it should be possible to sub-divide this long tradition into meaningful cultural units and to rely more closely on stylistic and technical attributes for comparative studies.

Additional work south of the Alaska range was conducted by Anne Shinkwin along the Copper River at Dakah De'Nin's Village, near Chitina (1974, 1975), where a nineteenth century Atna village was excavated in 1973. Tree ring dates of 1816-1838 were obtained by analyses of David Plaskett of the University of Alaska, which is supported by the absence of historic mention by early explorers. The village was apparently a main winter settlement, with semi-subterranean houses, sweat baths and caches. While horizontal distributional analyses of the within-structure dimension of artifacts has not been particularly rewarding ("At most, it can be said that the artifacts are concentrated along the eastern and western sections of the houses which may represent remains of activities conducted in front of the sleeping areas"—1974:63), there appeared to be significant variation in the frequency of copper artifacts among houses, which led Shinkwin to question the egalitarian picture presented by the ethnohistory of the area, suggesting that status differentiation may have meant that some families had no copper at all (1974:63). Pursuing this question with informants, she determined that "although anyone could collect copper, it 'belonged' to the chief" (1974:63), demonstrating the complementary nature of archaeological and ethnographic methodology in studying ethnohistoric problems (cf. VanStone 1955b).

Salvage excavations conducted by William Workman, Alaska Methodist University, for the Alyeska Pipeline Service company helped to round out our understanding of late prehistoric Ahtna subsistence patterns. Site GUL 077 is located in the upper Copper drainage on the Gulkana River and was partially excavated to allow use of the gravel deposits for pipeline construction. The site consisted mainly of clustered storage pits associated with a seasonal camp and a meagre artifact assemblage, dominated by copper projectile points, knives, perforators and ornaments. Stone tools were mostly burins and scrapers, while bone artifacts included barbed points and pins. A single winter house (unexcavated) and the faunal analysis suggested a late-winter/early spring occupation by small family groups during a period of severe and difficult subsistence (Workman 1976). Workman suggested dating ca. A.D. 1500-1700, prior to the introduction of European or Asian trade items. Several finds were worthy of mention, given the marginal state of our knowledge of the area, including sweatbath, cremation and birchbark baskets. We are fortunate that recent developments in federal historic preservation requirements prevented the further degradation of Alaska's heritage and that Alyeska acted responsibly in providing for the salvage of these data from an area very poorly known to date.

Further north along the route of the oil pipeline at the headwaters of the Gulkana River in Isabel Pass (Fish Creek), additional salvage excavations at a similar geomorphic feature (a glacial moraine overlooking a salmon river) were conducted in 1975 by the University of Alaska's Alyeska Archaeology Project (directed by John Cook). The Fish Creek Site (GUL-065) was excavated by Curtis Wilson under the direction of Raymond Newell and Wayne Wiersum. Three artifact clusters were excavated, containing microblades and cores, Donnelly burins, and side-notched, corner-notched and lanceolate projectile points. While the full analysis is not yet completed, information of importance to the understanding of behavioral clustering and variety in the Denali and Tangle Lakes complexes as well as more recent Athabascan complexes should be obtained (Newell and Wiersum in preparation). Further, these data have led to the refinement of techniques for establishing the behavioral integrity of analytic units within archaeological sites (Newell and Dekin in preparation).

As part of the increasing federal responsibility for managing cultural resources as one aspect of its long term planning processes, Linda Finn-Yarborough conducted an assessment of the Delta Land Management Study area (from the Alaska Range to the Yukon-Tanana uplands along the Tanana River) (Finn-Yarborough 1975b), noting 78 sites including 17 previously unknown sites. These sites represent a cross-section from historic to sites of unknown prehistoric age in a variety of locations, including numerous sites in lowland or upland spruce-hardwood forest overlooking lower brush-muskeg-bog areas. The majority of these were located adjacent to lakes or clear water streams (in contrast to the silty glacial-fed streams of the Alaska range). This study built on the earlier work of Cook et al. 1970 and Dixon

137

and Johnson 1972, essentially compiling management data rather than excavating
further samples from known sites. It is typical of management-related
studies which should be more prevalent as federal agencies expand their
planning considerations to cultural resources (cf. Dixon 1975b).

Additional information on the Campus site (on the University of Alaska's
Fairbanks campus) was compiled by Jeffrey Mauger in his study of Donnelly
Burins (Mauger 1970; see Hosley and Mauger 1967). In summation, these burins
are made on flakes (with a minimum of alteration on their original flake
surfaces), have an edge-struck burin facet right angles to the plane of the
flake, and have a unifacially flaked concavity adjacent to the point at which
the burin blow was struck (this is morphologically similar to "spokeshave"
concavities found on lithics in other areas). Replication experiments
suggested that these spalls were removed by direct percussion (1970:26) and
an analysis of "use flaking" suggested that these artifacts were used as
scrapers (1970:33), with wear from the ventral surface onto the burin scar.
The fact that some of these artifacts do not demonstrate this flake pattern
is seen as evidence for discard of the burin after it became too small to be
used efficiently (however, this smaller than usual size is not demonstrated
in this analysis). One of the major contributions of this paper is the
illustration and description of these burins, facilitated by photography
after coating with ammonian chloride smoke (Appendix B). While the interpretation that these are functional scrapers has widespread acceptance, it is
also possible that the burin spall results from the specific use of the adjacent
concavity as a spokeshave knife-scraper. Further intensive analysis of the
macroscopic and microscopic attributes of these artifacts, following the
directions indicated by Mauger in this analysis, will be necessary in order

138

to ascertain the various uses to which these burins were put.

North of Fairbanks along the oil pipeline, further survey and excavations were conducted by Alan Boraas (1971) as part of the University of Alaska's Alyeska Archaeology Project. An extensive series of sites on the tops of eroded ridges at Livengood were located and partially excavated, as were sites at the Tolovana river crossings (later excavated by David Derry) and the Hess Creek crossing (Boraas 1971-a Denali site with Donnelly burins).

The sites near the Tolovana River were located on or near outcrops of Livengood Chert, seemingly combining terrain observational characteristics with access to the characteristic black chert (Boraas 1971:438) (some of these sites were first reported in 1964 by M.A. Kegler, of the University of Alaska). The work by Boraas was principally site survey, resulting in numerous documented site locations, but limited excavation. However, artifacts characteristic of the Tuktu site from Anaktuvuk Pass and of the Denali complex were located and further work was conducted by David Derry in 1975. However, his death in an automobile accident following that field season was a tragic blow to this research potential and we can only hope that someone will continue the work to which he gave such an excellent start. Additional work in Livengood area was conducted during construction of the oil pipeline under the direction of Gordon Lothson, but the analysis of these sites, which included an extensive quarry site, is not yet completed.

Boraas also surveyed North of the Yukon River along the pipeline route, with extensive coverage of the area adjacent to the Kanuti River crossing and Caribou Mountain. Here sites were principally artifact scatters on the slightly raised portions of eroded granitic remnants along the Kanuti Valley or on eroded patches near or at the surrounding ridge tops. These sites included extensive use of locally available basalt, as well as obsidian and (rarely) chert.

139

In these locations (as described above) virtually every low eminence (rising above the surrounding tundra) contained cultural materials, albeit with varying densities. Several of these sites were excavated because they would be (or had been) impacted by pipeline construction in 1975, directed by Michael Yarborough and Albert Dekin. These results will be reported in the Alyeska final report by Yarborough, but core and blade complexes from Denali times on are apparently represented.

As part of the Alyeska survey, Charles E. Holmes conducted a survey along the pipeline corridor from Bonanza Creek across the Prospect Creek and Jim River drainages and along the South and North Forks of the Koyukuk River (1971). Following the extensive 1970 survey of this area, Holmes returned in 1971 supported by the University of Alaska, with transportation provided by the Alyeska Pipeline Service Company (1974b). These sites were located in similar circumstances to those in the upper Kanuti valley. These locales are found in the margin of the extensive uplands from which these creeks flow to the Koyukuk. The uplands separate the Koyukuk from the Chandalar drainage and are a major caribou winter habitat between the Brooks Range and the Yukon River.

Several sites were excavated in the Bonanza Creek Valley, but while some contained presumed diagnostic artifacts, many were clusters of artifacts which could not be directly related to known cultural complexes, because of their general nature. As an example, the K-4 site was a concentrated cluster of ca. 12' by 8' with an oval configuration. The collection of chert, obsidian and basalt artifacts included 35 microblades, a transverse burin and a spall, a microblade core and 3 tablets (raw materials matched the microblades), 4 biface fragments, 2 corners of projectile point bases, 4 blades and 5 end and side scrapers (Holmes 1971:334-339; cf. 1974b:36-38). While the clustering

140

appears to represent a single depositional event, there are no diagnostic characteristics which would allow the dating of this site or a clear statement of its cultural affinities. In general, most of the sites were located, surface collected, maybe a test excavation or two made, and then, its location noted for future pipeline avoidance or salvage, the survey party moved on (Holmes 1971:332-333). The 1971 work was concentrated at the Island Site (K-8), so named because it is a "woody island surrounded by a lake of tundra muskeg" (1974b:14). Four localities were sampled, all of which were surface sites with evidence of multiple occupations. While the data on flake distributions by raw material throughout these clusters are not presented (which might be useful in determining the integrity of the clusters), the rather tight cluster of artifacts at locality A demonstrates the association of 7 microblades, a burin spall, two projectile point fragments and a fluted point base (1974b:72), all concentrated within 3 feet of the intersection of 4 grid squares. This association of a fluted point and microblades is duplicated at locality C (1974b:75), where a burin is found in an adjacent square, apparently in the same artifact cluster. Locality A (but in a distribution of artifacts distinct from the one previously mentioned) also contains two clusters with notched points, separated by a distance of 15 feet, but linked by a "fit" between two fragments of the same projectile point. A fluted point was found in the space between these apparently related clusters, approximately 6 feet from the larger group (1974b:73). The presentation of the point provenience data on these tools is an appropriate demonstration of the data necessary to evaluate associations in surface sites, but the same attention to other artifacts which are more numerous (detritus) and which vary significantly in terms of raw material would allow the determination of the integrity of these behavioral episodes and the strength of the association

141

of their contents (cf. Newell and Dekin in preparation; Newell and Wiersum in preparation). However, the demonstration of association of fluted points and microblades is an important one. We will need obsidian hydration tests to determine whether or not obsidian microblades are really coeval with obsidian fluted points, but that testing may be accomplished soon, as more data are evaluated (note that such testing does not require the establishment of a rate of hydration for the region, but only that the relative hydration values be tested to determine if they could have been drawn from the same population).

Holmes also suggested that the Bonanza Creek notched points occurred in two morphological types (Bonanza Creek Tuktu and Tuktu-Palisades II notched points--1974b:58), varying in size of the neck and width of the base (being greater in Tuktu-Palisades II); however, the significance of this difference was not assessed. Holmes discusses the range of possibilities for dating the fluted points in these collections, concluding ". . .that Bonanza Creek Valley points are a part of the ASTt related material at K-8 Locality C" (1974b:61). Given the distance of this association (more than ca. 9 feet), the failure to demonstrate the integrity of the clusters, and the inability to define clusters of occupation, the field data do not demonstrate such an association, however well they demonstrate the association of fluted points and microblades. There are other associations of fluted points, burins (non ASTt), burin spalls and blades (cf. Humphrey 1966, 1970; Alexander 1974). As in other sites in interior Alaska, it will be essential to analyze fewer but better data on artifact associations within sites, if we are to assess the integrity of occupational episodes and to build meaningful cultural sequences. Holmes presents several alternate schemes of association and time in the valley, which differ largely in association and represent an objective and valiant effort to weave a

cultural-historical framework from such surface sites (1974b:67-69). Interestingly enough, his survey found no evidence of recent or late prehistoric
sites in this area, although 1975 excavations for Alyeska have revealed such
sites just to the south (Vick Rockshelter, to be reported by Michael Yarborough)
and possibly the Wiseman area (see Alyeska final report of excavations in 1975).

Extensive excavations at Prospect Creek on the Jim River were conducted
by Alyeska, under the supervision of Robert Gal in 1974, prior to the destruction of the site for a materials source for construction. This site was
apparently the location of an extensive fluted point occupation, with numerous
artifact concentrations, as well as notched point and other, often ill-defined,
occupations. There is an extremely large corpus of data from this site and
its analysis should provide extensive information on southern Brooks Range
cultural sequences from Paleo-Indian times on. Other sites were excavated
along the Jim River and at Grayling Lake to the north, which should provide
excellent data on the breadth of occupation and on variety of land-use patterns
in this north-south valley leading from the Yukon uplands to the foot of the
Brooks Range.

Another cluster of sites was located and excavated near the Middle Fork
of the Koyukuk River just south of Cathedral Mountain (Holmes 1971:374). These
were located on projections of the hills surrounding the "Cathedral Mountain
Flats" in circumstances similar to the setting of sites in the Bonanza Creek
valley and elsewhere. Others were found on the raised gravel features of the
flats, including its marginal and ground moraines and kame terraces. Most of
these were located during the corridor survey for the pipeline (Cook et al.
1970) and only a few were excavated subsequently (Holmes 1971) during the
construction phase (to be included in the Alyeska final report). Again, these

143

sites are problematic, as they contain ill-defined surface collections and are difficult to interpret above the level of the "diagnostic" artifact (see site K-34, Holmes 1971:374-377). Site K-9 was partially excavated in 1970 and more completely excavated in 1974 (in the face of the increased need for gravel by Alyeska), although the final analysis is not yet complete. The site appears to be a workshop site in conjunction with a chert-chalcedony source on Cathedral Mountain, less than two miles to the north (Holmes 1971:379). These artifacts represent a wide range of artifacts in various stages of manufacture and use from a wide range of cultural affinities, thus their interpretation will be extremely difficult. These problems were recognized by Holmes in his 1971 summary:

> In order to work out local and regional sequences one needs strict stratigraphic control which allows for a chronological series of components. When this control is absent one must turn to the assemblage and the individual artifacts themselves. Seriating components and separating components by horizontal isolation, if possible, should help in interpreting the sites (Holmes 1971:384).

With the increasing attention to the precision of data recording within sites, these problems should be increasingly faced directly. Hopefully, the final analyses of these data should reveal further efforts in this direction.

Extensive survey along the pipeline alignment north along the Koyukuk River revealed sites wherever terraces, moraines, and other glacial features were raised above the valley floor. Several of these sites were excavated in 1975, under the supervision of Michael Yarborough and Albert Dekin, some of which may relate to late and poorly known occupations of the southern Brooks Range. The pipeline corridor above Wiseman along the Dietrich River, across the Chandalar Shelf and Dietrich Pass and down into the Atigun River valley, was noteworthy for the dearth of archaeological sites discovered during survey and surveillance of construction. This stretch crosses the height of Brooks Range, marked by narrow valleys and high mountains, with limited permanent subsistence opportunities and relatively recently glaciated valleys of little variation in relief. This particular route does not cross gentle passes or high lake country, thus missing some of the significant ecological variation characteristic of some of the other passes through the Brooks Range (cf. Anaktuvuk Pass). Several isolated finds were discovered on the Chandalar Shelf, including a fluted point, but no extensive sites were located and no excavation was required prior to pipeline facilities construction. These finds and others located in conjunction with the pipeline will be reported in the final report on the Alyeska Archaeology Project of the University of Alaska.

Leaving the interior of Alaska for its north slope, the problem of undifferentiated collections from geomorphic features remains paramount and represents a barrier to our understanding larger than negative data. Perhaps the promise of new precise techniques of analysis, developed by the Alyeska archaeologists (Newell and Dekin in preparation; Newell and Wiersum in preparation) will provide some meaningful analytic units above the level of the individual artifact and its attributes in the absence of clear spatial stratification or perhaps we need a more refined set of observational variables (attributes) to factor out these complicated surface sites. Perhaps an understanding of the overall technological capability of Arctic populations, which recognizes that microblades have been around and represent a technology available for the last ten thousand years, thus which, in addition to burin techniques, are not diagnostic of any particular cultural period, per se would be advantageous. John Cook's summation in the 1971 Alyeska report is one of the earliest statements relevant to this problem:

145

> In other words, microblades——and other tools types——are/were
> used for different tasks within different cultures. Thus, the
> juxtaposition of stemmed, notched, and lanceolate projectile
> points, with or without microblades, and, if with, the various
> kinds of core and blade technology, should not cause wonder or
> skepticism but should force us to examine more deeply our
> typological concepts within a cultural context (Cook 1971a:464).

With the application of such a behavioral, as opposed to a normative, paradigm,

we may look forward to greater precision in excavation and greater attention

to the within-site analysis of artifacts and their associations.

The Atigun River valley in the vicinity of Galbraith Lake had been

surveyed by Alexander (see above; Alexander 1969a, 1969b) prior to work by

Cook and others (1971a, et al. 1970) in conjunction with Alyeska pipeline

construction (Campbell 1973). This area is physiographically comparable to

that of Cathedral Mountain (to the south; see above), as it marks the emergence

of a river flowing north-south out of the Brooks Range onto the Arctic foot-

hills and north slope. As such, it marks a transition between the high Brooks

Range (and its sharp mountain valleys) and adjacent uplands and lowlands, and

is an area of diverse physiography.

Extensive excavations were conducted at the Atigun Crossing site and at

the Aniganigurak Site (S-67), representing contact period Numamiut Eskimo.

Preliminary results were described in 1971 (Corbin 1971) while the data pro-

vided fuel for a much more extensive analysis (Corbin 1975). The site

consisted of the remains of moss houses, tent rings, meat rack supports, out-

door hearths, as corroborated by Eskimo informants (Corbin 1971:285-286), and

was dated to ca. 1880-1890.

Further north, Glenn Bacon surveyed numerous apparently recent tent

rings between the Itkillik River and the Kuparuk River divide at Murphy Lake

(Toolik Lake). Most of the rings were well marked, containing rather few

bone and stone fragments and virtually no prehistoric artifacts (Bacon 1971:264)

146

(one site contained large cores and blades similar to those from the Gallagher Flint Station—see below). These rings are thought to result from the early historic Nunamiut occupation of this area, being subsistence camps of short duration (Bacon 1971:269).

Additional excavations were conducted in the Atigun Valley near Galbraith Lake at the Mosquito Lake Site (S-63) directed by Michael Kunz and Dale Slaughter in 1974 and 1975 (Kunz 1976b,c,d), previously reported and partially excavated by Kunz in 1970 (Kunz 1971). This site represents a series of Arctic Small Tool related artifact clusters, thought by Kunz to relate to the earlier end of that developmental sequence (similar to some of the Proto-Denbigh artifacts from Onion Portage—Kunz 1976b,c,d). These site-clusters should yield extensive information and will provide one of the largest well-documented ASTt collections from northern Alaska.

In 1975, Kunz conducted a partial survey of the head of the Itkillik drainage at Itkillik Lake, with logistic support from the Alyeska Pipeline Service Company at its camp at Galbraith Lake (Kunz 1976a). Numerous sites were found in undisturbed condition and should provide a valuable testing ground for hypotheses generated during the course of analyses of the Alyeska corridor material to the east.

Unfortunately, late Eskimo sites have not so often escaped the impact of vandals, as a survey by Edwin S. Hall, Jr. in northwest Alaska demonstrated. "The activities of contractors working for the Navy and the various oil companies in the area have contributed heavily to their disturbance" (Hall 1975b:20). Obviously, the price of access to the resources of this region is to be eternal vigilance by those managers responsible for its cultural resources. Hall summarized the resources of the Noatak for such managers in 1974 (1974) and recently has conducted applied archaeological surveys in advance of oil exploration on the north slope.

Hall's surveys have contributed additional data on site locations representative of the known sequence of occupations of the western Brooks Range and north slope; however, he cautions us that "Most of the early cultural material recovered came from multi-component, single level open sites and hence is of limited use beyond establishing the distribution of specific artifact types" (Hall 1975b:19). The need for further methodological work aimed at establishing behaviorally meaningful analytic units within the boundaries of surface sites is as great in the far North as it is in the interior. Perhaps with this in mind, Hall suggested further work for the recent Eskimo sites in the area (with comparative data available from the Sagavirnirktok and Atigun rivers): "However, the large number of late Eskimo sites located, their size and the excellent preservation that may be expected offers hope for better understandings of the most recent occupation of the area" (Hall 1975b:19).

As the recent ethno-archaeological research of Lewis Binford in Anaktuvuk Pass has demonstrated (Binford 1974; Amsden 1972), the more detailed understanding of recent hunters has much to contribute to our general understanding of the technological behaviors of arctic hunters. Since they represent a wealth of well preserved and well studied (in some areas) sites, perhaps this combination of ethnographic, ethnohistoric and archaeological researches can be as productive as similar combinations in southwest Alaska (e.g., Lantis 1970a; Ackerman 1970; Koch 1968; and VanStone, various).

Of the numerous sites located and excavated along the Alyeska pipeline route, two of the more significant ones to be published to date lie in the far northern portion of the line. These are the Gallagher Flint Station

148

(Dixon 1971, 1972, 1975a, 1976) and the Putu Site (Alexander 1974), both of
which have caused a rethinking of our understanding of early occupations of
North America. The Putu Site is dated by its soil matrix at 8450± 130 B.P.
(WSU-318--Alexander 1974:25), containing 4 fluted points, transverse burins,
blades, a scraper on a blade core, cores and knife fragments (1974:24). The
artifacts are found within a buried stratum, isolated from a few scattered
artifacts and antlers on the surface representing a more recent occupation.
While Alexander considers the date to be somewhat problematical, this
association of artifacts is significant because of its stratigraphic integrity
and because it confirms associations found previously at surface sites
(Humphrey 1966, 1970). It is also important to note, for purposes of evaluating the efficacy of archaeological survey techniques in this region, that
the only surface indications were of recent origin and that the fluted point
complex was brought to light through the cooperation of a helpful ground
squirrel (may his kind increase?). While this site was close to the original
pipeline route, a realignment to avoid the construction problems of the
Atigun canyon has moved the pipeline away to the west, thus maintaining the
isolation which has preserved this and adjacent sites for so long.

        The Gallagher Flint Station was discovered in 1970 in conjunction with
the survey in advance of the pipeline route. It is located on a large and
prominent ice-contact kame northeast of Slope Mountain on the Sagavarnirktok
River. Following initial investigations and excavations in 1970 and 1971,
Alyeska revised the haul road alignment to by-pass this feature and abandoned
plans to utilize the gravel within it for construction purposes, making a
commitment to preserve this important site. While the research potential of
the Gallagher Flint Station is not yet fully realized by excavation or by

complete analysis, several papers and the Alyeska report have been published.
Three separate and distinctive occupations have been determined at this site
and are designated Localities I, IA, and II. "These three localities have been
distinguished on the basis of vertical stratigraphy, spatial relationships,
typological comparison and radiocarbon chronology" (Dixon 1975:68). Dixon's
summary statements follow:

> Locality I contains percussion-flaked cores, blades, platform
> flakes, unifacially retouched artifacts and waste flakes. . .
>
> Locality IA is characterized by bifacially chipped stone artifacts
> which have been fashioned from fine-grained cherts, as opposed to
> the mudstone characteristic of Locality I. The artifact inventory
> contains bifacial projectile points, a drill and waste flakes.
>
> Locality II consists of ten contiguous four-foot squares in the
> southeastern quadrant of the site. It differs greatly from
> Locality I, although it bears similarities to IA. Burins and
> bifacially chipped artifacts were distributed around two
> hearths (Dixon 1975:68).

Locality II dates ca. 3000 B.P. and may contain several components, dating to
a similar time but representing Norton occupation (on the basis of drills).
Two cores and numerous burins and burin spalls (transverse types), but no microblades were found. The burins vary greatly, with some comparable to proto-
Denbigh and others notched like Donnelly Burins (Dixon 1971:191,199). Dixon
related this southward facing locality to the spring movement of caribou to
their summer habitat, contrasting the other localities in northward exposure
for late summer and early fall southward movements of caribou (Dixon 1971:202).
Clearly, we have a complicated picture of several occupations representing
partial inventories of probably recognized complexes.

Locality I was seemingly a quarry and vantage point, lacking burins and
bifacially worked artifacts. It is comprised of cores, blades, platform flakes,
unifaces and debitage—all in congruence with the category quarry and flint

station. A radiocarbon date of 10,540+ 150 B.P. (SI-974--Dixon 1975:69) was
obtained from soil associated with these artifacts, but not apparently from
a well defined feature. Locality IA is apparently superimposed on the Locality I occupation, since it dates at 2620+ 175 B.P. (SI-975) from a higher
level in the site. The Locality I collection of cores and blades is extremely
large (1027 blades and blade fragments and more than 120 cores and core
fragments--Dixon 1975:69) and variable:

> Most of the cores from Locality I are multiplatformed,
> rotated specimens. No "type" core can be recognized at the
> site, although single specimens of several different types,
> as described in other site records, are present. The cores
> were apparently not used and have been manufactured solely for
> the production of blades and flakes. They can best be des-
> cribed as generalized. It appears that this kind of core and
> blade technology may be the technological ancestor of the more
> refined microblade and core traditions which developed later in
> the coastal areas of Alaska (Dixon 1975:69).

Given the lack of features, the inability to separate clusters of occupation
within each locale, the generalized nature of the collection of cores, the
obvious special function location of this site and the overall lack of integrity of the comparative and descriptive units, much of the interpretive
potential of this site is not yet realized, and it provides more questions
demanding answers from further field and analytic work than it provides
answers. Because of the significance attributed to the early radiocarbon
date (Dixon 1975) and subsequent comparisons with the American Paleo-Arctic
tradition and Anangula, some might even question the association of the radiocarbon date with the behaviors represented at the site, in the absence of both
clusters and features. Hopefully, those responsible for the stewardship of
this important site will insure that its data are wisely recovered, rather
than left to the vagaries of an increasingly populated Arctic. Further data
from this site are being analyzed by John Cook and we can look forward to a
more complete publication by Dixon and by Cook.

The trans-Alaska oil pipeline originates in Prudhoe Bay, and this northern terminus has produced a recent habitation site complete with available native informants for technical evaluation. The site was located in 1970, and while it would not be directly affected by planned construction, it would conceivably be altered by subsequent site development and impacted by vandals. It was excavated by David Derry in 1971 (Derry 1971, 1972). It is indeed tragic that an automobile accident while returning from the field claimed the life of Derry in 1975. His developmental work was done with insight, appreciation for those whom he studied, concern for methodology and caution in interpretation. This is nowhere better demonstrated than in his work at Prudhoe Bay, where he confronted archaeology as anthropology.

> The site is an excellent workshop for the testing of certain hypotheses. The typological method is of little value due to the nature of the tools at the site: a .30 caliber Winchester Center Fire shell casing is of dubious value as an "index fossil". Our discussion then must center not on tool types but on cultural debitage that reflects the sets of human behavioral patterns of the occupants (Derry 1971:15).

The site was composed of a small cabin, with lean-to, and associated caches, racks and other out-of-doors features, still recognizable on the surface. The site was apparently occupied ca. 1940 (Derry 1971:26-28).

Derry evaluated the evidence for the within-structure variation in behaviors, with particular attention to the archaeological evidence for maintenance of a sleeping area at the rear of the house (obviously analogous to the long and widespread sleeping platform among Eskimos) (1971:44). This and other interpretations were checked with informants and their significance evaluated by statistical inference wherever possible or necessary and were compared with other studies of similar material (e.g., Ackerman 1970). While several social interpretations were contradicted by informants, the general

structure of the behaviors at the site was confirmed, and the general methodology supported by the results (Derry 1971:98–105). Recently, the internal
structure of some of these features has been evaluated statistically by
Raymond Newell (personal communication) as part of an attempt to assess and
verify the use of statistical structures for the partitioning of archaeological
sites and features. It is my understanding that these data are providing a
useful proving ground for methodological developments and that Derry's contribution to our discipline continues.

In addition to the above summation of recent research contributions,
there have been a number of other changes which will affect the course of
Arctic archaeology. These include a willingness to re-think old concepts and
old problems (vide Clark 1976a, 1976b; Wilmsen 1964; Gordon 1970a; McGhee
1973, 1974b, 1976; McGhee and Tuck 1973, 1976) and a growing skepticism
regarding claims for "pre-projectile point" complexes in the Arctic (Wilmsen
1964; Schlesier 1967, 1968). These developments are symptomatic of a healthy
intellect among Arctic archaeologists, as we demonstrate a willingness to
debate often conflicting ideas.

New data structures are treated with increasing skepticism, and associations among artifacts and between artifact associations, features, clusters
and radiocarbon dates may be subject to a scrutiny which demands more from us
than an "Arctic Small Paper tradition". The growth in Arctic scholars has
been geometric as has the growth in the amount of archaeological research
conducted (compare the length of chapters in this historical essay!).
Hopefully, this work will contribute to increasing this growth and debate and
we shall see marked changes whenever the next "history and bibliography"
appears.

Having reviewed the history of Arctic archaeology, several problems of research and publication are outstanding. The literature of Arctic archaeology is composed largely of preliminary reports and analyses. The number of good monographs containing the artifactual data, their analysis and explanatory hypothesis and conclusions is relatively small. In partial compensation, the quality of the preliminary reports is high. An extremely low proportion of known and tested sites have been described and located in print, and the raw data are scattered in repositories from Alaska to Denmark.

One major problem is that of the ethnic identity of archaeologically known cultures. The problem of the use of the concept "Eskimo" will suffice as an example. Collins considered Denbigh to be Eskimo even though Giddings did not use the term Eskimo to refer to the Denbigh people or their culture: "The discoveries at Cape Denbigh have strengthened the hypothesis of the Mesolithic origin of Eskimo culture..." (Collins 1953:201). Margaret Lantis noted the conceptual confusion.

> Eskimo culture produces a paradox. Nearly every student of
> it in Alaska has classified and explained Eskimo culture in
> terms of one element or one small complex. Collins emphasized
> harpoon-heads for sea mammal hunting. Larsen and Rainey emphasized
> flintchipping and inland hunting. Now Giddings emphasizes
> fishing and use of birch, spruce, and willow. Yet the traits
> that characterize Eskimos and their culture, as William Laughlin
> has pointed out recently in an astute article, are their ver-
> satility, individualization of gear, experimentation, and
> resulting wide range of variation (Lantis 1954:55).

Recalling Collins's (1951b, 1953a) suggestions of the Mesolithic origins of "Eskimos", could we call this process a mesolithicization?

Meldgaard suggested that we may have been asking the wrong question: "From archaeological investigations, however, it gradually becomes clear that one can hardly talk about the origin of Eskimo culture" (Meldgaard 1960:65). Gordon Willey discusses the process of "Eskimo-ization" concluding that "...undoubtedly the changes from Pre-Dorset to Dorset in the East were a part of the same wave of early 'Eskimo-ization' that was going on in the Arctic at about the beginning of the first millenium B.C." (Willey 1966:442), although a later synthesis by Jesse Jennings considered that "...Dorset, although fully adapted to the Arctic, is non Eskimoid" (Jennings 1968:313) with a less specialized simpler technology. In addition, "Eskimo" has been used independently to refer to a specific population, a physical type, a language stock, an exploitative adaptation, a technological adaptation, a specific culture, and populations living in a particular geographic region. In the archtype of this concept, most of the above meanings of Eskimo coincide. Giddings presented a good review of the use of "Eskimo" (and the use of "migration") concluding that '...we shall have to depend upon mutual agreement, rather than upon factual information, for that point in prehistory when we cease to deal with 'Eskimos'" (1952:98). Eskimo is a heuristic concept which has proved useful to Arctic archaeologists, even though it remains a semantic problem.

In the Arctic, cultural changes have been attributed to migrations (Mathiassen 1935; Larsen and Meldgaard 1958:71), population spread (Giddings 1952b, 1960) and only occasionally to what was euphemistically called "diffusion". Giddings (1952) criticized the migration model introducing the concept of "population spread" yet retained a belief in the importances of diffusion (1952:100). In his historical article in 1951, Larsen raised the question of diffusion versus migration. "I do not deny that some of us, though well aware of the occurrence of trade pieces, may have underestimated the importance of diffusion as a means of distribution of culture elements. However, we must not go to the other extreme and underestimate the significance of migration" (1961:12). Taylor pointed out that "...anthropologists writing on the Canadian Arctic and Greenland have so often explained similarities by migration, and so rarely mentioned diffusion that one might wonder if something, perhaps low temperature, prohibited cultural flow by diffusion" (1968:7; see also 1959; and 1963:461-2). Rather than seeing migration and diffusion as a dichotomy, I am inclined to accept MacNeish's 1963 "Adaptive Complex Hypothesis of the peopling of the New World" as being applicable to most cultural and environmental contexts combining both processes of culture change.

> It would appear that there has been a steady flow of people and ideas back and forth across Bering Strait due to the movements of the rich food resources in the area and due to the fact that the Strait has never been a major barrier to animal or man. As far as the Bering Strait region is concerned, the ideas and peoples moving into it needed to change but little, apart from making local adaptations to the culture or cultures already there (except for the case of the first migrants). However, once ideas or peoples moved from that ecological zone to any of the many impinging ecological zones, changes had to occur if they were to survive. To survive in their new environment certain of the cultural activities already present would be maintained in terms of their adaptability, others be gradually discarded in favour of new concepts brought in, certain of them would readapt and a few originally adaptive inventions would occur. This process would ultimately develop a new cultural tradition or adaptive cultural complex that would be adjusted to particular environmental zones. Then this complex would start to spread relatively rapidly through the whole of the zone (that probably but barely extended eastward up to western Alaska). In this spread there would not only be movement of people with the complex but diffusion of the complex to people already there with a less effective complex as well as combinations of both processes. As might be expected as the tradition spread there would be some cultural changes within it due to inventions, cultural drift, adapting of traits from peoples within the zone, and diffusion into or through the zone. Generally speaking, however, it would maintain itself as a tradition, until either it was replaced by another tradition developed in a similar way and adapted to the same environment, or until the environment changed and forced the tradition to change. (Mac Neish 1963:106).

In the light of a lack of evidence for the utility of the concept of diffusion, except as a rather vague explanation for what was otherwise inexplicable, I would urge that we no longer use diffusion in our hypotheses or interpretations. If we want to use trade or ritual exchange or idea exchange through intermittent seasonal personal contacts, then let us be as precise as possible.

A good cultural chronology and knowledge of the general interpretations among excavated cultures is requisite for anthropological archaeology. Unfortunately, because of the vastness of the geography of the Arctic, the complexity of its cultures and their cultural dynamics over possibly 20,000 years of occupation, a well developed chronology has been long in coming. In its absence, archaeologists interested in problems of social organization, acculturation, etc. would have been forced into speculations which were not closely documented by good archaeological data. Anderson observed this emphasis on chronology and the "genetics" of burins or cores in a slightly different manner. To Anderson's "...knowledge few Arctic archaeologists have yet to see their material as remains left by social groups. One way of achieving this is by viewing the sites as composites of activity areas in which the structures are but of one kind of, or rather a compound form of, an activity sphere" (1968:397). Edwin Hall observed that "...much of the archaeological literature on Northern Alaska has not...paid enough attention to the possibility of reconstructing human behavior from the archaeological remains" (1967:2). The number of possible interpretations of archaeological material increases when trying to do Anthropology, and this sensitization to the increased alternatives cannot help but improve our hypotheses, our field techniques, our methods of interpretation and might even elicit an explanation or two—all things which our Social Science should value. Students of

157

social organizations and socio-cultural change should look closely at the reported "communal dwellings" or larger houses reported from Dorset sites and from late prehistoric Eskimo sites in Canada and Greenland, respectively. What (and why) really happened to Thule? Why did Dorset smell of the forest? We know the how of the change from Pre-Dorset to Dorset at Lake Harbour--why was this change evolutionary at Lake Harbour and revolutionary at Igoolik? What was the nature of this transition elsewhere in the Eastern Arctic? Is the internal structure of finds in Pre-Dorset houses indicative of a change in social organization and if so, why? What was going on culturally in the Eastern Aleutians and in Southwestern Alaska at A.D. 1000 that produced widespread culture change and marks a morphological shift in Aleut craniology? Does the inland-coastal dichotomy of Denbigh Flint Complex sites in Alaska follow the model of the Nunamiut-Taremiut or are they seasonal occupations of the same people? Were there ecologically adaptive changes during the evolutionary continuum from Birnirk to Thule?

One of the important legacies that Giddings and his colleagues in Alaska have left us is a vast number of sites reported but not excavated because they did not fit the problems that these men were pursuing. If archaeology in the Arctic is to become anthropology in the Arctic we must turn new insights, methods and techniques on these rich archaeological resources, building on the chronologies and regional sequences that are the achieved goal of an earlier generation of scholars. Only when this is done, may we then say that anthropological archaeology has developed in the Arctic.

VII. Current Trends and Problems

In previous sections, we have seen that many of the major contributions to Arctic archaeology have been answers to questions of what, where, who and when with regard to the region's culture history. In recent years, we have seen a shift in the intellectual concerns of Arctic archaeologists and increasing attention to questions of how and why. To a great degree, this shift is made possible only by successful (or at least operational) answers to the first four questions, for without an adequate space-time framework of accepted behavioral units (i.e., "cultures"), it is difficult to pose meaningful questions of human adaptation and resource exploitation or explanations of culture process.

While the last half-dozen years or so have seen major attempts to deal with these more sophisticated questions in a formal manner, there have also continued to be major contributions in content and new and significant answers to questions of what, where, who and when. In each region of the Arctic, new finds have caused a rethinking of previously held interpretations and even the revitalization of old concepts. While some have tried to build sophisticated castles in the intellectual air, others have busily altered the data base on which these castles must be built. The winds of intellectual change are blowing across the Arctic. This is a time of interpretive and synthetic flux. It is clearly not a time to draw historically meaningful lines between periods of intellectual development. Perhaps it is best to seek evidence of interpretive change and to point in directions toward which Arctic archaeologists may be tending. The rate of ideational change is increasing as is the number of archaeologists working in the area. There is a greater diversity of ideas and a greater number of directions in which we may head. With full awareness that hindsight is an easier approximation to 20/20 vision than foresight, the following trends appear to characterize the present state of Arctic archaeology.

1. Archaeologists are taking broader perspectives on their work, moving beyond the reconstruction of local/regional culture history as a primary goal to attempt projects of wider intellectual interest. The rate of borrowing of models and methods from other disciplines has concomitantly increased.

2. The precise formulation of testable ideas and models is increasing, along with an increase in problem oriented explicit hypothesis testing research (paralleling the trend towards more explicitly hypothetico-deductive research methods in the "new archaeology").

3. Field data collection and depiction techniques are increasingly precise, both the within-site dimension and the among-site dimension. With this increased precision, more sophisticated data manipulation techniques are being applied.

4. There is an increasing concern for sampling methods and techniques and for the evaluation of the effects of sample bias on present and past archaeological field research, both at the site location (i.e., survey) and artifact collection stages of research.

5. Archaeological research is increasingly sponsored by or coordinated with native and governmental interests, both those which are related to the elucidation and management of their historic resources and those which relate to planning for future development. There is an increased direct involvement by federal agencies other than those which have traditionally sponsored academic research interests. More archaeological research is being done in

an applied cultural resource management framework than in traditional settings.

This shift in sponsorship of archaeological research and its conduct in what is becoming more explicitly an "applied" institutional context is related to the increase in northern development and federal insistence that such development be in harmony with the region's resources, specifically including historical and archaeological resources.

6. Arctic archaeologists are increasing in number and diversity of background and interests, thus the discipline may be said to be evolving. With the expansion of archaeological management positions in federal agencies and the increase in applied archaeological research opportunities, more Arctic archaeologists are becoming Arctic residents than has been the case in the past, and the trend of summer-only residents is somewhat reversed.

7. On the research front, the trend of multi-disciplinary studies with archaeological foci continues, along with the increased application of archaeological research in other programs of applied research, in support of land management decisions. Increasingly, archaeological research is used to provide the time depth so sorely needed for long term land management research.

8. New scholarly journals and new publication series are symptomatic of new efforts to alleviate the Arctic Small Paper tradition and the parochialism which occasionally impaired the effective flow of archaeological information.

VIII. Bibliography

Ackerman, Robert E.

1959   Archaeological Survey of St. Lawrence Island, Alaska.
Philadelphia Anthropological Society Bulletin 12(1).

1961   Archaeological Investigations into the Prehistory of St.
Lawrence Island, Alaska. Ph.D. dissertation. University of
Pennsylvania.

1962   Culture Contact in the Bering Sea: Birnirk-Punuk Period. In:
Prehistoric Cultural Relations Between the Arctic and Temperate
Zones of North America. John M. Campbell, ed. pp. 27–35. Arctic
Institute of North America, Technical Paper No. 11. Montreal.

1964a Lichens and the Patination of Chert in Alaska. American Antiquity
29(3):386–387.

1964b Prehistory in the Kuskokwim-Bristol Bay Region, Southwestern
Alaska. Laboratory of Anthropology Report of Investigations, No.
26. Washington State University. Pullman.

1964c Archaeological Survey, Glacier Bay National Monument, Southeastern
Alaska. Laboratory of Anthropology Report of Investigations 28(1).
Washington State University. Pullman.

1965a Archaeological Survey, Glacier Bay National Monument, Southeastern
Alaska. Laboratory of Anthropology Report of Investigations 36
(2). Washington State University. Pullman.

1965b Art or Magic: The Incised Pebbles from Southern Alaska. The
Michigan Archaeologist 11(3–4):181–188.

1967   Prehistoric Art of the Western Eskimos. The Beaver 298:67–71.

1968a The Archaeology of the Glacier Bay Region, Southeastern Alaska.
Laboratory of Anthropology Report of Investigations, No. 44.
Washington State University. Pullman.

1968b Review: The Ethnoarchaeology of Crow Village, Alaska, by W. H.
Oswalt and J. W. VanStone. Smithsonian Institution Bureau of
American Ethnology Bulletin, No. 199. Washington, D. C., 1967.
American Anthropologist 70(3):633–634.

1968c Review: Ancient Men of the Arctic, by J. Louis Giddings, Jr.
Alfred A. Knopf. New York, 1967. American Journal of
Archaeology 72:298.

1969   Review: Tikchik Village: A Nineteenth Century Riverine Community
in Southwestern Alaska, by James W. VanStone. Fieldiana
Anthropology, Vol. 56 No. 3. Chicago: Field Museum of Natural
History, 1968. American Antiquity 34(4):488–489.

1970   Archaeology, Ethnoarchaeology, and the Problems of Past
       Cultural Patterning. In: Ethnohistory in Southwestern Alaska and
       the Southern Yukon. Margaret Lantis, ed. pp. 11-48. Studies in
       Anthropology No. 7. University of Kentucky Press. Lexington.

1971a Review: Eskimo Prehistory, by Hans-Georg Bandi. University of
       Alaska Press. College, 1969. American Journal of Archaeology 75:
       354-355.

1971b Review: Historical Settlement Patterns in the Nushagak River
       Region, Alaska, by James W. VanStone. Fieldiana Anthropology,
       Vol. 61. Chicago: Field Museum of Natural History, 1971. His-
       torical Archaeology 1971(5):126-127.

1973   Review: Nushagak: An Historic Trading Center in Southwestern
       Alaska, by James W. VanStone. Fieldiana Anthropology, Vol. 62.
       Chicago: Field Museum of Natural History, 1972. Arctic 26(3):
       265-267.

1974   Post Pleistocene Cultural Adaptations on the Northern Northwest
       Coast. In: International Conference on the Prehistory and
       Paleoecology of Western North American Arctic and Subarctic.
       Scott Raymond and Peter Schledermann, eds. pp. 1-20. University
       of Calgary Archaeological Association. Alberta.

1975a Review: Beluga Hunters: An Archaeological Reconstruction of the
       History and Culture of the Mackenzie Delta Kittegaryumiut, by
       Robert McGhee. University of Toronto Press. Toronto, 1974.
       Arctic 28(4):304-305.

1975b Technological Perspectives in Northern Northwest Coast Prehistory:
       Aspects of the Lithic Industry of the GHB2 Site, Southeastern
       Alaska. Paper presented to the Symposium on Correlation of
       Ancient Cultures. Novosibirsk, U.S.S.R., October.

Aigner, Jean S.

1966   Bone Tools and Decorative Motifs from Chaluka, Umnak Island.
       Arctic Anthropology 3(2):57-83.

1970   The Unifacial, Core and Blade Site on Anangula Island,
       Aleutians. Arctic Anthropology 7(2):59-88.

1972   Carved and Incised Stones from Chaluka and Anangula. Anthropolo-
       gical Papers of the University of Alaska 15(2):39-51.

1974   Studies in the Early Prehistory of Nikolski Bay: 1937-1971.
       Anthropological Papers of the University of Alaska 16(1):9-25.

1976a Aleutian Archaeology Symposium: Introduction. Arctic Anthropology
       13(2):31.

1976b Early Holocene Evidence for the Aleut Maritime Adaptation. Arctic
       Anthropology 13(4):32-45.

Aigner, Jean S. and Douglas M. Bieber, Jr.

1976 Preliminary Analysis of Stone Tool Distributions and Activity
Zonation at Anangula, an 8500 B. P. Coastal Village in the Aleutian
Islands, Alaska. Arctic Anthropology 13(4):46-59.

Aigner, Jean S. and Bruce Fullem

1976 Cultural Implications of Core Distribution and Use Patterns at
Anangula, 8500-8000 B. P. Arctic Anthropology 13(4):71-82.

Aigner, Jean S., Bruce Fullem, Douglas Veltre and Mary Veltre

1976 Preliminary Reports on Remains from Sandy Beach Bay, a 4300-5600
B. P. Aleut Village. Arctic Anthropology 13(4):83-90.

Aigner, Jean S. and Douglas Veltre

1976 The Distribution and Pattern of Umqan Burial on Southwest Umnak
Island. Arctic Anthropology 13(4):113-127.

Aigner, Jean S., Douglas Veltre, Bruce Fullem and Mary Veltre

1976 An Infant Burial from Southwest Umnak Island. Arctic Anthropology
13(4):128-131.

Aigner, Jean S., William S. Laughlin and Robert F. Black

1971 Early Racial and Cultural Identifications in Southwestern Alaska.
Science 171(3966):87-88.

Alaska Office of Statewide Cultural Programs

1975a Report of Archaeological Investigations in the Vicinity of the
Proposed Airstrips at Akhiok, Ambler, Karluk, Larsen Bay, Newtok
and Portage Creek to the Alaska Division of Aviation. Alaska
Office of Statewide Cultural Programs. Division of Parks Bulletin,
No. 8. Anchorage.

1975b Report of Archaeological Investigations in the Vicinity of the
Proposed Noatak and Kivalina Water Systems to the U. S. Public
Health Service under Contract No. 243-75-0528. P. Bowers and J.
Turney. Alaska Office of Statewide Cultural Programs. Division
of Parks Bulletin, No. 9. Anchorage.

1975c Report of Archaeological Investigations along the Copper River,
Tasnuna River to Chitna to the Department of Highways. Alaska
Office of Statewide Cultural Programs. Division of Parks Bulletin,
No. 10. Anchorage.

1975d Report of Archaeological Investigations in the Vicinity of the
Proposed Snettisham Power Transmission Line, Bishop to Thane,
Alaska to the U. S. Army Corps of Engineers under Contract No.
NPSAW 75-745. Alaska Office of Statewide Cultural Programs.
Division of Parks Bulletin, No. 11. Anchorage.

1975e Report of Archaeological Investigations at Arctic Village, Alaska
to the Alaska Department of Highways. (Rural Trails and Highways
Project G-20209). Alaska Office of Statewide Cultural Programs.
Division of Parks Bulletin, No. 12. Anchorage.

1975f Archaeological and Historical Investigations along the Taylor
Highway; Report to the Alaska Department of Highways. P. M.
Bowers, J. H. Turney and T. Cole. Alaska Office of Statewide
Cultural Programs. Division of Parks Bulletin, No. 13.
Anchorage.

1975g Heritage Resources along the Upper Susitna River; a Study Pre-
pared for the U. S. Army Corps of Engineers under Contract DA
CW85-75-C-0041. Glenn Bacon, ed. Alaska Office of Statewide
Cultural Programs. Division of Parks Bulletin, No. 14. Anchorage.

Alaska Packers Association

1917 Petroglyphs on Kodiak Island, Alaska. American Anthropologist
19:320-322.

Alexander, Herbert L., Jr.

1969a Alaska: Archaeology in the Atigun Valley. Expedition 11(1):35-37.

1969b Prehistory of the Central Brooks Range--An Archaeological
Analysis. Ph.D. dissertation. University of Oregon.

1974 The Association of Aurignacoid Elements with Fluted Point Complexes in North America. In: International Conference on the Prehistory and Paleoecology of Western North American Arctic and
Subarctic. Scott Raymond and Peter Schledermann, eds. pp. 21-32.
University of Calgary Archaeological Association. Alberta.

Allen, G. M.

1939 Dog Skulls from Uyak Bay, Kodiak Island. Journal of Mammology
20:336-340.

Amdrup, Georg Carl

1909 The Former Eskimo Settlement on the East Coast of Greenland Between Scoresby Sound and the Angmassalik District. Meddelelser om
Grønland 28:285-328.

Amsden, Charles W.

1971 Review: Tichik Village, a Nineteenth Century Riverine Community
in Southwestern Alaska, by James W. VanStone. Fieldiana: Anthropology, Vol. 56, No. 3. Chicago: Field Museum of Natural History,
1968. Historical Archaeology 1971(5):123-124.

167

1972   But What Happened in Between?: Nunamiut Settlement and Exploita-
        tive Patterns - 1900 to 1970. A Paper presented at the Symposium
        on the Late Prehistoric/Historic Eskimos of Interior Alaska. 37th
        Annual Meeting of the Society for American Archaeology. Miami,
        5 May.

Anderson, Douglas D.

1962   Cape Krusenstern Ipiutak Economic and Settlement Patterns.
        Master's thesis. Brown University.

1966a   Preliminary Report on the Onion Portage Site. Paper presented at
        the 31st Annual Meeting of the Society for American Archaeology.
        Reno, Nevada, 5 May.

1966b   Review: Urgeschichte der Eskimo, by Hans-Georg Bandi. B. F.
        Verlag. Stuttgart, 1965. American Antiquity 31(6):881-882.

1967   Dating and Archaeology of the Onion Portage Site, Alaska: Con-
        tinuing Excavations. Report to the National Science Foundation.

1968a   A Stone Age Campsite at the Gateway to America. Scientific
        American 218(6):24-33.

1968b   Review: The Ethnoarchaeology of Crow Village, Alaska, by Wendell
        Oswalt and James W. VanStone. Bureau of American Ethnology
        Bulletin, No. 199. Washington, D.C., 1968. American Antiquity
        33(3):396-397.

1968c   The American Paleo-Arctic Tradition: New Evidence for Early Man
        in Alaska. Paper presented at the 33rd Annual Meeting of the
        Society for American Archaeology. Santa Fe, May.

1970a   Athabaskans in the Kobuk Arctic Woodlands, Alaska? Canadian
        Archaeological Association Bulletin 2:3-12. (English Edition).

1970b   Akmak: An Early Archaeological Assemblage from Onion Portage,
        Northwest Alaska. Acta Arctica, Fasc. 16.

1970c   Microblade Traditions in Northwestern Alaska. Arctic Anthropology
        7(2):2-16.

1972   An Archaeological Survey of the Noatak Drainage, Alaska. Arctic
        Anthropology 9(1):66-117.

1975   Trade Networks Among the Selawik Eskimos, Northwestern Alaska
        During the Late 19th and Early 20th Centuries. Folk 16-17:63-72.

Anderson, James E. and Charles F. Merbs

1962   A Contribution to the Human Osteology of the Canadian Arctic.
        Occasional Paper, No. 4. Royal Ontario Museum, Art and
        Archaeology Division. Toronto.

Anderson, James E., and James A. Tuck

    1974   Osteology of the Dorset People. Man in the Northwest 8:89-97.

Anderson, Svent T. and Theodore P. Bank, II

    1952   Pollen and Radiocarbon Studies of Aleutian Soil Profiles.
          Science 116(3004):84-86.

Andrews, James T., Robert McGhee and Lorna McKenzie-Pollock

    1971   Comparison of Elevations of Archaeological Sites and Calculated
          Sea Levels in Arctic Canada. Arctic 24(3):210-228.

Archaeological Research, Inc.

    1970   Archaeological Report, Amchitka Island, Alaska 1969-1970. Report
          to Holmes and Narver, Inc., contractors for the U. S. Atomic
          Energy Commission (R. J. Desautels, A. J. McCurdy, M. D. Flynn,
          R. R. Ellis). Costa Mesa, California. (See Desautels, et. al.)

Archaeology Division, National Museum of Man

    1969   Newsletter No. 6. National Museum of Canada. Ottawa.

    1970   Newsletter No. 7. National Museum of Canada. Ottawa.

Arundale, Wendy H.

    1976a A Discussion of Two Models Related to Climatic Change in the
          Eastern Arctic. Paper presented at the 41st Annual Meeting of
          the Society for American Archaeology. St. Louis, Missouri, 8 May.

    1976b The Archaeology of the Nanook Site: An Explanatory Approach. Ph.D.
          dissertation. Michigan State University.

Arutiunov, S. and D. Sergeev

    1973   Stability and Adaptability in the Evolution of Ancient Eskimo
          Hunting Tools. Paper presented to the 9th International Congress
          of Anthropological and Ethnological Sciences. Chicago.

    1975   Stability and Adaptability in the Evolution of Hunting Tools in
          Ancient Eskimo Culture. In: Prehistoric Maritime Adaptations of
          the Circumpolar Zones. William W. Fitzhugh, IV, ed. pp. 159-166.
          Mouton and Company. Paris.

Bacon, Glenn H.

    1971   Archaeological Survey and Excavation Near Murphy Lake in the
          Arctic Foothills. In: Final Report of the Archaeological Survey
          and Excavations along the Alyeska Pipeline Service Company Pipe-
          line Route. John P. Cook, ed. pp. 208-271. Department of
          Anthropology. University of Alaska.

1972 Archaeological Survey and Excavation near Murphy Lake in the
Arctic Foothills, Northern Alaska. Master's thesis. University
of Alaska.

1975 Preliminary Testing at the Long Lake Archaeological Site. Paper
Presented at the 2nd Alaskan Anthropology Conference. University
of Alaska. March.

Bacon, Glenn H., Terrence Cole and E. James Dixon, Jr.

1975 Heritage Resources Along the Upper Susitna River. A Study Prepared for the U. S. Army Corps of Engineers under Contract
DACW85-75-C-0041. Edited by Glenn Bacon, under the general
supervision of Douglas Reger. Office of Statewide Cultural Programs, Alaska Division of Parks.

Bandi, Hans-Georg

1963 The Burins in the Eskimo Area. In: Early Man in the Western
Arctic, A Symposium. Anthropological Papers of the University
of Alaska 10(3):19-28.

1967 Preliminary Report on the "St. Lawrence Island Archaeological
Field Project 1967" of the University of Berne, Switzerland and
the University of Alaska.

1969 Eskimo Prehistory. University of Alaska Press. College.

Bandi, Hans-Georg and Jørgen Meldgaard

1952 Archaeological Investigations on Clavering, Northeast Greenland.
Meddelelser om Grønland 126(4).

Bank, Theodore P., II

1953a Cultural Succession in the Aleutians. American Antiquity 19(1):
40-49.

1953b Ecology of Prehistoric Aleutian Village Sites. Ecology 34:246-64.

1958 The Aleuts. Scientific American 199 (5):112-120.

Barre, Georges

1970 Reconnaissance Archeologique dans la Region de la Baie de Wakeham
(Nouveau-Quebec). Societe d'Archeologie Prehistorique du Quebec.
Montreal.

Bartovics, Albert Foster

1970 A Procedure for Studying Small Scale Artifact Distributions.
Master's thesis. Department of Sociology and Anthropology. Brown
University.

Bass, William M.

    1966 Review: The Most Ancient Eskimos, by Lawrence Oschinsky.
        Canadian Resources Centre for Anthropology. University of Ottawa,
        1964. Anthropologica 8:164-165.

Beals, C. S.

    1968 Science, History and Hudson Bay. Queen's Printer. Ottawa.
        (2 Vols.) (Ed.)

Bentham, Robert and Diamond Jenness

    1941 Eskimo Remains in Southeast Ellesmere Island. Proceedings and
        Transactions of the Royal Society of Canada 2:41-55. Meeting of
        the Royal Society of Canada. Ottawa, May.

Beregovaya, N. A.

    1953 Harpoon Heads From Ancient Settlements on Cape Barrow. Excava-
        tions of the Kolyma Expedition, 1946. In: Paleolithic and Neo-
        lithic of U.S.S.R. 39:421-445. Moscow. (In Russian)

Binford, Lewis R.

    1974 Forty Seven Trips. A Case Study in the Character of Some Forma-
        tion Processes of the Archaeological Record. Paper Presented at
        the 1974 Biennial Conference of the Australian Institute of
        Aboriginal Studies. Canberra.

Bird, Junius B.

    1945 Archaeology of the Hopedale Area, Labrador. Anthropological Papers
        of the American Museum of Natural History 39(2):117-188.

Birket-Smith, Kaj

    1929 The Caribou Eskimos. Report of the 5th Thule Expedition, 1921-24
        5(1) and 5(2). Copenhagen.

    1930a The Question of the Origin of Eskimo Culture: A Rejoinder.
        American Anthropologist 32(4):608-624.

    1930b On the Origin of Eskimo Culture. Proceedings of the 23rd Inter-
        national Congress of Americanists. pp. 470-475. New York, 1928.

    1930c Folk Wanderings and Culture Drifts in Northern North America.
        Paper Presented at the 18th Scandinavian Naturalist Congress.
        Societe des Americanists de Paris N.S. 22:1-32. Paris.

    1940 Anthropological Observations on the Central Eskimos. Report of
        the 5th Thule Expedition, 1921-24 3(2). Copenhagen.

1951   Recent Achievements in Eskimo Research. Journal of the Royal Anthropological Institute 32(4):145-157.

1958   Boulder-Chip Scrapers in the Eastern Arctic. Man 58:113-114.

1959   The Eskimos. Methuen. London.

Birket-Smith, Kaj and Frederica deLaguna

1938   The Eyak Indians of the Copper River Delta, Alaska. Munksgaard. Copenhagen.

Black, Robert F.

1966   Late Pleistocene to Recent History of Bering Sea-Alaska Coast and Man. Arctic Anthropology 3(2):7-22.

1974a Geology and Ancient Aleuts, Amchitka and Umnak Islands, Aleutians. Arctic Anthropology 11(2):126-140.

1974b Late-Quaternary Sea Level Changes, Umnak Island, Aleutians-- Their Effects on Ancient Aleuts and Their Causes. Quaternary Research 4(3):264-281.

1975   Late Quaternary Geomorphic Processes: Effects on the Ancient Aleuts of Umnak Island in the Aleutians. Arctic 28(3):159-169.

1976   Geology of Umnak Island, Eastern Aleutian Islands As Related to the Aleuts. Arctic and Alpine Research 8(1):7-35.

Black, Robert F. and William S. Laughlin

1964   Anangula: A Geological Interpretation of the Oldest Archaeological Site in the Aleutians. Science 143:1321-1322.

Blake, Weston, Jr.

1966   End Moraines and Deglaciation Chronology in Northern Canada with Special Reference to Southern Baffin Island. Geological Survey of Canada, Department of Mines and Technical Survey Paper, No. 66-26. Ottawa.

1970   Studies of Glacial History of Arctic Canada. I. Pumice, Radio- carbon Dates, and Differential Postglacial Uplift in the Eastern Queen Elizabeth Islands. Canadian Journal of Earth Sciences 7(2): 634-664. Ottawa.

Boas, Franz

1901   The Eskimo of Baffin Land and Hudson Bay. American Museum of Natural History Bulletin 15(1).

1902   Some Problems in North American Archaeology. American Journal of Archaeology (second series) 6:1-6.

1907　The Eskimo of Baffin Land and Hudson Bay.　American Museum of
　　　　Natural History Bulletin 15(2).

Bockstoce, John R.

1973a A Prehistoric Population Change in the Bering Strait Region.
　　　　Polar Record 16(105):793-803.

1973b Aspects of the Archaeology of Cape Nome, Alaska: 2000 Years of
　　　　Cultural Change at Bering Strait.　D. Phil. Thesis.　University
　　　　of Oxford.

Bogoras, Waldemar

1925　Early Migrations of the Eskimo between Asia and America.　Pro-
　　　　ceedings of the 21st International Congress of Americanists 2:216-
　　　　235.　Göteborg.

Boraas, Alan S.

1971　Archaeological Survey Results in a Transect Between Livengood and
　　　　Fish Creek.　In: Final Report of the Archaeological Survey and
　　　　Excavations Along the Alyeska Pipeline Service Company Pipeline
　　　　Route.　John P. Cook, ed.　pp. 401-450.　Department of Anthro-
　　　　pology.　University of Alaska.

Borden, Charles E.

1951　Facts and Problems of Northwest Coast Prehistory.　Anthropology in
　　　　British Columbia 2:35-52.　Victoria.

1952a A Uniform Site Designation Scheme for Canada.　Anthropology in
　　　　British Columbia, No. 3.　Victoria.

1952b Results of Archaeological Investigations in Central British
　　　　Columbia.　British Columbia Provincial Museum Publication, No. 3.

1960　DjRi3, An Early Site in the Fraser Canyon, British Columbia.　Con-
　　　　tributions to Anthropology, 1957.　National Museum of Canada
　　　　Bulletin 162:101-118.　Ottawa.

1962　West Coast Cross Ties With Alaska.　In: Prehistoric Cultural Rela-
　　　　tions Between the Arctic and Temperate Zones of North America.
　　　　John M. Campbell, ed.　pp. 9-19.　Arctic Institute of North
　　　　America, Technical Paper No. 11.　Montreal.

1968　New Evidence of Early Cultural Relations Between Eurasia and
　　　　Western North America.　Paper Presented at the 8th International
　　　　Congress of Anthropological and Ethnological Sciences.　Tokyo.

1969　Early Population Movements from Asia into Western North America.
　　　　Syesis 2(1&2):2-13.　British Columbia Provincial Museum.
　　　　Victoria.

Brant, Charles S.

    1972 Review: The History of Greenland. Volume I: Earliest Times to
           1700, by Finn Gad. Queens University Press. Montreal, 1971.
           American Anthropologist 74(4):890-892.

Brierly, J. and F. G. Parsons

    1906 Notes on a Collection of Ancient Eskimo Skulls. Journal of the
           Royal Anthropological Institute 36:104-120.

Bröste, K. and K. Fischer-Møller

    1944 The Mediaeval Norsemen at Gardar. Anthropological Investigations.
           (With a Chapter on Dentition by P. O. Pederson.) Meddelelser om
           Grønland, Bd. 89.

Brown, Craig Canavan

    1973 Trace Element Analysis of Obsidian by Instrumental Neutron Activa-
           tion. Report for the degree Master of Science in Chemistry.
           University of Wisconsin.

Bruun, Daniel

    1918 The Icelandic Colonization of Greenland and the Finding of Vine-
           land. (With a preface by Finnur Jonsson) Meddelelser om
           Grønland 57(10).

Bryan, Alan L.

    1969 Early Man in America and the Late Pleistocene Chronology of
           Western Canada and Alaska. Current Anthropology 10(4):339-365.

Burch, Ernest S., Jr.

    1972 The Caribou/Wild Reindeer as a Human Resource. American Antiquity
           37(3):339-368.

Burkitt, M. C.

    1956 The Old Stone Age. New York University Press. New York.

Byers, Douglas S.

    1957 The Bering Bridge--Some Speculations. Ethnos 1-2:20-26.

    1962 New England and the Arctic. In: Prehistoric Cultural Relations
           Between the Arctic and Temperate Zones of North America. John M.
           Campbell, ed. pp. 143-153. Arctic Institute of North America,
           Technical Paper No. 11. Montreal.

Cadzow, Donald D.

    1928 Archaeological Work With the Putnam Baffin Island Expedition. Museum of the American Indian. Indian Notes 5:98-106.

Campbell, John M.

    1959 The Kayuk Complex of Arctic Alaska. American Antiquity 25(1):94-105.

    1961a The Tuktu Complex of Anaktuvuk Pass. Anthropological Papers of the University of Alaska 19(2):61-80.

    1961b The Kogruk Complex of Anaktuvuk Pass, Alaska. Anthropologica 3(1):3-20. Ottawa.

    1962a Cultural Succession at Anaktuvuk Pass, Arctic Alaska. In: Prehistoric Cultural Relations Between the Arctic and Temperate Zones of North America. John M. Campbell, ed. pp. 39-54. Arctic Institute of North America, Technical Paper No. 11. Montreal.

    1962b Prehistoric Cultural Relations Between the Arctic and Temperate Zones of North America. Arctic Institute of North America, Technical Paper No. 11. Montreal. (Ed.)

    1962c Review: Contributions to Anthropology 1957, National Museum of Canada Bulletin 162. Ottawa, 1960. American Antiquity 27(4): 600-601.

    1962d Anaktuvuk Prehistory: A Study in Environmental Adaptation. Ph.D. dissertation. Yale University.

    1962e An Anthropologist Looks at the Arctic National Wildlife Range. In: Science in Alaska, 1961. Proceedings of the 12th Alaskan Science Conference, Alaska Division, American Association for the Advancement of Science. George Dahlgren, Jr., ed. pp. 53-58.

    1962f Notes and News, Arctic. American Antiquity 27(3):442-446.

    1963a Current Research, Arctic. American Antiquity 28(4):576-581.

    1963b Ancient Alaska and Paleolithic Europe. Anthropological Papers of the University of Alaska 10(2):19-49.

    1964a Current Research, Arctic. American Antiquity 29(4):535-539.

    1964b Ancient Man in a Cold Climate: Eskimo Origins. Review: The Archaeology of Cape Denbigh, by J. Louis Giddings. Brown University Press. Providence, 1964. Science 145:913-915.

    1965a Review: The Cultural Affinities of the Newfoundland Dorset Eskimo, by Elmer E. Harp, Jr. In: Anthropology Series, No. 67. National Museum of Canada Bulletin 200. Ottawa, 1964. American Antiquity 31(2):288-289.

1965b Current Research, Arctic. American Antiquity 31(2:1):290-295.

1966a Radiocarbon Dating and Far Northern Archaeology. Proceeding of the 6th International Conference of Radiocarbon and Tritium Dating. pp. 179-186. Pullman, 1965.

1966b Current Research, Arctic. American Antiquity 31(6):895-899.

1967 Current Research, Arctic. American Antiquity 32(4):560-564.

1968a The Kavik Site of Anaktuvuk Pass, Central Brooks Range, Alaska. Anthropological Papers of the University of Alaska 14(1):32-42.

1968b Territoriality Among Ancient Hunters: Interpretations from Ethnography and Nature. In: Anthropological Archaeology in the Americas. pp. 1-21. Anthropological Society of Washington Lecture Series, 1966-67. Washington, D.C.

1970 Current Research, Arctic. American Antiquity 35(2):239-244.

1973 Archaeological Studies Along the Proposed Trans-Alaska Oil Pipeline Route. Arctic Institute of North America, Technical Paper No. 26. Montreal.

1976 The Soviet-American Siberian Expedition. Arctic 29(1):3-6.

Campbell, John M. and Ellen M. Cummings

1975 A Field Guide to the Recognition of Archaeological Materials Along the Trans-Alaska Pipeline. Ecology and Environment, Inc. Anchorage.

Candela, P. B.

1939 Blood Group Determinations upon the Bones of Thirty Aleutian Mummies. American Journal of Physical Anthropology 16(4):451-462.

Cardinal, Elizabeth A.

n.d. The Faunal Remains from Unalakleet, Alaska. Manuscript.

Carignan, Paul

1975 The Beaches: A Multi-Component Habitation Site in Bonavista Bay. Mercury Series. Archaeological Survey of Canada Paper, No. 39. National Museums of Canada. Ottawa.

n.d. Prehistoric Cultural Tradition at the Beaches Site, DeAk-1, Bonavista Bay. Master's thesis. Memorial University of Newfoundland.

Carlson, Roy L.

    1954 Archaeological Investigations in the San Juan Islands. Master's thesis. University of Washington, Pullman.

    1960 Chronology and Culture Change in the San Juan Islands. American Antiquity 25(4):562-586.

Carter, Wilbert K.

    1953a Archaeological Survey of Eskimo, or Earlier, Material in the Vicinity of Point Barrow, Alaska. Status Report submitted to the Office of Naval Research, by the Arctic Institute of North America. Manuscript.

    1953b Archaeological Survey of Eskimo, or Earlier, Material in the Vicinity of Point Barrow, Alaska. Final Report to the Office of Naval Research. Manuscript.

    1962 Archaeological Survey of Eskimo, or Earlier, Material in the Vicinity of Point Barrow, Alaska. Status Report submitted to the Office of Naval Research, by the Arctic Institute of North America. Manuscript.

    1966 Archaeological Survey of Eskimo, or Earlier, Material in the Vicinity of Point Barrow, Alaska. Final Report to the Office of Naval Research, by the Arctic Institute of North America. Manuscript.

Chard, Chester S.

    1955a Eskimo Archaeology in Siberia. Southwestern Journal of Anthropology 11(2):150-177.

    1955b An Early Pottery Site in the Chukchi Peninsula. American Antiquity 20(3):283-284.

    1956 The Oldest Sites of Northern Siberia. American Antiquity 21(4): 405-409.

    1957 The Southwestern Frontier in Northeast Asia and Alaska. American Antiquity 22(3):304-305.

    1958a An Outline of the Prehistory of Siberia: Part I. The Pre-Metal Periods. Southwestern Journal of Anthropology 14(1):1-33.

    1958b Regional Reports: Northeast Asia. Asian Perspectives 2(1):13-21.

    1958c Mesolithic Sites in Siberia. Asian Perspectives 2(1):118-127.

    1958d Organic Tempering in Northeast Asia and Alaska. American Antiquity 24(2):193-194.

1958e New World Migration Routes. Anthropological Papers of the University of Alaska 7(1):23-26.

1959a The Age of Feather Tempering in Alaska. American Antiquity 24 (4): 429.

1959b New World Origins: A Reappraisal. Antiquity 33(129):44-49.

1960a Northwest Coast - Northeast Asiatic Similarities: A New Hypothesis. Selected Papers of the 5th International Congress of Anthropological and Ethnographic Sciences. pp. 235-40. Philadelphia, 1956.

1960b Review: Eskimo Prehistory in the Vicinity of Point Barrow, Alaska, by James A. Ford. Anthropological Papers of the American Museum of Natural History 47(1). New York, 1959. American Journal of Archaeology 64:122-123.

1960c Additional Materials from Lake El'gytkhyn, Chukchi Peninsula. Anthropological Papers of the University of Alaska 9(1):1-12.

1960d Maritime Culture in the North Pacific: Age and Origin. Proceedings of the 34th International Congress of Americanists. pp. 279-283. Vienna.

1960e Routes to Bering Straits. American Antiquity 26(2):283-285.

1960f Reviews. American Antiquity 26(1):121-123. (Ed.)

1960g Recent Archaeological Work in the Chukchi Peninsula. Anthropological Papers of the University of Alaska 8(2):119-120.

1961 Eskimo Remains from Shalanrova Island, Siberia. In: Notes and News. Anthropological Papers of the University of Alaska 10(1): 73-76.

1962a Northeast Asia. Asian Perspectives 5(1):16-20.

1962b New Developments in Siberian Archaeology. Asian Perspectives 5(1): 118-126.

1967 Arctic Anthropology in America. In: The Philadelphia Anthropological Society Papers Presented on its Golden Anniversary. Jacob W. Gruber, ed. pp. 77-106. Columbia University Press. New York.

1969 Review: Eskimo Prehistory, by Hans-Georg Bandi. University of Alaska Press, College, 1969. Science 165:1247.

Chard, Chester S. and B. P. Merbs

1964 The Alaska Situla Ware: An East Asiatic Transplant in the New World. Proceedings of the 35th International Congress of Americanists 1(11):16. Mexico, 1962.

Chard, Chester S. and William B. Workman

    1965   Soviet Archaeological Radiocarbon Dates: II. Arctic Anthropology
           3(1):146–150.

Cinq-Mars, Jacques

    1973   Preliminary Archaeological Study, MacKenzie Corridor. Environmental-
           Social Program, Northern Pipelines, Report No. 73–10.
           Information Canada.

    1974   Second Preliminary Archaeological Study, MacKenzie Corridor,
           Environmental-Social Program, Northern Pipelines, Report No. 74–11.
           Information Canada.

Clark, A. McFadyen

    1970   The Athabaskan-Eskimo Interface. Canadian Archaeological Associa-
           tion Bulletin 2:13–23. (English Edition).

    1972   Review: Ethnohistory in Southwestern Alaska and the Southern Yukon:
           Method and Content, by Margaret Lantis, ed. Studies in Anthro-
           pology No. 7. University of Kentucky Press. Lexington, 1970.
           Arctic 25(2):164–165.

Clark, A. McFadyen and Donald W. Clark

    1974   Koyukon Athapaskan Houses as Seen Through Oral Tradition and Through
           Archaeology. Arctic Anthropology 11 (suppl.):29–38.

Clark, Donald W.

    1956   Upper Station Site. In: Archaeology of the Uyak Site Kodiak
           Island, Alaska (appendix), by Robert F. Heizer. University of
           California Anthropological Records 17(1):94–97.

    1960a A Decorated Stone Lamp for the Kodiak Area. Anthropological
           Papers of the University of Alaska 9(1):58–60.

    1960b Kizhuyak Bay Excavation: Archaeological Excavation at Kizhuyak
           Bay, Kodiak Island, Alaska. Kodiak and Aleutian Islands Historical
           Society Publication. Kodiak.

    1964   Incised Figurine Tablets from Kodiak Island. Arctic Anthropology
           2(1):118–134.

    1966a Perspective in the Prehistory of Kodiak Island, Alaska. American
           Antiquity 31(3):358–371.

    1966b Two Late Prehistoric Pottery-Bearing Sites on Kodiak Island,
           Alaska. Arctic Anthropology 3(2):157–184.

    1968   Koniag Prehistory. Ph.D. dissertation. University of Wisconsin.
           Madison.

1970a The Late Kachemak Tradition at Three Saints and Crag Point, Kodiak Island, Alaska. Arctic Anthropology 6(2):73-111.

1970b Archaeology of the Batza Tena Obsidian Source, West Central Alaska. Report of the National Museum of Man, Archaeological Division. National Museums of Canada. Ottawa.

1970c Archaeological Surveys on the Koyukuk and Anderson Rivers: A Narrative of Fieldwork Undertaken in 1970. Report of the National Museum of Man, Archaeological Division. National Museums of Canada. Ottawa.

1970d Petroglyphs on Afognak Island, Kodiak Group, Alaska. Anthropological Papers of the University of Alaska 15(1):13-18.

1972a Archaeology of the Batza Tena Obsidian Source, West-Central Alaska. Anthropological Papers of the University of Alaska 15(2):1-21.

1972b Review: Akmak: An Early Archaeological Assemblage from Onion Portage, Northwestern Alaska, by Douglas D. Anderson. (Appendix by Thomas D. Hamilton). Acta Arctica, Fasc., 16. Copenhagen: Munksgaard, 1970. Arctic 25(1):67-68.

1973 Koniag Prehistory. Tubingen Monographien Zur Urgeschichte, I. Tubingen, Germany.

1974a Archaeological Collections from Norutak Lake on the Kobuk-Alatna River Portage, Northwestern Alaska. Mercury Series. Archaeological Survey of Canada Paper, No. 18. National Museums of Canada. Ottawa.

1974b The Earliest Prehistoric Cultures of Kodiak Island, Alaska: 1971 Field Work, Preliminary Report. Arctic Anthropology 11(1):41-46.

1974c Highlights of Archaeological Surveys in Northern Interior District of Mackenzie, N.W.T. Canadian Archaeological Association Bulletin 6:48-91.

1974d Filaments of Prehistory on the Koyukuk River, Northwestern Interior Alaska. In: International Conference on the Prehistory and Paleoecology of Western North American Arctic and Subarctic. Scott Raymond and Peter Schledermann, eds. pp. 33-46. University of Calgary Archaeological Association. Alberta.

1975a Archaeological Reconnaissance in Northern Interior District of Mackenzie, 1969, 1970, and 1972. Mercury Series. Archaeological Survey of Canada Paper, No. 27. National Museums of Canada. Ottawa.

1975b Technological Continuity and Change Within a Persistent Maritime Adaptation: Kodiak Island, Alaska. In: Prehistoric Maritime Adaptations of the Circumpolar Zone. William W. Fitzhugh, IV, ed. pp. 203-228. Mouton and Company. Paris.

1975c Koniag-Pacific Eskimo Bibliography. Mercury Series. Archaeological Survey of Canada Paper, No. 35. National Museums of Canada. Ottawa.

1976a The Pacific Origin of Eskimos. Paper presented at the 3rd Annual Conference of the Alaska Anthropological Association. Anchorage.

1976b Progress Report on a Reexamination of the Engigstciak Site Collections. Manuscript.

Clark, Donald W. and Annette McFadyen Clark

1973 Fluted Points at the Batza Tena Obsidian Source, Northwestern Interior Alaska. 9th International Congress of Anthropological and Ethnological Sciences. Chicago. (Preprint No. 2129.)

1975 Fluted Points from the Batza Tena Obsidian Source of the Koyukuk River Region, Alaska. Anthropological Papers of the University of Alaska 17(2):31-38.

Clark, Donald W. and Frederick Milan

1974 Contributions to the Later Prehistory of Kodiak Island, Alaska. Mercury Series. Archaeological Survey of Canada Paper, No. 20. National Museums of Canada. Ottawa.

Clark, Gerald H.

1968 The Archaeology of the Takli Site, Katmai National Monument, Alaska. Master's thesis. University of Oregon.

1974 The Prehistory of the Pacific Coast of Katmai National Monument. Ph.D. dissertation. University of Oregon.

Clark, John Grahame Douglas

1969 World Prehistory: A New Outline. Cambridge University Press. London. (2nd Edition)

Collins, Henry B., Jr.

1928a Check-Stamped Pottery from Alaska. Journal of the Washington Academy of Science 18(9):254-256.

1928b The Eskimo of Western Alaska. Explorations and Fieldwork of the Smithsonian Institution in 1927. Smithsonian Institution Bulletin. pp. 149-156.

1929a Prehistoric Art of the Alaskan Eskimo. Smithsonian Miscellaneous Collection 81(14).

1929b The Ancient Eskimo Culture of Northwestern Alaska. Explorations and Fieldwork of the Smithsonian Institution in 1928. Smithsonian Institution Bulletin 3011:141-150.

1930   Prehistoric Eskimo Culture in Alaska. Explorations and Fieldwork
        of the Smithsonian Institution in 1929. Smithsonian Institution
        Bulletin. pp. 147-156.

1931   Ancient Culture of the St. Lawrence Island, Alaska. Explorations
        and Fieldwork of the Smithsonian Institution in 1930. Smith-
        sonian Institution Bulletin 3111:135-144.

1932a   Prehistoric Eskimo Culture on St. Lawrence Island. Geographical
        Review 22:107-119.

1932b   Archaeological Investigations in Northern Alaska. Explorations
        and Fieldwork of the Smithsonian Institution in 1931.
        Smithsonian Institution Bulletin. pp. 103-112.

1933   Archaeological Investigations at Point Barrow, Alaska. Explora-
        tions and Fieldwork for the Smithsonian Institution in 1932.
        Smithsonian Institution Bulletin. pp. 45-48.

1934a   Review: Inugsuk, A Mediaeval Eskimo Settlement in Upernivik Dis-
        trict, West Greenland, by Therkel Mathiassen. Meddelelser om
        Grønland 77:4, 1930. and Ancient Eskimo Settlements in the
        Kangamiut, by Therkel Mathiassen. Meddelelser om Grønland 91:1,
        1931. American Anthropologist 36(1):118-124.

1934b   Eskimo Archaeology and Somatology. American Anthropologist 36(2):
        309-313.

1934c   Archaeology of the Bering Sea Region. Proceedings of the 5th
        Pacific Science Congress of Canada, 1933 (4):2825-2839. Toronto.

1935   Archaeology of the Bering Sea Region. Smithsonian Annual Report
        for 1933. pp. 453-468.

1937a   Archaeology of St. Lawrence Island. Smithsonian Institution
        Miscellaneous Collection 96(1):1-431.

1937b   Culture Migrations and Contacts in the Bering Sea Region.
        American Anthropologist 39(3):375-384.

1937c   Archaeology Excavations at Bering Strait. Explorations and Field-
        work for the Smithsonian Institution in 1936. Smithsonian
        Institution Bulletin. pp. 63-68.

1940   Notes and News, Arctic. American Antiquity 5(3):233-234.

1941   Outline of Eskimo Prehistory. In: Essays in Historical Anthro-
        pology of North America. Smithsonian Institution Miscellaneous
        Collections 100:533-592.

1943   Eskimo Archaeology and Its Bearing on the Problem of Man's
        Antiquity in America. Proceedings of the American Philosophical
        Society 86(2):220-235. Philadelphia.

1945a Review: The Anthropology of Kodiak Island, by Ales Hrdlicka. Wistar Institute of Anatomy and Biology. Philadelphia, 1944. American Journal of Physical Anthropology 3(4):355-361.

1945b Review: The Aleutian and Commander Islands and Their Inhabitants, by Ales Hrdlicka. Wistar Institute of Anatomy and Biology. Philadelphia, 1945. American Journal of Physical Anthropology 3 (4):355-361.

1950 Excavations at Frobisher Bay, Baffin Island, N.W.T. Annual Report to the National Museum of Canada for 1948-49. National Museum of Canada Bulletin 118:18-43. Ottawa.

1951a The Origin and Antiquity of the Eskimo. Smithsonian Annual Report for 1950. pp. 423-467.

1951b Excavations at Thule Culture Sites Near Resolute Bay, Cornwallis Island, N.W.T. Annual Report of the National Museum of Canada for 1949-50. National Museum of Canada Bulletin 123:49-63. Ottawa.

1952 Archaeological Excavations at Resolute, Cornwallis Island, N.W.T. Annual Report of the National Museum of Canada for 1950-51. National Museum of Canada Bulletin 126:48-63. Ottawa.

1953a Recent Developments in the Dorset Culture Area. Memoirs of the Society of American Archaeology 9:32-39.

1953b Radiocarbon Dating in the Arctic. American Antiquity 18:197-213.

1954a "Arctic Area". Program of the History of America. Comission de Historia 1(2):152. Mexico City.

1954b Archaeological Research in the North American Arctic. Arctic 7(3 and 4):296-306.

1954c The Position of Ipiutak in Eskimo Culture - Reply. American Antiquity 20(1):79-84.

1955a Excavations of Thule and Dorset Culture Sites at Resolute, Cornwallis Island, N.W.T. National Museum of Canada Bulletin 136:22-35. Ottawa.

1955b Dorset Dwellings. Science 122(3175):866-867.

1956a The T-1 Site at Native Point Southhampton Island, N.W.T. Anthropological Papers of the University of Alaska 4(2):63-89.

1956b Review: The Arctic Woodland Culture of the Kobuk River, by J. Louis Giddings. University Museum Monograph. University of Pennsylvania, 1952. American Antiquity 22(2):199-201.

1956c Archaeological Investigations on Southhampton and Coats Islands, N.W.T. Annual Report of the National Museum of Canada for 1954-55. National Museum of Canada Bulletin 142:82-113. Ottawa.

1957a Archaeological Investigations on Southhampton and Walrus Islands, N.W.T. Annual Report of the National Museum of Canada for 1956. National Museum of Canada Bulletin 147:22-61. Ottawa.

1957b Archaeological Work in Arctic Canada. Smithsonian Annual Report for 1956. pp. 509-528. Smithsonian Institution Publication.

1958 Present Status of the Dorset Problem. Proceedings of the 32nd International Congress of Americanists. pp. 557-560. Copenhagen, 1956.

1959 An Okvik Artifact from Southwest Alaska and Stylistic Resemblances between Early Eskimo and Paleolithic Art. Polar Notes 1:126-139.

1960a Recent Trends and Developments in Arctic Archaeology. Proceedings of the 6th International Congress of Anthropology and Ethnographic Sciences, Vol. 1. Paris.

1960b Comment on: The Archaeology of Bering Strait, by J. Louis Giddings. Current Anthropology 1(2):131-136.

1962a Eskimo Cultures. Encyclopedia of World Art. (Vol. 5.) McGraw-Hill Book Co. New York.

1962b Bering Strait to Greenland. In: Prehistoric Cultural Relations Between the Arctic and Temperate Zones of North America. John M. Campbell, ed. pp. 126-139. Arctic Institute of North America. Technical Paper No. 11. Montreal.

1963 Paleo-Indian Artifacts in Alaska: An Example of Cultural Retardation in the Arctic. Anthropological Papers of the University of Alaska 10(2):13-18.

1964 The Arctic and Subarctic. In: Prehistoric Man in the New World. Jesse D. Jennings and Edward Norbeck, eds. pp. 85-114. University of Chicago Press.

1967 Diamond Jenness and Arctic Archaeology. Beaver 298(2):78-79.

1970 The Okvik Figurine: Madonna or Bear Mother. Folk 11-12:125-132.

1971 Composite Masks: Chinese and Eskimo. In: Pilot Not Commander. J. and P. Lotz, eds. Anthropologica N.S. 13(1-2).

1973 Eskimo Art. In: The Far North, 2000 Years of American Eskimo and Indian Art. Henry B. Collins, Jr., et al. pp. 1-25. National Gallery of Art. Washington.

1975 Additional Examples of Early Eskimo Art. Folk 16-17:55-62.

Collins, Henry B., Jr., and Frederica deLaguna, Edmund Carpenter, and
   Peter Stone

   1973 The Far North, 2000 Years of American Eskimo and Indian Art.
         National Gallery of Art. Washington.

Collins, Henry B., Jr., and William E. Taylor, Jr.

   1970 Diamond Jenness (1886-1969). Arctic 23(2):71-81.

Comer, George

   1910 A Geographical Description of Southhampton Island and Notes Upon
         Eskimo. American Geographical Society Bulletin 32:84-90.

Conrad, Geoffrey W.

   n.d. The Archaeological Potential of Indian House Lake, Quebec.
         (mimeographed)

Cook, John P.

   1964 Early Groundstone Artifacts of Northern North America. Master's
         thesis. Brown University.

   1968 Some Microblade Cores from the Western Boreal Forest. Arctic
         Anthropology 5(1):121-127.

   1969 The Early Prehistory of Healy Lake, Alaska. Ph.D. dissertation.
         University of Wisconsin. Madison.

   1971a Final Report of the Archaeological Survey and Excavations along
         the Alyeska Pipeline Service Company Pipeline Route. Department
         of Anthropology. University of Alaska. (Ed.)

   1971b Hogan Hill to Livengood. In: Final Report of the Archaeological
         Survey and Excavations along the Alyeska Pipeline Service Company
         Pipeline Route. John P. Cook, ed. pp. 451-456. Department of
         Anthropology. University of Alaska.

   1971c Review: Kijik: An Historic Tanaina Indian Settlement, by James W.
         VanStone and Joan B. Townsend. Fieldiana Anthropology, Vol. 59.
         Chicago: Field Museum of Natural History, 1970. American Anthro-
         pologist 73(6):1408-1409.

Cook, John P., E. James Dixon, Jr. and Charles E. Holmes

   1972 Archaeological Report, Site 49 Rat 32, Amchitka Island, Alaska.
         United States Atomic Energy Commission. Las Vegas.

Cook, John P. and Robert A. McKennan

   1970a The Village Site of Healy Lake, Alaska: An Interim Report. Paper
         Presented at the 35th Annual Meeting of the Society for American
         Archaeology. Mexico City, May.

1970b   The Athapaskan Tradition: A View from Healy Lake in the Yukon-
         Tanana Upland. Paper read by Robert A. McKennan at the 10th
         Annual Meeting of the Northeastern Anthropological Association,
         Ottawa, Canada, 7-9 May.

Cook, John P. and W.J. Stringer

1974   Feasibility Study for Locating Archaeological Village Sites by
        Satellite Remote Sensing Techniques. Final Report for Contract
        NAS5-21833, ERTS Project 110-N. Prepared for National Aeronautics
        and Space Administration. Geophysical Institute, University of
        Alaska.

Cook, John P., et al.

1970   Report of Archaeological Survey and Excavations along the Alyeska
        Pipeline Service Company Haulroad and Pipeline Alignments.
        Department of Anthropology. University of Alaska.

Corbin, James A.

1971   Aniganigurak (S-67): A Contact Period Nunamiut Eskimo Village in
        the Brooks Range. In: Final Report of the Archaeological Survey
        and Excavations along the Alyeska Pipeline Service Company Pipe-
        line Route. John P. Cook, ed. pp. 272-296. Department of
        Anthropology. University of Alaska.

1975   Aniganigaruk: A Study in Nunamiut Archaeology. Ph.D. dissertation.
        Washington State University.

Cranz, David

1967   The History of Greenland: containing a description of the country,
        and its inhabitants. . . J. Dodsley. London.

Cressman, Luther S. and Don E. Dumond

1962   Research on Northwest Prehistory: Prehistory in the Naknek Drain-
        age, Southwestern Alaska. Final Report to the National Science
        Foundation. University of Oregon.

Crowe, Keith J.

1974   A History of the Original Peoples of Northern Canada. Arctic
        Institute of North America. McGill-Queen's University Press.
        Montreal.

Daifuku, Hiroshi

1952   The Pit House in the Old World and in Native North America.
        American Antiquity 18(1):1-7.

Dall, William H.

1873   Notes on Prehistoric Remains in the Aleutian Islands. Proceedings
        of the California Academy of Science 4:283-287. (1868-1872).

1875a On Further Examinations of the Amaknak Cave, Captain's Bay,
       Unalashka. Proceedings of the California Academy of Sciences 5:
       196-200. (1873-1874).

1875b Notes on Some Aleut Mummies. Proceedings of the California
       Academy of Science 5:399-400. (1873-1874).

1875c Alaskan Mummies. American Naturalist 9(8):433-440.

1877 On the Succession of Shell-heaps in the Aleutian Islands. In:
       Tribes of the Extreme Northwest, Contributions to North American
       Ethnology 1(2):41-91.

1878 On the Remains of Later Prehistoric Man Obtained from Caves in the
       Catherina Archipelago, Alaska Territory, and Especially from the
       Caves of the Aleutian Islands. Smithsonian Contributions to
       Knowledge 22(6):1-40.

Davis, Wilbur A.

1954 Archaeological Investigations of Inland and Coastal Sites of the
       Katmai National Monument, Alaska. Microcard Publications of
       Archaeology and Anthropology of the University of Wisconsin, No. 4.

Debetz, George F.

1959 The Skeletal Remains of the Ipiutak Cemetery. Actas del 33 Con-
       gresso International de Americanists 2:157-164. San Jose, Costa
       Rica, 1958.

1960 Problems of Physical Anthropology in Arctic Regions. Report of
       the Circumpolar Conference 1958. Acta Arctica 12:61-65.

Deevey, E. S. and R. F. Flint

1957 Postglacial Hypsithermal Interval. Science 125:182-184.

Deberbøl, Magnus

1934 Animal Bones from the Norse Ruins at Brattahlid. Meddelelser om
       Grønland 88(1)149-155.

1936a Animal Remains from the West Settlement in Greenland. With special
       Reference to Livestock. Meddelelser om Grønland, Bd. 88.

1936b The Former Eskimo Habitation in the Kangerdlugssuak District,
       East Greenland. Meddelelser om Grønland 104(10).

Dekin, Albert A., Jr.

1967 The Closure Site: A Pre-Dorset Site on Southern Baffin Island.
       Paper Presented at the 32nd Annual Meeting of the Society for
       American Archaeology. Ann Arbor, 4 May.

1968   Hypotheses on Cultural Interaction in the Eastern American Arctic.
        Paper Presented to the Michigan Academy of Science, Arts and
        Letters, Grand Valley State College. Grand Valley, Michigan,
        22 March.

1969   Paleo-Climate and Prehistoric Cultural Interaction in the Eastern
        Arctic. Paper Presented at the 34th Annual Meeting of the Society
        for American Archaeology. Milwaukee, May.

1970   Paleo-Climate and Paleo-Ecology of the Eastern North American
        Arctic During Its Occupancy by Man (2500 BC to date). Paper Pre-
        sented at the 3rd Annual Meeting of the Canadian Archaeological
        Association. Ottawa, March.

1971a   Prehistoric Climatic Change and Human Ecology--Evidence from the
        Eastern Arctic. Paper Presented to the Symposium on Late
        Pleistocene and Holocene Climatic Changes and their Human Ecologi-
        cal Implications at the 36th Annual Meeting of the Society for
        American Archaeology. Norman, Oklahoma, 6 May.

1971b   Review: Akulivikchuk: A Nineteenth Century Eskimo Village on the
        Nushagak River, Alaska, by James W. VanStone. Fieldiana: Anthro-
        pology, Vol. 60. Chicago: Field Museum of Natural History, 1970.
        Historical Archaeology 5:125-126.

1972a   Climate and Culture in Greenlandic Prehistory: An Explicitly
        Scientific Approach. Paper Presented at the 5th Annual Meeting of
        the Canadian Archaeological Association. Symposium on Prehistoric
        Climatic and Cultural Change in Eastern Canada and Adjacent
        Regions. St. John's: Memorial University of Newfoundland.

1972b   Climatic Change and Cultural Change: A Correlative Study from
        Eastern Arctic Prehistory. Polar Notes 12:11-31.

1972c   Review: Fort Chimo and Payne Lake, Ungava Peninsula Archaeology,
        1965, by Thomas E. Lee. Collection, Travaux Divers, No. 16.
        Centre d'Etudes Nordiques. Universite Laval. Quebec, 1967. and
        Archaeological Discoveries, Payne Bay Region, Ungava, 1966, by
        Thomas E. Lee. Collection, Travaux Divers, No. 20. Centre d'
        Etudes Nordiques. Universite Laval. Quebec, 1968. and
        Archaeological Findings: Gyrfalcon to Eider Islands, Ungava, 1968,
        by Thomas E. Lee. Collection, Travaux Divers, No. 27. Centre d'
        Etudes Nordiques. Universite Laval. Quebec, 1969. American
        Anthropologist 74(6):1501-1504

1973a   The Arctic. In: The Development of North American Archaeology.
        James E. Fitting, ed. pp. 14-48. Anchor Press/Doubleday. Garden
        City, New York.

1973b   Preliminary Paper and Discussion. School of American Research
        Advanced Seminar on Pre-Dorset--Dorset Problems. Santa Fe.

1973c   Reply to Lee. American Anthropologist 75(6):2040-2041.

1974 The Walrus and the Polished Burin: A Possible Dynamic Duo from Eastern Arctic Prehistory. Paper Presented at the 39th Annual Meeting of the Society for American Archaeology. Washington, D.C., 3 May.

1975 Models of Pre-Dorset Culture: Towards an Explicit Methodology. Ph.D. dissertation. Michigan State University.

1976a Elliptical Analysis: An Heuristic Technique for the Analysis of Artifact Clusters. In: Eastern Arctic Prehistory: Paleoeskimo Problems. Moreau S. Maxwell, ed. pp. 79-88. Memoirs of the Society for American Archaeology, No. 31.

1976b The Arctic Small Tool Horizon: A Behavioral Model of the Dispersal of Human Populations into an Unoccupied Niche. In: Eastern Arctic Prehistory: Paleoeskimo Problems. Moreau S. Maxwell, ed. pp. 156-163. Memoirs of the Society for American Archaeology, No. 31.

In preparation Reports on Archaeological Excavations Conducted in the Wiseman Area, Koyukuk Valley, Interior Alaska for the Alyeska Pipeline Service Company by the University of Alaska, ed. by John P. Cook.

deLaguna, see Laguna, Frederica de

Denniston, Glenda G.

1966 Cultural Change at Chaluka, Umnak Island: Stone Artifacts and Features. Arctic Anthropology 3(2):84-124.

1972 Ashishik Point: An Economic Analysis of a Prehistoric Aleutian Community. Ph.D. dissertation. University of Wisconsin. Madison.

1974 The Diet of the Ancient Inhabitants of Ashishik Point, An Aleut Community. Arctic Anthropology 11(Suppl.):143-152.

Denniston, Glenda B. and Allen P. McCartney

1963 Eastern Aleutian Prehistory: An Analysis of Chaluka Midden, Umnak Island. Paper Presented at the Annual Meeting of the Society for American Archaeology. Boulder, May.

Derry, David E.

1971 The Archaeology and Anthropology of a Recent Eskimo Habitation at Prudhoe Bay, Alaska. In: Final Report of the Archaeological Survey and Excavations along the Alyeska Pipeline Service Company Pipeline Route. John P. Cook, ed. pp. 6-116. Department of Anthropology. University of Alaska.

1972 The Archaeology and Anthropology of a Recent Eskimo Habitation at Prudhoe Bay, Alaska. Master's thesis. University of Alaska.

1974   Bone Tools from the Umingmak Site: The Musk-Ox Way Revisited?
        Manuscript.

Desautels, Roger J., et. al.

1970   Archaeological Report, Amchitka Island, Alaska, 1969-1970. Report
        by Archaeological Research, Inc. to the U. S. Atomic Energy Com-
        mission. Las Vegas, Nevada.

Dixon, E. James Jr.

1971   The Gallagher Flint Station and Other Sites Along the Sagavanirktok
        River. In: Final Report of the Archaeological Survey and Excava-
        tions along the Alyeska Pipeline Service Company Pipeline Route.
        John P. Cook, ed. pp. 117-207. Department of Anthropology.
        University of Alaska.

1972   The Gallagher Flint Station, an Early Man Site on the North Slope,
        Arctic Alaska. Master's thesis. University of Alaska.

1975a   The Gallagher Flint Station, an Early Man Site on the North Slope,
        Arctic Alaska, and its Role in Relation to the Bering Land Bridge.
        Arctic Anthropology 12(1):68-75.

1975b   Final Report, Archaeological Probability Modeling. Submitted to
        Bureau of Land Management under Contract #52500-CT4-114.
        Fairbanks, Alaska.

1976   The Pleistocene Prehistory of Arctic North America. Paper Pre-
        pared for Presentation at the 11th International Congress of Pre-
        historic and Protohistoric Sciences. Nice, France, 13-18
        September.

Dixon, R. Greg and William F. Johnson

1972   Survey of the Prehistoric and Historic Values of 48 Waysides of the
        Alaska State Park System. Manuscript.

Donahue, P. F.

1973a   Middle Porcupine River Survey: A Note. Canadian Archaeological
        Association Bulletin 5:127-129.

1973b   A Bibliography of Circumpolar Prehistory. University of Manitoba
        Anthropology Papers, No. 2. University of Manitoba. Winnipeg.

Drucker, Philip

1943   Archaeological Survey on the Northern Northwest Coast. Bureau of
        American Ethnology Bulletin 133(20):17-142.

Dubbs, Patrick J.

1971   Review: Kijik: An Historic Tanaina Indian Settlement, by James W. VanStone and Joan B. Townsend. Fieldiana Anthropology, Vol. 59. Chicago: Field Museum of Natural History, 1970. Historical Archaeology 1971(5):124–125.

Dumond, Don E.

1962a Blades and Cores in Oregon. American Antiquity 27(3):419–424.

1962b Human Prehistory in the Naknek Drainage, Alaska. Ph.D. dissertation. University of Oregon.

1962c Prehistory of the Naknek Drainage: A Preliminary Statement. In: Research on Northwest Prehistory: Prehistory in the Naknek Drainage, Southwest Alaska, by Luther S. Cressman and Don E. Dumond. Anthropological Papers of the University of Oregon.

1963   Two Early Phases from the Naknek Drainage. Arctic Anthropology 1(2):93–102.

1964   A Note on the Prehistory of Southwestern Alaska. Anthropological Papers of the University of Alaska 12(1):33–45.

1965a On Eskaleutian Linguistics, Archaeology and Prehistory. American Anthropologist 67:1231–1257.

1965b Review: The Archaeology of Cape Denbigh, by J. Louis Giddings. Brown University Press. Providence, 1964. American Antiquity 30(4):520–521.

1966   Review: The Most Ancient Eskimo, by Lawrence Oschinsky. The Canadian Research Centre for Anthropology. Ottawa, 1964. American Antiquity 31(4):598–599.

1968a On the Presumed Spread of Slate Grinding in Alaska. Arctic Anthropology 5(1):82–91.

1968b Toward a Prehistory of Alaska. In: Frontier Alaska, R. A. Frederick, ed. Proceedings of a Conference on Alaskan History, 1967. Alaska Methodist University, Anchorage.

1969a Prehistoric Cultural Contacts in Southwestern Alaska. Science 166:1108–1115.

1969b The Prehistoric Pottery of Southwestern Alaska. Anthropological Papers of the University of Alaska 14(2):19–42.

1969c Toward a Prehistory of the Na-Dene, with a General Comment on Population Movements Among Nomadic Hunters. American Anthropologist 75(5):857–863.

1970a Eskimos and Aleuts. Proceedings of the 8th International Congress of Anthropological and Ethnological Sciences 3:102-107. Tokyo, 1968.

1970b Review: Eskimo Prehistory, by Hans-Georg Bandi. University of Alaska Press. College, 1969. American Anthropologist 72(4):941-943.

1971a A Summary of Archaeology in the Katmai Region, Southwestern Alaska. Anthropological Papers of the University of Oregon, No. 2.

1971b Rejoinder to "Early Racial and Cultural Identifications in Southwestern Alaska", by Jean S. Aigner, William S. Laughlin and Robert F. Black. Science 171(3966):88-90.

1971c Review: Historic Settlement Patterns in the Nushagak River Region, Alaska, by James VanStone. Fieldiana Anthropology, Vol. 61. Chicago: Field Museum of Natural History, 1970. Arctic 24(4):314-315.

1972a Prehistoric Population Growth and Subsistence Change in Eskimo Alaska. In: Population Growth: Anthropological Implications. Brian Spooner, ed., pp. 311-328. MIT Press. Cambridge.

1972b Review: Akmak: An Early Archaeological Assemblage from Onion Portage, Northwest Alaska, by Douglas D. Anderson. Acta Arctica, Fasc., 16. Copenhagen, 1970. American Anthropologist 74(6):1504-1505.

1972c The Alaska Peninsula in Alaskan Prehistory. In: For the Chief: Essays in honor of L. S. Cressman. F. W. Voget and R. S. Stevenson, eds. University of Oregon Anthropological Papers, No. 4.

1973a Review: Kijik: An Historic Tanaina Indian Settlement, by James W. VanStone and Joan B. Townsend. Fieldiana Anthropology, Vol. 59. Chicago: Field Museum of Natural History, 1970. and Akulivkchuk: A Nineteenth Century Eskimo Village on the Nushagak River, Alaska, by James W. VanStone. Fieldiana Anthropology, Vol. 60. Chicago: Field Museum of Natural History, 1970. American Antiquity 38(2):247-248

1973b Review: Copper Eskimo Prehistory, by Robert McGhee. National Museums of Canada, National Museum of Man Publications in Archaeology, No. 2. Ottawa, 1972. Arctic 26(3):264=265.

1974a Some Uses of R-Mode Analysis in Archaeology. American Antiquity 39(2):253-270.

1974b Remarks on the Prehistory of the North Pacific: To Lump or Not to Lump. In: International Conference on the Prehistory and Paleo-ecology of Western North American Arctic and Subarctic. Scott Raymond and Peter Schledermann, eds. pp. 47-56. University of Calgary Archaeological Association. Alberta.

1974c Prehistoric Ethnic Boundaries on the Alaska Peninsula. Anthropological Papers of the University of Alaska 16(1):1-7.

1975 Coastal Adaptation and Cultural Change in Alaskan Eskimo Prehistory. In: Prehistoric Maritime Adaptations of the Circumpolar Zone. William W. Fitzhugh, IV, ed. pp. 167-180. Mouton and Company. Paris.

Dumond, Don E., Leslie Conton and Harvey M. Shields

1975 Eskimos and Aleuts on the Alaska Peninsula: A Reappraisal of Port Moller Affinities. Arctic Anthropology 12(1):49-67.

Dumond, Don E. and Robert L. A. Mace

1968 An Archaeological Survey Along Knik Arm. Anthropological Papers of the University of Alaska 14(1):1-21.

Emmons, George T.

1908 Petroglyphs in Southeastern Alaska. American Anthropologist 10: 221-230.

Eyerdam, W. J.

1936 Mammal Remains From an Aleut Stone Age Village. Journal of Mammology 17:61.

Fawcett, Francis L.

1971 Review: Ethnohistory in Southwestern Alaska and the Southern Yukon: Method and Content, by Margaret Lantis, ed. Studies in Anthropology No. 7. University Press of Kentucky. Lexington, 1970. Man N.S. 6(3):511.

Fedirchuk, G.

1970 Recent Archaeological Investigations at Fisherman Lake: The Julian Site. In: Early Man and Environments in Northwest North America. R. A. Smith and J. W. Smith, eds. pp. 105-116. Proceedings of the 2nd Annual Paleo-Environmental Workshop of the University of Calgary Archaeological Association. Students' Press. Calgary.

Finnegan, Michael

1974 A Migration Model for Northwest North America. In: International Conference on the Prehistory and Paleoecology of Western North American Arctic and Subarctic. Scott Raymond and Peter Schledermann, eds. pp. 57-74. University of Calgary Archaeological Association. Alberta.

Finn-Yarborough, Linda

   1975a Preliminary Archaeology Survey of the Port Lions Water Improve-
         ments. EDA Title 10 Project, #07-31-005. Manuscript.

   1975b Archaeology in the Delta Land Management Planning Study Area. A
         Report for the Alaska State Division of Parks and the U. S.
         Government, under Contract #CC10-0825.

Fischer-Møller, Knud

   1937 Skeletal Remains of the Central Eskimos. Report of 5th Thule
        Expedition, 1921-24 3(1).

   1938 Skeletons from Ancient Greenland Graves. Meddelelser om Grønland
        119(4).

   1942 Mediaeval Norse Settlements in Greenland. Anthropological Inves-
        tigations. Meddelelser om Grønland, Bd. 89.

Fitzhugh, William W., IV

   1969 Prehistoric Labrador: Archaeology Opens a New Frontier. Science
        Forum, Dec. 1969. pp. 31-34. University of Toronto Press.

   1970a Environmental Archaeology and Culture Systems in Hamilton Inlet,
         Labrador: A Survey of the Central Labrador Coast from 3000 B.C.
         to the Present. Ph.D. dissertation. Department of Anthropology.
         Harvard University.

   1970b Cultural Traditions of the Central Labrador Coast--3000 B.C. to
         the Present. Paper Presented at the 3rd Annual Meeting of the
         Canadian Archaeological Association. Ottawa, 12-15 March.

   1972 Environmental Archaeology and Cultural Systems in Hamilton Inlet,
        Labrador: A Survey of the Central Labrador Coast from 3000 B.C. to
        the Present. Smithsonian Contributions to Anthropology, No. 16.
        Smithsonian Institution Press. Washington, D.C.

   1973 Preliminary Paper and Discussion. School of American Research
        Advanced Seminar on Pre-Dorset--Dorset Problems. Santa Fe.

   1975a Prehistoric Maritime Adaptations of the Circumpolar Zone. Mouton
         and Company. Paris. (Ed.)

   1975b Introduction. In: Prehistoric Maritime Adaptations of the Circum-
         polar Zone. William W. Fitzhugh, IV, ed. pp. 1-20. Mouton and
         Company. Paris.

   1975c A Comparative Approach to Northern Maritime Adaptations. In: Pre-
         historic Maritime Adaptations of the Circumpolar Zone. William W.
         Fitzhugh, IV, ed. pp. 339-386. Mouton and Company. Paris.

1975d Preliminary Culture History of Nain, Labrador: Smithsonian
       Fieldwork for 1975. Manuscript.

1976a Paleoeskimo Occupations of the Labrador Coast. In: Eastern Arctic
       Prehistory: Paleoeskimo Problems. Moreau S. Maxwell, ed. pp. 103-
       118. Memoirs of the Society of American Archaeology, No. 31.

1976b Environmental Factors in the Evolution of Dorset Culture: A Mar-
       ginal Proposal for Hudson Bay. In: Eastern Arctic Prehistory:
       Paleoeskimo Problems. Moreau S. Maxwell, ed. pp. 139-149.
       Memoirs of the Society for American Archaeology, No. 31.

Forbis, Richard S.

1961   Early Point Types from Acasta Lake, N.W.T., Canada. American
       Antiquity 27(1):112-113.

Ford, James A.

1932a Archaeological Work in Alaska. Science 75(1935):9.

1932b Studying Eskimo Mounds in Alaska. El Palacio 32(10&11):155-156.

1932c Eskimo Burial Customs. El Palacio 33(21&22):198-199.

1952   Measurements of some Prehistoric Design Developments in the South-
       eastern States. Anthropological Papers of the American Museum of
       Natural History 44(3).

1959   Eskimo Prehistory in the Vicinity of Point Barrow Alaska. Anthro-
       pological Papers of the American Museum of Natural History 47(1):
       272.

Fradkin, E. E.

1970   Polykonic Sculpture from the Upper Paleolithic Site of Kostenki I.
       Arctic Anthropology 7(7):129-136.

Fredericksen, Demaris L.

n.d.   The Platinum Sites. Manuscript. Copy on file at the Danish.
       National Museum. Copenhagen.

Friedmann, Herbert

1932   The Birds of St. Lawrence Island, Bering Sea. Proceedings of the
       United States National Museum 80(12):1-31.

1933   The Chinese Cormorant on Kodiak Island, Alaska. Condor 35:30-31.

1934a Bird Bones from Eskimo Ruins on St. Lawrence Island, Bering Sea.
       Journal of the Washington Academy of Science 24(2):83-96.

1934b Bird Bones from old Eskimo Ruins in Alaska. Journal of the
      Washington Academy of Science 24(5):230-237.

1935 Avian Bones from Prehistoric Ruins on Kodiak Island, Alaska.
      Journal of the Washington Academy of Science 25(1):44-51.

1937 Bird Bones from Archaeological Sites in Alaska. Journal of the
      Washington Academy of Science 27(10):431-438.

1941 Bird Bones from Eskimo Ruins at Cape Prince of Wales, Alaska.
      Journal of the Washington Academy of Science 31(9):404-409.

Gad, Finn

1970 The History of Greenland I; Earliest Times to 1700. (Trans. from
      the 1967 Danish Edition by Ernst Dupont.) C. Hurst & Co. London.

Gehr, Elliot A.

1970 A Description of the Artifact Collection from Kukak Bay, Alaska.
      Master's thesis. Department of Anthropology. University of
      Oregon.

Geist, Otto W.

1962 Collecting Pleistocene Fossils and Natural History Material in
      Arctic Alaska River Basins, 1959, 1960 and 1961. Final Report to
      the Office of Naval Research by the Arctic Institute of North
      America. Manuscript.

Geist, Otto W. and Froelich Rainey

1936 Archaeology Excavations at Kukulik, St. Lawrence Island, Alaska.
      Miscellaneous Publication of the University of Alaska, Vol. 2.

Gibson, William

1939 Prehistoric Wanderings of the Eskimos. Beaver 270(3):18-23.

Giddings, J. Louis, Jr.

1938a Buried Wood from Fairbanks, Alaska. Tree Ring Bulletin 4(4):3-5.

1938b Recent Tree-Ring Work in Alaska. Tree Ring Bulletin 5(2):16.

1940 The Application of Tree Ring Dates to Arctic Sites. Tree Ring
      Bulletin 7(2):10-14.

1941a Dendrochronology in Northern Alaska. Master's thesis. University
      of Arizona.

1941b Dendrochronology in Northern Alaska. University of Alaska Publica-
      tion, No. 4.

1941c Rock Paintings in Central Alaska. American Antiquity 7(1):69-70.

1941d Ethnographic Notes, Kobuk River Region, Alaska. The Kiva 6(7):25-28.

1942 Dated Sites on the Kobuk River, Alaska. Tree Ring Bulletin 9(1): 2-8.

1943a Some Climatic Aspects of Tree Growth in Alaska. Tree Ring Bulletin 9(4):26-32.

1943b A Plan for Mapping Arctic Sea Currents. Geographic Review 33:326-327.

1944 Dated Eskimo Ruins of an Inland Zone. American Antiquity 10(2): 113-134.

1947 Mackenzie River Delta Chronology. Tree Ring Bulletin 13(4):26-29.

1948a Chronology of the Kobuk-Kotzebue Sites. Tree Ring Bulletin 14(4): 26-32.

1948b Diagonal Flaking from Kotzebue, Alaska. American Antiquity 14(2): 127.

1949 Early Flint Horizons on the North Bering Sea Coast. Journal of the Washington Academy of Sciences 39(3):85-90.

1950a Problems of Early Man in Alaska. Proceedings of the Alaska Scientific Conference. Washington, 9-11 Nov. National Research Council Bulletin 122(50).

1950b Early Man on the Bering Sea Coast. Annals of the New York Academy of Science (Ser. II) 13(1):18-21.

1950c Traces of Early Man on the North Bering Sea Coast. University of Pennsylvania Museum Bulletin 14(4):3-13. Philadelphia.

1950d New Light on Early Man in Alaska. Bulletin of the Philadelphia Anthropological Society 3(2):2-4. Philadelphia.

1951a The Denbigh Flint Complex. American Antiquity 16(3):193-203.

1951b The Arctic Woodland Culture of the Kobuk River. Ph.D. dissertation. University of Pennsylvania.

1951c Review: Ipiutak and the Arctic Whale Hunting Culture, by Helge Larsen and Froelich Rainey. Anthropological Papers of the American Museum of Natural History, No. 4. New York, 1948. American Antiquity 17(2):158-160.

1951d The Forest Edge at Norton Bay, Alaska. Tree Ring Bulletin 18(1).

1951e The Museum of the University of Alaska at Fairbanks. Museum 4(2): 115-117.

1952a The Arctic Woodland Culture of the Kobuk River. Monograph of the University of Pennsylvania Museum.

1952b Ancient Bering Strait and Population Spread. In: Science in Alaska. Henry Collins, ed. Special Publication of the Arctic Institute of North America 1:85-102.

1952c Driftwood and Problems of Arctic Sea Currents. Proceedings of the American Philosophical Society 96(2):129-142.

1952d Observations on the "Eskimo Type" of Kinship and Social Structure. Anthropological Papers of the University of Alaska 1(1):5-10.

1953a Yukon River Spruce Growth. Tree Ring Bulletin 20(1):2-5.

1953b A Holiday with the Padlimiut. Bulletin of the Philadelphia Anthropological Society 7(1):3-5.

1954a Tree Ring Dating in the American Arctic. Tree Ring Bulletin 20 (3&4):23-25.

1954b Early Man in the Arctic. Scientific American 190(6):82-88.

1955 The Denbigh Flint Complex Is Not Yet Dated. American Antiquity 21(3):255-268.

1956a A Flint Site in Northernmost Manitoba. American Antiquity 21(3): 255-268.

1956b The Burin Spall Artifact. Arctic 9(4):229-237.

1956c "Pillows" and Other Rare Flints. Anthropological Papers of the University of Alaska 4(2):117-120.

1956d Forest Eskimos: An Ethnographic Sketch of the Kobuk River People in the 1880's. Bulletin of the University of Pennsylvania Museum 20(2).

1957a Review: Archaeology of the Uyak Site, Kodiak Island, by Robert Heizer. Anthropological Records, Vol. 17, No. 1. Berkeley, 1956. American Anthropologist 59(2):371-372.

1957b Round Houses in the Western Arctic. American Antiquity 23(2):121-135.

1957c The Tenuous Beaufort Sea Archaeology. In: Science in Alaska, 1954. Proceedings of the 5th Alaskan Science Conference. Fairbanks.

1959 Archaeological Studies of Kotzebue Sound, Alaska. Year Book of the American Philosophical Society for 1959. pp. 513-514. Philadelphia.

1960a A View of Archaeology about Bering Strait. Acta Arctica 12:27-33.

1960b First Traces of Man in the Arctic. Natural History 69(9):10-19.

1960c The Archaeology of Bering Strait. Current Anthropology 1(2):121-138.

1961a Cultural Continuities of Eskimos. American Antiquity 27(2):155-173.

1961b Review: Archaeological Investigations of Inland and Coastal Sites of the Katmai National Monument, Alaska, by Wilbur Davis. Microcard Publications of Archaeology and Anthropology of the University of Wisconsin, No. 4. Madison, 1954. American Antiquity 27(1):126.

1961c Kobuk River People. Studies of Northern Peoples, No. 1. University of Alaska.

1961d Alaskan Aboriginal Culture History. National Survey of Historical Sites and Buildings. United States National Park Service Bulletin.

1962a Onion Portage and Other Flint Sites of the Kobuk River. Arctic Anthropology 1(1):6-27.

1962b Seven Discoveries of Bering Straits. Proceedings of the American Philosophical Society 106(2):89-93. Philadelphia.

1962c Side-Notched Points Near Bering Straits. In: Prehistoric Cultural Relations Between the Arctic and Temperate Zones of North America. John M. Campbell, ed. pp. 35-38. Arctic Institute of North America Technical Paper No. 11. Montreal.

1962d Eskimos and Old Shorelines. The American Scholar 31(4):585-594.

1962e Alaska Aboriginal Culture. The National Survey of Historic Sites & Buildings. Theme 16. National Park Service.

1963 Some Arctic Spear Points and Their Counterparts. Anthropological Papers of the University of Alaska 10(2):1-12.

1964 The Archaeology of Cape Denbigh. Brown University Press. Providence.

1965a A Long Record of Eskimos and Indians at the Forest Edge. In: Context and Meaning in Cultural Anthropology. M. E. Spiro, ed. pp. 89-205. The Free Press. New York.

1965b Part 2: Archaeology. In: The Quaternary Geology and Archaeology of Alaska, by T. L. Pewe, D. M. Hopkins and J. L. Giddings. In: The Quarternary of the United States. H. E. Wright and D. G. Frey, eds. pp. 355-374. (Review Volume of the VII Congress of the International Association of Quaternary Research).

1966 Cross-Dating the Archaeology of Northwestern Alaska. Science
      153(3732):127-135.

1967 Ancient Men of the Arctic. Alfred A. Knopf. New York.

Giddings, J. Louis, Jr. and Hans-Georg Bandi

1962 Eskimo-archaeologische Strandwalluntersuchungen auf Kap
      Krusenstern Nordwest-Alaska. Germania 40(1):1-21.

Giddings, J. Louis, Jr. and David M. Hopkins

1953 Geological Background of the Iyatayet Archaeological Site, Cape
      Denbigh, Alaska. Smithsonian Miscellaneous Collection 121:11.
      Smithsonian Institution, Washington, D. C.

Giddings, J. Louis, Jr. and Ivar Skarland

1948 Flint Stations in Central Alaska. American Antiquity 14(2):116-120.

Giddings, Ruth W.

1970 Review: Tikchik Village: A 19th Century Riverine Community in
      Southwestern Alaska, by James W. VanStone. Fieldiana Anthropology,
      Vol. 56, No. 3. Chicago: Field Museum of Natural History, 1968.
      American Anthropologist 72(2):451-453.

Gjessing, Gutorm

1944 Circumpolar Stone Age. Acta Arctica, Fasc. 2.

1948 Some Problems in Northwestern Archaeology. American Antiquity
      13(4):298-302.

Glob, P. V.

1935 Eskimo Settlements in Kempe Fjord and King Oscar Fjord.
      Meddelelser om Grønland 102:2.

Gordon, Bryan C.

1970a Recent Archaeological Investigations on the Arctic Yukon Coast:
      Including a Description of the British Mountain Complex at Trout
      Lake. In: Early Man and Environments in Northwest North America.
      R. A. Smith and J. W. Smith, eds. pp. 67-86. Proceedings of the
      2nd Annual Paleo-Environmental Workshop of the University of
      Calgary Archaeological Association. Students' Press. Calgary.

1970b Bison Antiquus from the Northwest Territories. Arctic 23(2):132-
      133.

1972 Interim Report, Upper Thelon River Archaeological-Botanical Pro-
      ject. University of Calgary Department of Archaeology.
      Mimeographed.

1974a Mackenzie Delta Archaeology-1972. In: International Conference on the Prehistory and Paleoecology of Western North American Arctic and Subarctic. Scott Raymond and Peter Schledermann, eds. pp. 75-86. University of Calgary Archaeological Association. Alberta.

1974b Of Men and Herds in Barrenland Prehistory. Ph.D. dissertation. Department of Archaeology. University of Calgary.

1975 Of Men and Herds in Barrenland Prehistory. Mercury Series. Archaeological Survey of Canada Paper, No. 28. National Museums of Canada. Ottawa.

1976a Antler Pseudo-Tools Made by Caribou. In: Primitive Art and Technology. J. S. Raymond, B. Loveseth, C. Arnold and G. Reardon, eds. pp. 121-128. Archaeological Association of the University of Calgary. Alberta.

1976b Report of 1975 Fieldwork. The Calgary Archaeologist 4:9-10. University of Calgary.

Gordon, Bryan C. and Howard Savage

1974 Whirl Lake: A Stratified Indian Site Near the Mackenzie Delta. Arctic 27(3):175-188.

Gosselin, A., P. Plumet, P. Richard and J. P. Salaun

1974 Recherches Archeologiques et Paleoecologiques au Nouveau Quebec. Paleo-Quebec No. 1. Trois-Rivieres: Universite du Quebec a Trois-Rivieres.

Grant, J. C. B.

1929 Anthropometry of the Cree and Salteaux Indians in Northeastern Manitoba. Anthropological Series of the National Museum of Canada 59(13). Ottawa.

1930 Anthropometry of the Chipewyan and Cree Indians of the Neighborhood of Lake Athapaska. Anthropological Series of the National Museum of Canada 64(14). Ottawa.

Gray, Norman H. and David R. Yesner

n.d. Effects of Human exploitation on Predator-Prey Interactions: an Example from the Aleutian Islands. Manuscript.

Grayson, Donald K.

1969 The Tigalda Site: An Eastern Aleutian Midden. Master's thesis. University of Oregon.

Green, Dee F.

    1975   Cluster Analysis of Silumiut Houses. Arctic Anthropology 12(1):
             82-89.

Greengo, Robert E.

    1972   Review: BC Studies, Special Issue. Archaeology in British Colum-
             bia: New Discoveries, by Roy L. Carlson, ed. BC Studies, 6 and 7.
             Vancouver: University of British Columbia, 1970. American Anthro-
             pologist 74(4):959-960.

Griffin, James B.

    1953   A Preliminary Statement on the Pottery from Cape Denbigh, Alaska.
             In: Asia and North America: Transpacific Contacts. Marian W.
             Smith, ed. Society for American Archaeology Memoirs, No. 9.
             American Antiquity 18(3):2:40-42.

    1960   Some Prehistoric Connections Between Siberia and America.
             Science 131(3403):801-812.

    1962   A Discussion of Prehistoric Similarities and Connections Between
             the Arctic and Temperate Zones of North America. In: Prehistoric
             and Cultural Relations Between the Arctic and Temperate Zones of
             North America. John M. Campbell, ed. pp. 154-163. Arctic Insti-
             tute of North America, Technical Paper No. 11. Montreal.

    1971   Review: Archaeological Investigations in the Grand Rapids,
             Manitoba, Reservoir 1961-62, by William J. Mayer-Oakes. Univer-
             sity of Manitoba Press. Winnipeg, 1970. Arctic 24(4):309-310.

Griffin, James B. and Roscoe H. Wilmeth, Jr.

    1964   The Ceramic Complexes at Iyatayet. In: The Archaeology of Cape
             Denbigh (Appendix), by J. Louis Giddings, Jr., Brown University
             Press. Providence.

Griffin, James B., G. A. Wright and A. A. Gordus

    1969a Obsidian Samples from Archaeological Sites in Northwestern Alaska:
             A Preliminary Report. Arctic 22(2):152-156.

    1969b Preliminary Report on Obsidian Samples from Archaeological Sites
             in Northwestern Alaska. Arctic 22(2):152-156.

Guggenheim, P.

    1945   An Anthropological Campaign on Amchitka. Scientific Monthly 61:
             21-32.

Hadleigh-West, Frederick

1958 Distributions of Certain Economic Plants and Their Relations to
Culture History in the Aleutian Islands. Oriental Geographer 2(1).
Dacca.

1959 Exploratory Excavations at Sitka National Monument. Final Report
Submitted to the National Park Service.

1960 A Report of an Archaeological Survey at Ogotoruk Creek, Alaska.
Interim Final Report Submitted to the U. S. Atomic Energy
Commission.

1963a Early Man in the Western American Arctic: A Symposium. Anthropological Papers of the University of Alaska 10:2. (Ed.)

1963b Leaf-Shaped Points in the Western Arctic. Anthropological Papers
of the University of Alaska 10(2):51-62.

1965 Excavations at Two Sites on the Teklanika River, Mount McKinley
National Park, Alaska. Report to the National Park Service.

1966a Otto William Geist, 1888-1963. American Anthropologist 68(1):132-
133.

1966b Archaeology of Ogotorok Creek. In: Environment of the Cape
Thompson Region, Alaska. Norman J. Wilimovsky and John N. Wolfe,
eds. pp. 927-968. U. S. Atomic Energy Commission. Division of
'Technical Information. PNE-481. Springfield.

1967a A System of Archaeological Sites Designation for Alaska. American
Antiquity 32(1):107.

1967b The Donnelly Ridge Site and the Definition of an Early Core and
Blade Complex in Central Alaska. American Antiquity 32(3):360-
382.

1971 Archaeological Reconnaissance of Denali State Park, Alaska. Report to the Division of Parks, State of Alaska.

1972 Archaeological and Paleoecological Research in the Tangle Lakes,
Central Alaska, 1966-1972: A Report of Progress. Manuscript.

1974 The Significance of Typologically Early Site Collections in the
Tangle Lakes, Central Alaska: A Preliminary Consideration. In:
International Conference on the Prehistory and Paleoecology of
Western North American Arctic and Subarctic. Scott Raymond and
Peter Schledermann, eds. pp. 217-238. University of Calgary
Archaeological Association. Alberta.

1975 Dating the Denali Complex. Arctic Anthropology 12(1):76-81.

Hadleigh-West, Frederick and H. G. Bandi and J. V. Matthews

    1965   Archaeological Survey and Excavations in the Proposed Rampart Dam
           Impoundment, 1963–64. Report to the National Park Service.

Hadleigh-West, Frederick and William B. Workman

    1970   A Preliminary Archaeological Evaluation of the Southern Part of
           the Route of the Proposed Trans-Alaska Pipeline System: Valdez to
           Hogan's Hill. Manuscript.

Hall, Edwin S., Jr.

    1966   Kangiguksuk: A Cultural Reconstruction of a 16th Century Eskimo
           Site in Northern Alaska. Ph.D. dissertation. Department of
           Anthropology. Yale University.

    1968   An Addition to Eskimo Material Culture. Anthropological Papers of
           the University of Alaska 14(1):23-26.

    1969a Avian Remains from the Kangiguksuk Site, Northern Alaska. Condor
           71(1):66-67.

    1969b Speculations on the Late Prehistory of the Kutchin Athapaskans.
           Ethnohistory 16(4):317-333.

    1970a Excavations at Tukuto Lake: The Late Prehistoric/Early Historic
           Eskimos of Interior Northwest Alaska. Mimeographed.

    1970b Review: The Arnapik and Tyara Sites: An Archaeological Study of
           Dorset Culture Origins, by William E. Taylor, Jr. Memoirs of the
           Society for American Archaeology, No. 22. American Antiquity 33
           (4):1-129. American Anthropologist 72(4):943-944.

    1970c The Late Prehistoric Early Historic Eskimo of Interior Northern
           Alaska: An Ethnoarchaeological Approach: Anthropological Papers
           of the University of Alaska 15(1):1-12.

    1971   Kangiguksuk: A Cultural Reconstruction of a Sixteenth Century
           Eskimo Site in Northern Alaska. Arctic Anthropology 8(1):1-101.

    1973a Archaeological Investigations in the Noatak River Valley--Summer
           1973. Mimeographed.

    1973b Archaeological and Recent Evidence for Expansion of Moose Range in
           Northern Alaska. Journal of Mammalogy 54(1):294=295.

    1974   Known Archaeological Resources of the Noatak River Basin, Northern
           Alaska, as of October 1974. Prepared for the National Park Service,
           U. S. Department of the Interior.

1975a Review: Historic Settlement Patterns in the Nushagak River Region, Alaska, by James W. VanStone, Fieldiana Anthropology, Vol. 61. Chicago: Field Museum of Natural History, 1971. <u>and</u> Nushagak: An Historic Trading Center in Southwestern Alaska, by James W. VanStone, Fieldiana Anthropology, Vol. 62. Chicago: Field Museum of Natural History, 1972. American Antiquity 40(4):502-504.

1975b An Archaeological Survey of Interior Northwest Alaska. Anthropological Papers of the University of Alaska 17(2):13-30.

n.d. Technological Change in Northern Alaska. Manuscript.

Hall, Edwin S., Jr. and Robert A. McKennan

1973 An Archaeological Survey of the Old John Lake Area, Northern Alaska. Polar Notes 13:1-31.

Hamilton, Thomas D.

1970 Geological Relations of the Akmak Assemblage, Onion Portage, Alaska. Appendix to Akmak: An Early Archaeological Assemblage from Onion Portage, Northwest Alaska, by Douglas D. Anderson. Acta Arctica, Fasc. 16.

Hammerich, Louis L.

1958 The Origin of the Eskimo. Proceedings of the 32nd International Congress of Americanists. pp. 640-644. Copenhagen, 1956.

Hanable, William S., Karen W. Workman and William A. Sachack

1974 Lower Copper and Chitina Rivers: An Historic Resource Study. Alaska Office of Statewide Cultural Programs. History and Archaeology Series, Miscellaneous Publications, No. 5. Alaska Division of Parks. Anchorage.

Hantzsch, Bernhard

1908 Uber Eskimo-Steingraber im nordostlichen Labrador und das Sammein Anthropologischen Materials aus solchen. Abhandlungen und Berichte des Kgl. Zoologischen und Anthropologisch-Ethnographischen Museums zu Dresden 12:55-58. Dresden. (Printed as translated by M.B.A. Anderson, 1930.)

1930 Eskimo Stone Graves in North-Eastern Labrador and the Collection of Anthropological Material from Them. Canadian Field-Naturalist 44:180-182. (Translated by M.B.A. Anderson.)

Harp, Elmer, Jr.

1951 An Archaeological Reconnaissance in the Straits of Belle Isle Area. American Antiquity 16(3):203-221.

1952 The Cultural Affinities of the Newfoundland Dorset Eskimo. Ph.D. dissertation. Harvard University.

1953 New World Affinities of Cape Dorset Culture. Anthropological Papers of the University of Alaska 1(2):37-54.

1958 Prehistory in the Dismal Lake Area. Arctic 11(4):218-249.

1959a The Moffatt Archaeological Collection from the Dubawnt Country, Canada. American Antiquity 24(1):412-422.

1959b Ecological Continuity on the Barren Grounds. Polar Notes 1:48-56.

1960 Archaeological Research in Arctic North America: 1958-1960. Anthropologica 2(2):228-239.

1961a Notes and News, Arctic. American Antiquity 26(4):580-582.

1961b The Archaeology of the Lower and Middle Thelon, N.W.T. Arctic Institute of North America, Technical Paper No. 8.

1962 The Cultural History of the Central Barren Grounds. In: Prehistoric Cultural Relations Between the Arctic and Temperate Zones of North America. John M. Campbell, ed. pp. 69-75. Arctic Institute of North America, Technical Paper No. 11. Montreal.

1963 Evidence of Boreal Archaic Culture in Southern Labrador and Newfoundland. Contributions to Anthropology, 1961-1962. National Museum of Canada Bulletin 193(1):184-261.

1964a The Cultural Affinities of the Newfoundland Dorset Eskimo. National Museum of Canada Bulletin, No. 200. Queen's Printer. Ottawa.

1964b The Prehistoric Indian and Eskimo Cultures of Labrador and Newfoundland. Paper Presented at the 7th International Congress of Anthropological and Ethnological Sciences. Moscow, U.S.S.R., August.

1964c World Arctic Archaeology. In: The Unbelievable Land. I. Norman Smith, ed. pp. 49-54. Publication of the Department of Northern Affairs and Natural Resources and the Northern Service of the CBC. Ottawa.

1965 Review: The Archaeology of Cape Denbigh, by J. Louis Giddings, Jr. Brown University Press. Providence, 1964. American Anthropologist 67(2):578-579.

1968a Anthropological Interpretation from Color. In: Manual of Color Aerial Photography. J. T. Smith, ed. American Society of Photogrammetry. Fall's Church, Virginia.

206

1968b Optimum Scales and Emulsions in Air Photo Archaeology. Proceedings of the 8th International Congress of Anthropological and Ethnological Sciences 3:163-165. Tokyo.

1968c Review: Ancient Men of the Arctic, by J. Louis Giddings, Jr. Alfred A. Knopf. New York, 1967. American Anthropologist 70(5): 1018.

1970 Late Dorset Eskimo Art from Newfoundland. Folk 11&12:109-124.

1972 Review: The Arctic Small Tool Tradition in Manitoba, by Ronald J. Nash. Department of Anthropology Papers, No. 2. University of Manitoba Press. Winnipeg, 1969. American Anthropologist 74 (1-2):134-135.

1973a Review: An Archaeological Survey Between Cape Parry and Cambridge Bay, N.W.T., Canada in 1963, by William E. Taylor, Jr. Mercury Series. Archaeological Survey of Canada Paper, No. 1. National Museum of Man. Ottawa, 1972. Arctic 26(2):175-176.

1973b Preliminary Paper and Discussion. School of American Research Advanced Seminar on Pre-Dorset--Dorset Problems. Santa Fe.

1974 Threshold Indicators of Culture in Air Photo Archaeology: A Case Study in the Arctic. In: Aerial Photography in Anthropological Field Research. E. Z. Vogt, ed. pp. 14-27. Harvard University Press.

1975a A Late Dorset Copper Amulet from Southeastern Hudson Bay. Folk 16-17:33-44.

1975b Aerial Photography for the Arctic Archaeologist. In: Aerial Remote Sensing Techniques in Archaeology. Thomas R. Lyons and Robert K. Hitchcock, eds. Prescott College Press. Prescott, Arizona.

1976 Dorset Settlement Patterns in Newfoundland and Southeastern Hudson Bay. In: Eastern Arctic Prehistory: Paleoeskimo Problems. Moreau S. Maxwell, ed. pp. 119-138. Memoirs of the Society for American Archaeology, No. 31.

Harp, Elmer, Jr. and David R. Hughes

1968 Five Prehistoric Burials from Port au Choix, Newfoundland. Polar Notes 8:1-47.

Harris, David R.

1976 Review: Prehistoric Maritime Adaptations of the Circumpolar Zone, by William W. Fitzhugh, IV, ed. Papers from a Congress, Chicago, 1973. Mouton, The Hague, 1975. Science 193:755-756.

Hartweg, Raoul and Patrick Plumet

1974   Archeologie du Nouveau-Quebec: Sepultures et Squelettes de l'
       Ungava. Paleo-Quebec, No. 3. Universite du Quebec a Trois-
       Rivieres. Trois-Rivieres.

Hatt, Gudmund

1934   North American and Eurasian Culture Connections. Proceedings of
       the 5th Pacific Science Congress 4:2755-2765. Victoria and
       Vancouver, B. C.

1953   Early Intrusion of Agriculture in the North Atlantic Subarctic
       Region. Anthropological Papers of the University of Alaska 2(1):
       51-107.

Hattersley-Smith, G.

1973   An Archaeological Site on the North Coast of Ellesmere Island.
       Arctic 26(3):255-256.

Haury, Emil W., et. al.

1956   An Archaeological Approach to the Study of Cultural Stability.
       In: Seminars in Archaeology: 1955. R. Wauchope, ed. Memoirs of
       the Society for American Archaeology, No. 11. American
       Antiquity 32:31-57.

Hayashi, Kensaku

1968   The Fukui Microblade Technology and its Relationships in Northeast
       Asia and North America. Arctic Anthropology 5(1):128-190.

Haynes, C. Vance, Jr.

1966   Elephant Hunting in North America. Scientific America 214(6):
       104-112.

1969   New Developments on the Earliest Americans. Science 166:709-715.

1971   Time, Environment, and Early Man. Arctic Anthropology 8(2):3-14.

Heizer, Robert F.

1944   Artifact Transport by Migratory Animals and Other Means.
       American Antiquity 9(4):395-400.

1947   The Petroglyphs from Southwestern Kodiak Island, Alaska. Pro-
       ceedings of the American Philosophical Society 91(3):194-293.

1949   Pottery from the Southern Eskimo Region. Proceedings of the
       American Philosophical Society 93(1):48-56.

1951   The Sickle in Aboriginal Western North America. American Antiquity 16(3):247-252.

1952a   Incised Slate Figurines from Kodiak Islands, Alaska. American Antiquity 17(3):266.

1952b   Notes on Koniag Material Culture. Anthropological Papers of the University of Alaska 1(1):11-19.

1956   Archaeology of the Uyak Site, Kodiak Island, Alaska. Anthropological Records 17:1. Berkeley.

1957   Review: Chugach Prehistory: The Archaeology of Prince William Sound, Alaska, by Frederica deLaguna. University of Washington Publications in Anthropology, Vol. 13. Pullman, 1956. American Antiquity 59(2):370-371.

Helm, June

1973   Subarctic Athabascan Bibliography, 1973. University of Iowa. Iowa City.

Helmuth, H.

1975   Osteology of Eskimo Skulls from Kittigarjuit, Mackenzie Delta, N.W.T., Canada. Arctic Anthropology 12(1):90-103.

Hemstock, C. Anne and Geraldine A. Cooke

1973   Yukon Bibliography: Update 1963-1970. Occasional Publication of the Boreal Institute for Northern Studies 8(1). University of Alberta. Edmonton.

Henderson, Gerald Mitchell

1952   A Neo-Eskimo House Excavation at the Iyatayet Site on Cape Denbigh. Master's thesis. University of Pennsylvania.

Henn, Winfield

1975   Current Research on Eskaleut Prehistory in the Ugashik River Drainage, Alaska Peninsula. Paper Presented at the Annual Meeting of the American Anthropological Association. San Francisco, November.

Henoch, W. E. S.

1964   Preliminary Geomorphological Study of a Newly Discovered Dorset Culture Site on Melville Island, N.W.T. Arctic 17(2):119-125.

Heusser, Calvin J.

1963   Postglacial Palynology and Archaeology in the Naknek River Drainage Area, Alaska. American Antiquity 29(1):74-81.

Hewes, Gordon Winaut

    1947   Aboriginal Use of Fishery Resources in Northwestern North America.
            Ph.D. dissertation. University of California.

Hibben, Frank C.

    1941   Archaeological Aspects of Alaskan Muck Deposits. New Mexico
            Anthropologist 5(4):151-157.

    1943   Evidences of Early Man in Alaska. American Antiquity 8(3):254-259.

Hickey, Clifford G.

    1968   The Kayak Site: An Analysis of the Spatial Aspect of Culture as an
            Aid to Archaeological Inference. M.A. thesis. Brown University.

    1974   Effects of Treeline Shifts on Human Societies: Crazy Quilt Varia-
            bility vs. Macrozonal Adaptation. In: International Conference on
            the Prehistory and Paleoecology of Western North American Arctic
            and Subarctic. Scott Raymond and Peter Schledermann, eds. pp. 87-
            100. University of Calgary Archaeological Association. Alberta.

Hill, Beth and Ray Hill

    1975   Indian Petroglyphs of the Pacific Northwest. University of
            Washington Press. Seattle.

Hirsch, David I.

    1954   Glottochronology and Eskimo and Eskimo-Aleut Prehistory.
            American Anthropologist 56:825-38.

Hlady, Walter M.

    1970   Ten Thousand Years: Archaeology in Manitoba. Manitoba
            Archaeological Society. Winnipeg. (Ed.)

Hoffman, B.G.

    1952   Implications of Radiocarbon Datings for the Origin of Dorset
            Culture. American Antiquity 18(1):15-17.

Holm, Gustav

    1924   Small Additions to the Vinland Problem. In Consequence of Pro-
            fessor H.P. Steensby's Norsemen's Route from Greenland to Wine-
            land. Meddelelser om Grønland, Bd. 59.

Holmes, Charles E.

    1971   The Prehistory of the Upper Koyukuk River Region in North-Central
            Alaska. In: Final Report of the Archaeological Survey and Exca-
            vations along the Alyeska Pipeline Service Company Pipeline Route.
            John P. Cook, ed. pp. 326-400. Department of Anthropology.
            University of Alaska.

1974a Preliminary Testing of a Microblade Site at Lake Minchumina,
Alaska. In: International Conference on the Prehistory and
Paleoecology of Western North American Arctic and Subarctic.
Scott Raymond and Peter Schledermann, eds. pp. 99-113. Univer-
sity of Calgary Archaeological Association. Alberta.

1974b The Archaeology of Bonanza Creek Valley, North-Central Alaska.
Master's thesis. University of Alaska.

Holtved, Erik

1939 Archaeological Investigations in the Thule District. 2nd International Congress of Anthropological and Ethnological Sciences,
Copenhagen, 1938. Comtes Rendus. Copenhagen.

1944 Archaeological Investigations in the Thule District. Meddelelser
om Grønland 141(1&2).

1954 Archaeological Investigations in the Thule District, III.
Nugdlit and Comer's Midden. Meddelelser om Grønland 146(3).

Hopkins, David M.

1952 Age of the Denbigh Flint Complex. Science 116:513.

1959 Cenozoic History of the Bering Land Bridge. Science 129:1519-
1528.

1967 ·The Bering Land Bridge. Stanford University Press. Stanford.
(Ed.)

Hopkins, David M. and J. Louis Giddings, Jr.

1953 Geological Background of the Iyatayet Archaeological Site, Cape
Denbigh. Smithsonian Miscellaneous Collections 121(11).
Smithsonian Institution.

Hosley, Edward H.

1967 Grant No. 4083--Penrose Fund (1964), $1,500. The McGrath Ingalik
Indians, Central Alaska. Year Book of the American Philosophical
Society for 1967. pp. 544-547.

1972 Archaeological Evaluation of Ancient Habitation Site, Point Hope,
Alaska. Survey Report, Point Hope Beach Erosion, Point Hope,
Alaska. Alaska District, Corps of Engineers, Anchorage.

Hosley, Edward and Jeffrey Mauger

1967 The Campus Site Excavations--1966. Paper Presented at the Annual
Meeting of the Society for American Archaeology. Ann Arbor,
Michigan, 4 May.

Hough, Walter

    1898a The Lamp of the Eskimo. Annual Report of the U. S. National
           Museum for 1896. pp. 1025-1057.

    1898b The Origin and Range of the Eskimo Lamp. American Anthropologist
           11:116-122.

Howells, William W.

    1941 Review: Anthropometric Observations on the Eskimos and Indians of
          Labrador, by T. Dale Stewart. In: Fieldiana Anthropology, Vol.
          31, No. 1. Chicago: Field Museum of Natural History, 1939.
          American Antiquity 7(1):90-92.

Hrdlicka, Ales

    1924 Catalog of Human Crania in the United States National Museum
          Collections: The Eskimo, Alaskan and Related Indians, Eastern
          Asiatics. Proceedings of the United States National Museum
          63(12):1-51.

    1927 Anthropological Work in Alaska. Explorations and Fieldwork of
          the Smithsonian Institution in 1926. pp. 137-158. Smithsonian
          Institution Bulletin.

    1930a Anthropological Survey in Alaska. 46th Annual Report of the
           Bureau of American Ethnology--1929. pp. 19-374.

    1930b The Ancient and Modern Inhabitants of the Yukon. Explorations
           and Fieldwork of the Smithsonian Institution in 1929. pp. 137-
           146. Smithsonian Institution Bulletin.

    1931 Anthropological Work on the Kuskokwim River, Alaska. Explora-
          tions and Fieldwork of the Smithsonian Institution in 1930.
          pp. 123-134. Smithsonian Institution Bulletin.

    1932 Anthropological Work in Alaska. Explorations and Fieldwork of the
          Smithsonian Institution in 1931. pp. 91-102. Smithsonian
          Institution Bulletin.

    1933 Anthropological Explorations on Kodiak Island, Alaska. Explora-
          tions and Fieldwork of the Smithsonian Institution in 1932.
          pp. 41-44. Smithsonian Institution Bulletin.

    1935a Archaeological Excavations on Kodiak Island, Alaska. Explora-
           tions and Fieldwork of the Smithsonian Institution in 1934.
           pp. 47-52. Smithsonian Institution Bulletin.

    1935b A Leaf from the Prehistory of Kodiak Island, Alaska. The American
           Scholar 4:496-503.

1936 Archaeological Expedition to Kodiak Island, Alaska. Explorations and Fieldwork of the Smithsonian Institution in 1935. pp. 47-53. Smithsonian Institution Bulletin.

1937 Archaeological Explorations on Kodiak and the Aleutian Islands. Explorations and Fieldwork of the Smithsonian Institution in 1936. pp. 57-62. Smithsonian Institution Bulletin.

1940 Ritual Ablation of Front Teeth in Siberia and America. Smithsonian Miscellaneous Collections 99:3. Smithsonian Institution.

1941a Artifacts on Human and Seal Skulls from Kodiak Island. American Journal of Physical Anthropology 28:411-421.

1941b Diseases of and Artifacts on Skulls and Bones from Kodiak Island. Smithsonian Miscellaneous Collection 101(4):1-14.

1941c Exploration of Mummy Caves in the Aleutian Islands. Part I-- Previous Knowledge of Such Caves, Original Investigations. Scientific Monthly Jan.-Feb., 1941.

1942a Crania of Siberia. American Journal of Physical Anthropology 29(4):435-581.

1942b Catalog of Human Crania in the United States National Museum Collections: Eskimo in General. Proceedings of the United States National Museum 91(3131):169-429.

1944 The Anthropology of Kodiak Island. Wistar Institute of Anatomy and Biology. Philadelphia.

1945 The Aleutian and Commander Islands and their Inhabitants. Wistar Institute of Anatomy and Biology. Philadelphia.

Hughes, Charles C.

1973 Review: Ethnohistory in Southwestern Alaska and the Southern Yukon, by Margaret Lantis, ed. Studies in Anthropology No. 7. University of Kentucky Press. Lexington, 1970. American Anthropologist 75 (2):417-418.

Hughes, David R.

1968 Further Observations on the Human Remains from Sugluk and Mansel Islands. Contributions to Anthropology, 1967. National Museum of Canada Publication.

Humphrey, Robert L., Jr.

1966 The Prehistory of the Utukok River Region. Current Anthropology 7(5):586-588.

1970   The Prehistory of the Arctic Slope of Alaska: Pleistocene Cultural Relationships Between Eurasia and North America. Ph.D. dissertation. Department of Anthropology. University of New Mexico.

Humphrey, Robert L., Jr., et al.

1975/76   A Study of Archaeological and Historic Potential Along the Trans-Alaskan Natural Gas Pipeline Routes. Related to an Application Filed in Docket Number CP75-96, et al. September 24, 1974. Volumes I and II. Iroquois Research Institute.

Hurt, Wesley R., Jr.

1950   Artifacts from Shemya, Aleutian Islands. American Antiquity 16(1):69.

Ingstad, Anne Stine

1970   The Norse Settlement at L'Anse Aux Meadows, Newfoundland: A Preliminary Report from the Excavations 1961-1968. Acta Archaeologica 41:109-154.

Irving, William N.

1951   Archaeology in the Brooks Range of Alaska. American Antiquity 17(1):52-53.

1952   An Archaeological Reconnaissance of the Lower Colville River and Delta Regions. University of Alaska and ONR-ARL Libraries. (Mimeo)

1953a   An Archaeological Reconnaissance of the Lower Colville River and Delta Regions. Final Report Submitted to the Office of Naval Research, by the University of Alaska. Manuscript.

1953b   Evidence of Early Tundra Cultures in Northern Alaska. Anthropological Papers of the University of Alaska 1(2):55-85.

1954   Preliminary Report of an Archaeological Reconnaissance in the Western Brooks Range, Alaska. (Mimeo)

1955   Burins from Central Alaska. American Antiquity 20(4):380-383.

1957   An Archaeological Survey of the Susitna Valley. Anthropological Papers of the University of Alaska 6(1):37-52.

1962a   A Provisional Comparison of Some Alaskan and Asian Stone Industries. In: Prehistoric Culture Relations Between the Arctic and Temperate Zones of North America. John M. Campbell, ed. pp. 58-68. Arctic Institute of North America, Technical Paper No. 11. Montreal.

1962b   Field Work in the Western Brooks Range, Alaska: A Preliminary Report. Arctic Anthropology 1(1):76-83.

1963a Northwest North American and Central United States: A Review. Anthropological Papers of the University of Alaska 10(2):63–71.

1963b Review: The Archaeology of the Lower and Middle Thelon, N.W.T., by Elmer Harp, Jr. Arctic Institute of North America, Technical Paper No. 3. Montreal, 1961. Anthropologica 5:95–99.

1964 Punyik Point and the Arctic Small Tool Tradition. Ph.D. dissertation. Department of Anthropology. University of Wisconsin, Madison.

1966a Review: The Archaeology of Cape Denbigh, by J. Louis Giddings. Brown University Press. Providence, 1964. American Journal of Archaeology 70:210–213.

1966b Blade and Burin Industries in Northwest North America: A Summary of Current Research. Paper Presented at the 11th Annual Pacific Science Conference. Symposium 52:10. Tokyo.

1967 Klo-Kut: A Late Prehistoric Kutchin Site in Northern Yukon Territory. Paper Presented at the 32nd Annual Meeting of the Society for American Archaeology. Ann Arbor, May.

1968a The Barren Grounds. In: Science, History, and Hudson Bay, Vol. I. C. S. Beals, ed. pp. 26–54. Queen's Printer, Ottawa.

1968b Legend and Prehistory in the Brooks Range. Paper Presented at the 2nd Annual Meeting of the Canadian Archaeological Association, Toronto.

1968c Review: The Bering Land Bridge, by David M. Hopkins, ed. Stanford University Press. Stanford, 1967. American Anthropologist 70(4): 816.

1970 The Arctic Small Tool Tradition. Proceedings of the 8th International Congress of Anthropological and Ethnological Sciences 3:340–342. Tokyo and Kyoto, 1968.

1971a Review: Aghvook, White Eskimo: Otto Geist and Alaska Archaeology, by Charles J. Keim. University of Alaska Press. College, 1969. American Anthropologist 73(2):419–420.

1971b Recent Early Man Research in the North. Arctic Anthropology 8(2):68–82.

n.d. Preliminary Report on an Archaeological Reconnaissance in the Western Part of the Brooks Range of Alaska. Manuscript.

Irving, William N. and Harumi Befu

1961 Review: Tarukishi Remains. Hakodate Municipal Museum Research Bulletin, No. 4. Hakodate, 1956, and Tachikawa: Pre-Ceramic Stone Industries at the Tachikawa Site, Southern Kokkaido. Hakodate Municipal Museum, Research Bulletin, No. 6. Hakodate, 1960. American Antiquity 26(4):578–579.

Irving, William N. and Jacques Cinq-Mars

    1974   A Tentative Archaeological Sequence for Old Crow Flats, Yukon
           Territory. Arctic Anthropology 11(Suppl.):65-81.

Irving, William N. and C. Richard Harington

    1970   Pleistocene Radiocarbon Dated Artifacts from Northern Yukon Terri-
           tory. Paper Presented at the 3rd Annual Meeting of the Canadian
           Archaeological Association. Ottawa, 1970.

    1973   Upper Pleistocene Radiocarbon-Dated Artifacts from the Northern
           Yukon. Science 179:335-340.

Irving, William N. and William J. Mayer-Oakes

    n.d.   The Twin Lakes Pre-Dorset Site, Near Churchill, Manitoba.
           Manuscript.

Janes, Robert R. and Timothy C. Losey

    1974   Recent Discoveries in Fur Trade Archaeology of Upper and Central
           Mackenzie River Regions. Canadian Archaeological Association
           Bulletin 6:92-120.

Jelinek, Arthur

    1971   Early Man in the New World: A Technological Perspective. Arctic
           Anthropology 8(2):15-21.

Jenness, Diamond

    1923a Origin of the Copper Eskimos and their Copper Culture. Geographi-
           cal Review 13:540-541.

    1923b The Life of the Copper Eskimo. Report of the Canadian Arctic
           Expedition, 1913-1918, Vol. 12. Ottawa.

    1925   A New Eskimo Culture in Hudson Bay. Geographical Review 15:428-
           437.

    1928a Archaeological Investigations in Bering Strait, 1926. Annual Re-
           port to the National Museum of Canada for 1926. National Museum
           of Canada Bulletin 50:71-80.

    1928b The National Museum of Canada. American Anthropologist 30(1):
           178-180.

    1928c Ethnological Problems of Arctic America. In: Problems of Polar
           Research. American Geographical Society Special Publication
           7:167-175.

    1929a Little Diomede Island, Bering Strait. Geographical Review 19(1):
           78-86.

1929b Notes on the Beothuk Indians of Newfoundland. Annual Report to the
       National Museum of Canada. National Museum of Canada Bulletin
       57:36–39. Ottawa.

1932   Fifty Years of Archaeology in Canada. In: Fifty Years Retrospect,
       Anniversary Volume, 1882–1932. pp. 71–76. Publication of the
       Royal Society of Canada. Ottawa.

1933a The American Aborigines, Their Origin and Antiquity. University
       of Toronto Press. Toronto. (Ed.)

1933b The Problem of the Eskimo. In: The American Aborigines, Their
       Origin and Antiquity. Diamond Jenness, ed. pp. 373–396. Univer-
       sity of Toronto Press. Toronto.

1938   Review: Archaeology of St. Lawrence Island, by Henry B. Collins,
       Jr. Smithsonian Institution Miscellaneous Collection 96:1.
       Washington, D. C., 1937. American Antiquity 4(2):173–176.

1940   Prehistoric Culture Waves from Asia to America. Journal of the
       Washington Academy of Science 30(1):1–15.

1941a An Archaeological Collection from the Belcher Islands in Hudson
       Bay. Annals of the Carnegie Museum 28:189–206. Pittsburg.

1941b Prehistoric Culture Waves from Asia to America. Smithsonian
       Annual Report for 1940. Smithsonian Institution Bulletin.
       pp. 383–396.

1941c Wintemberg, William John--1876–1941. American Antiquity 7:64–66.

nnings, Jessie D.

1968   Prehistory of North America. McGraw-Hill Book Company. New York.

chelson, W. Vladimir

1906   Past and Present Subterranean Dwellings of the Tribes of North-
       eastern Asia and Northwestern America. Proceedings of the Inter-
       national Congress of Americanists 15(2):115–123.

1925   Archaeological Investigations in the Aleutian Islands. Carnegie
       Institute of Washington Publication, No. 367.

1928   Archaeological Investigations in Kuchatka. Carnegie Institute of
       Washington Publication, No. 388.

hnson, Donald McI.

1927   The Eskimo Remains. Cambridge Expedition to East Greenland in
       1926, Appendix 6. Geographical Journal 70:254–260.

1933   Observations on the Eskimo Remains on the East Coast of Greenland
       Between 72° and 75° North Latitude. Meddelelser om Grønland 92:6.

Johnson, Frederick

    1946a An Archaeological Survey Along the Alaska Highway, 1944. American Antiquity 11(3):183-186.

    1946b Man in Northeastern North America. Papers of the Robert S. Peabody Foundation for Archaeology, Vol. 3. (Ed.)

    1952 Archaeological Survey Along the Alaska Highway in Southwestern Yukon. Paper Presented to the Society of American Archaeology. Columbus, Ohio.

Johnson, Lionel

    1975 The Great Bear Lake: Its Place in History. Arctic 28(4):231-244.

Jones, Dorothy M. and John R. Wood

    1975 An Aleut Bibliography. Report Series No. 44. Institute for Social, Economic and Geographic Research. University of Alaska.

Jordan, Richard H.

    1974 Preliminary Report on Archaeological Investigations of the Labrador Eskimo in Hamilton Inlet in 1973. Man in the Northeast 8:77-89.

    1975 Pollen Studies at Hamilton Inlet, Labrador, Canada, and Implications for Environmental Prehistory. Ph.D. dissertation. University of Minnesota.

Jørgensen, J. B.

    1953 The Eskimo Skeleton: Contributions to the Physical Anthropology of the Aboriginal Greenlanders. Meddelelser om Grønland 146:2.

Kegler, Mary Ann

    1971 Archaeological Field Studies: Kachemak Bay State Park, Chugach State Park, Hatcher Pass Study Area, Lake Louise Study Area. Manuscript.

Keim, Charles J.

    1969 Aghvook, White Eskimo: Otto Geist and Alaskan Archaeology. University of Alaska Press. College.

Keithahn, Edward L.

    1940 The Petroglyphs of Southeastern Alaska. American Antiquity 6(2): 123-132.

    1953a About Slate Figurines. American Antiquity 19(1):81.

1953b The Tools of the Petroglyph Mason. Proceedings of the 4th Alaska Science Conference. pp. 250-252.

1962 Stone Artifacts from Southeastern Alaska. American Antiquity 28(1):66-77.

Kellogg, R.

1936 Mammals from a Native Village Site on Kodiak Island. Proceedings of the Biological Society of Washington 49:37-38.

Kent, Frederick J., John V. Matthews and Frederick Hadleigh-West

1964 An Archaeological Survey of the Portions of the Northwestern Kenai Peninsula. Anthropological Papers of the University of Alaska 12(2):101-134.

Knuth, Eigil

1948 Pearyland Eskimoerne. Fra Nationalnuseets Arbejdsmark. pp. 28-37. Copenhagen.

1951 Et Umiak-fund i Pearyland. Fra Nationalnuseets Arbejdsmark. pp. 28-36. Copenhagen.

1952 An Outline of the Archaeology of Pearyland. Arctic 5(1):17-33.

1954 The Paleo-Eskimo Culture of Northeast Greenland Elucidated by Three New Sites. American Antiquity 19(4):367-381.

1958 Archaeology of the Farthest North. Proceedings of the 32nd International Congress of Americanists in 1956. pp. 561-73. Copenhagen.

1965 Second and Third Danish Pearyland Expeditions, 1963 and 1964. Polar Record 12(81):733-738.

1967a The Ruins of the Musk Ox Way. Folk 8&9:191-219.

1967b Archaeology of the Musk Ox Way. Contributions du Centre d'Etudes Arctiques et Finno Scandinaves, No. 5. Paris.

1968 The Independence II Bone Artifacts and the Dorset-Evidence in North Greenland. Folk 10:61-80.

n.d. Report on Arctic Archaeological Research, Summer 1965. 12 Manuscript Pages on File in the Archaeological Division of the National Museum of Canada. Ottawa.

Kobayashi, Tatsuo

1970 Microblade Industries in the Japanese Archipelàgo. Arctic Anthropology 7(2):38-58.

Koch, Walton B.

1968   An Inventory Analysis of a Late Historic Eskimo House in Southwestern Alaska, and Insights into Sources of Error in Archaeological Interpretations. Master's thesis. Washington State University.

Koldewey, K.

1873   Die Zweite Deutsche Nord Polarfahrt in den Jahren 1869 und 1879.
I. Leipsig.

Kowta, Makoto

1963   Old Togiak in Prehistory. Ph.D. dissertation. University of
California. Los Angeles.

Kreiger, Alex D.

1961   Review: Late Pleistocene Environments of North Pacific North
America, by Calvin J. Heusser. Publication of the American Geographical Society. Washington, D.C., 1960. American Antiquity
27(2):249.

1964   Early Man in the New World. In: Prehistoric Man in the New World,
Jesse D. Jennings and Edward Norbeck, eds. pp. 23-31. University
of Chicago Press. Illinois.

Kreiger, H. W.

1927   Archaeological and Ethnological Studies in Southwest Alaska. Explorations and Fieldwork of the Smithsonian Institution in 1926.
Smithsonian Institution Miscellaneous Collection 78(7).

Kunz, Michael

1971   The Mosquito Lake Site (S-63) in the Galbraith Lake Area. In:
Final Report of the Archaeological Survey and Excavations along
the Alyeska Pipeline Service Company Pipeline Route. John P. Cook,
ed. pp. 297-324. Department of Anthropology. University of
Alaska.

1976a Archaeological Survey in the Region of Itkillik Lake, Alaska. A
Report to the Bureau of Land Management and the National Park
Service. Manuscript.

1976b Athapaskan/Eskimo Interfaces in the Central Brooks Range, Alaska.
Paper Presented at the University of Calgary Archaeology Conference. 4-7 November.

1976c Mosquito Lake. Paper Prepared for Presentation at an Informal
Seminar at the University of Alaska. Manuscript.

1976d The Mosquito Lake Site, Atigun Valley, Alaska. Paper Presented at
the 3rd Annual Conference of the Alaska Anthropological Association. Anchorage.

Kunz, Michael, William Evans and Charles Diters

1970 TAPS Archaeological Survey Preliminary Report: Hogan Hill to
Black Rapids Glacier. Manuscript.

Laguna, Frederica de

1932 A Comparison of Eskimo and Paleolithic Art. (Part I) American
Journal of Archaeology 36(4):477-551.

1933a A Comparison of Eskimo and Paleolithic Art. (Part II) American
Journal of Archaeology 37(1):77-107.

1933b Mummified Heads from Alaska. American Anthropologist 35:742-744.

1934 The Archaeology of Cook Inlet, Alaska. University of Pennsylvania
Press. Philadelphia.

1936 An Archaeological Reconnaissance of the Middle and Lower Yukon
Valley, Alaska. American Antiquity 2(1):6-12.

1938 Review: Archaeology of St. Lawrence, Alaska, by Henry B. Collins.
Smithsonian Institution Miscellaneous Collection, Vol. 96, No. 1.
Washington, ·D. C., 1937. American Anthropologist 40(2).

1939a A Pottery Vessel from Kodiak Island, Alaska. American Antiquity
4(4):334-353.

1939b Review: Archaeological Excavations at Kukulik, St. Lawrence
Island, Alaska, by Otto W. Geist and Froelich Rainey. Publica-
tion of the University of Alaska. College, 1936. American
Antiquity 4(3):288-291.

1940 Eskimo Lamps and Pots. Journal of the Royal Institute for
Anthropology of Great Britain and Ireland 50(1):53-76.

1946 The Importance of the Eskimo in Northeastern Archaeology. In:
Man in Northeastern North America. Papers of the Robert S.
Peabody Foundation 3:106-142.

1947 The Prehistory of Northern North America as Seen from the Yukon.
Memoirs of the Society for American Archaeology, No. 3.

1949 Review: Archaeologie du Pacifique-Nord, by A. Leroi-Gourhan.
Travaux et Memoires de L'Institut d'Ethnologie, No. 47. Paris,
1946. American Anthropologist 51:645-647.

1953 Some Problems in the Relationship Between Tlingit Archaeology and
Ethnology. Memoirs of the Society for American Archaeology,
No. 9.

1956a Chugach Prehistory: The Archaeology of Prince William Sound, Alaska. Publication in Anthropology 13(9-10):289. University of Washington.

1956b Review: Archaeology of the Uyak Site, Kodiak Island, Alaska, by Robert F. Heizer. Anthropological Records of the University of California, Vol. 17, No. 1. Berkeley, 1956. American Antiquity 22(2):202.

1958 Geological Confirmation of Native Traditions, Yakutat, Alaska. American Antiquity 23(4):434.

1960 The Story of a Tlingit Community: A Problem in the Relationship Between Archaeological, Ethnological and Historical Methods. Bureau of American Ethnology Bulletin, No. 172.

1962 Intemperate Reflections on Arctic and Subarctic Archaeology. In: Prehistoric Cultural Relations Between the Arctic and Temperate Zones of North America. John M. Campbell, ed. pp. 164-169. Arctic Institute of North America, Technical Paper No. 11. Montreal.

1973 Athabaskan Art. In: The Far North, 2000 Years of American Eskimo and Indian Art. Henry B. Collins, Jr., et al. pp. 133-134. National Gallery of Art. Washington.

Laguna, Frederica de, F. A. Riddell, D. F. McGeein, K. S. Lane, J. A. Freed and C. Osborne

1964 Archaeology of the Yakutat Bay Area, Alaska. Bureau of American Ethnology Bulletin, No. 192.

Lantis, David W.

1955 A Habitat of Early Man in Alaska. Geographical Review 45(1):113-114.

Lantis, Margaret

1938a The Alaskan Whale Cult and Its Affinities. American Anthropologist 40:438-464.

1938b The Alaskan Whale Cult and Its Affinities, Addendum. American Anthropologist 42:366-368.

1954 Research on Human Ecology of the American Arctic. Arctic Institute of North America. (Mimeo)

1956 Problems of Human Ecology in the North American Arctic. In: Arctic Research. D. Rowley, ed. Special Publication, No. 2. pp. 195-208. Arctic Institute of North America. Montreal.

1970a Ethnohistory in Southwestern Alaska and the Southern Yukon.
Studies in Anthropology No. 7. University of Kentucky Press.
Lexington. (Ed.)

1970b The Methodology of Ethnohistory (the introduction). In: Ethnohistory in Southwestern Alaska and the Southern Yukon. Margaret
Lantis, ed. pp. 3-10. Studies in Anthropology No. 7. University
of Kentucky Press. Lexington.

1970c The Aleut Social System, 1750 to 1810, from Early Historical
Sources. In: Ethnohistory in Southwestern Alaska and the Southern
Yukon: Method and Content. Margaret Lantis, ed. pp. 138-301.
Studies in Anthropology No. 7. University of Kentucky Press.
Lexington.

Larsen, Helge

1934 Dødemandsbugten, and Eskimo Settlement on Clavering Island.
Meddelelser om Grønland 102(1).

1938 Archaeological Investigations in Knud Rasmussen's Land.
Meddelelser om Grønland 119(8).

1940 Point Hope Expedition. American-Scandinavian Review 28(3):210-
222.

1950 Archaeological Investigations in Southwestern Alaska. American
Antiquity 15(3):177-186.

1951 De Dansk-Amerikanske Alaska Ekspeditioner, 1949-1950. Geografisk
Tidsskrift 51:69-93.

1952 The Ipiutak Culture: Its Origin and Relationships. Selected
Papers Presented to the 29th International Congress of
Americanists. pp. 22-30. Chicago.

1953 Archaeological Investigations in Alaska Since 1939. Polar Record
6(45):593-607.

1954 The Position of Ipiutak in Eskimo Culture. American Antiquity
20(1):74-79.

1955 Recent Developments in Eskimo Archaeology. Actes du IV Congres
International des Sciences Anthropologiques et Ethnologiques.
(Tome II) pp. 316-319. Vienna, 1952.

1958 The Material Culture of the Nunamiut and Its Relation to Other
Forms of Eskimo Culture in Northern Alaska. Proceedings of the
32nd International Congress of Americanists. pp. 574-582.
Copenhagen, 1956.

1960a Eskimo Archaeological Problems in Greenland. Acta Arctica, Fasc.
12.

1960b Paleo-Eskimo in Disko Bay, West Greenland. Proceedings of the International Congress of Anthropological and Ethnological Sciences, 1956. pp. 574-579.

1961 Archaeology in the Arctic, 1935-1960. American Antiquity 27(1): 7-15.

1962 The Trail Creek Caves on Seward Peninsula, Alaska. Proceedings of the 34th International Congress of Americanists. pp. 284-291. Vienna, 1960.

1966 J. Louis Giddings, Jr., 1909-1964. American Antiquity 31(3):398-401.

1968a The Eskimo Culture and Its Relation to Northern Eurasia. Proceedings of the 8th International Congress of Anthropological and Ethnological Sciences 3:338-340.

1968b Trail Creek, Final Report on the Excavation of Two Caves on Seward Peninsula, Alaska. Acta Arctica 15:7-79.

1968c Near Ipiutak and Uwelen-Okvik. Folk 10:81-90.

Larsen, Helge and Jorgen Meldgaard

1958 Paleo-Eskimo Cultures in Disko Bugt, West Greenland. Meddelelser om Grønland 161(2):1-75.

Larsen, Helge and Froelich G. Rainey

1948 Ipiutak and the Arctic Whale Hunting Culture. Anthropological Paper, No. 42. American Museum of Natural History. New York.

Laufer, Berthold

1915 The Eskimo Screw as a Culture-Historical Problem. American Anthropologist, Vol. 18.

Laughlin, Sara B., William S. Laughlin and Mary E. McDowell

1975 Anangula Blade Site Excavations, 1972 and 1973. Anthropological Papers of the University of Alaska 17(2):39-48.

Laughlin, William S.

1949 The Physical Anthropology of Three Aleut Populations: Attu, Atka and Nikolski. Ph.D. dissertation. Harvard University.

1950 Blood Groups, Morphology and Population Size of the Eskimos. Cold Spring Harbor Symposia on Quantitative Biology 15:165-173.

1951a The Physical Anthropology of the American Indians. Viking Fund, Inc. (Ed.)

1951b The Alaska Gateway Viewed from the Aleutian Islands. In: The
Physical Anthropology of the American Indians. William S.
Laughlin, ed. pp. 98-126. Viking Fund, Inc.

1951c Notes on an Aleutian Core and Blade Industry. American
Antiquity 17(1):52-55.

1952a Contemporary Problems in Anthropology of Southern Alaska. In:
Science in Alaska, Arctic Institute of North America Special
Publication 1:66-84.

1952b The Aleut-Eskimo Community. Anthropological Papers of the
University of Alaska 1:25-46.

1952c Supplementary Notes on the Aleutian Core and Blade Industry.
American Antiquity 18(1):69-70.

1955 Review: Arctic Area, by Henry B. Collins. Program of the History
of America, Commission de Historia 1(2):1-152. Mexico City, 1954.
American Antiquity 21(2):189-190.

1956 Human Skeletal Material from Kawumkan Springs Midden. Proceedings of the American Philosophical Society 46(4):475-480.

1958 Neo-Aleut and Paleo-Aleut Prehistory. Proceedings of the 32nd
International Congress of Americanists. pp. 516-530.
Copenhagen, 1956.

1962a Generic Problems and New Evidences in the Anthropology of the
Eskimo-Aleut Stock. In: Prehistoric Cultural Relations Between
the Arctic and Temperate Zones of North America. John M.
Campbell, ed. Arctic Institute of North America, Technical Paper
No. 11. pp. 110-112. Montreal.

1962b Bering Strait to Puget Sound: Dichotomy and Affinity Between
Eskimo Aleuts and American Indians. In: Prehistoric Cultural
Relations Between the Arctic and Temperate Zones of North America.
John M. Campbell, ed. Arctic Institute of North America,
Technical Paper No. 11. pp. 113-125. Montreal.

1962c Archaeological Investigation on Umnak Island, Aleutians. Arctic
Anthropology 1(1):108-110.

1963a Addendum: Excavations at Anangula Island, 1962. Anthropological
Papers of the University of Alaska 10(2):90-91.

1963b Eskimos and Aleuts: Their Origins and Evolution. Science 142:
633-645.

1963c Review: Archaeological Investigations on Agattu, Aleutian
Islands, by Albert C. Spaulding. Anthropological Papers of the
Museum of Anthropology, No. 18. University of Michigan, 1962.
American Antiquity 29:244-245.

1963d The Earliest Aleuts. Anthropological Papers of the University of Alaska 10(2):633-645.

1965a Review: The Archaeology of Cape Denbigh, by J. Louis Giddings, Jr. Brown University Press. Providence, 1964. Arctic 18(1):61-64.

1965b Review: The Arctic and Subarctic, by Henry B. Collins. In: Prehistoric Man in the New World. Jesse D. Jennings and Edward Norbeck, eds. pp. 85-114. University of Chicago Press. Chicago, 1964. American Antiquity 30(4):501-503.

1966a Genetical and Anthropological Characteristics of Arctic Populations. In: The Biology of Human Adaptability. J. Weiner and P. Baker, eds. pp. 469-495. Oxford University Press.

1966b Introduction (Aleutian Studies). Arctic Anthropology 3(2):23-27.

1966c Paleo-Aleut Crania from Port Moller, Alaska Peninsula. Arctic Anthropology 3(2):159.

1966d Eskimos and Aleuts: Their Origins and Evolution. In: New Roads to Yesterday. J. D. Caldwell, ed. pp. 247-276. Basic Books Inc. New York (Reprint of 1963 Article in Science 142:633-645).

1967 Human Migration and Permanent Occupation in the Bering Sea Area. In: The Bering Land Bridge. David M. Hopkins, ed. pp. 409-450. Stanford University Press. Stanford.

1970 Aleutian Ecosystem. Science 169:1107-8.

1975a Aleuts: Ecosystem, Holocene History, and Siberian Origin. Science 189:507-515.

1975b Holocene History of Nikolski Bay, Alaska and Aleut Evolution. Folk 16-17:95-116.

Laughlin, William S., A. P. Okladnikov, A. P. Derevyanko, A. B. Harper and I. V. Atseev

1976 Early Siberians from Lake Baikal and Alaskan Population Affinities. American Journal of Physical Anthropology 45(3):651-660.

Laughlin, William S. and Jean S. Aigner

1966 Preliminary Analysis of the Anangula Unifacial Core and Blade Industry. Arctic Anthropology 3(2):41-56.

1974 Burial of an Aged Chaluka Adult Male. Arctic Anthropology 11(1):47-60.

1975 Aleut Adaptations and Evolution. In: Prehistoric Maritime Adaptations of the Circumpolar Zones. William W. Fitzhugh, IV, ed. pp. 181-202. Mouton and Company. Paris.

Laughlin, William S. and Gordon H. Marsh

    1951   A New View of the History of the Aleutians. Arctic 4:75-88.

    1954   The Lamellar Flake Manufacturing Site on Anangula Island in the
           Aleutians. American Antiquity 20(1):27-39.

    1956   Trends in Aleutian Chipped Stone Artifacts. Anthropological
           Papers of the University of Alaska 5(1):5-21.

Laughlin, William S., G. H. Marsh and J. W. Leach

    1952   Supplementary Note on the Aleutian Core and Blade Industry.
           American Antiquity 18(1):69-70.

Laughlin, William S. and W. C. Reeder

    1962a Revision of Aleutian Prehistory. Science 137:856-857.

    1962b Rationale for the Collaborative Investigation of Aleut-Konyag
           Prehistory and Ecology. Arctic Anthropology 3(2):41-56.

    1966   Studies in Aleutian Kodiak Prehistory, Ecology and Anthropology.
           Arctic Anthropology 3(2):1-240). (Eds.)

Laughlin, William S. and William E. Taylor, Jr.

    1960   A Cape Dorset Culture Site on the West Coast of Ungava Bay. In:
           Contributions to Anthropology in 1958. National Museum of Canada
           Bulletin 168:1-28.

Leakey, Louis S. B., R. Simpson and T. Clement

    1968   Archaeological Investigations in the Calico Mountains, California:
           Preliminary Report. Science 160:1022-1023.

Lee, Thomas E.

    1965   Archaeological Investigations at Lake Abitibi, 1964. Collection,
           Travaux Divers No. 10. Centre d'Etudes Nordiques. Universite
           Laval. Quebec.

    1966a The Norse in Ungava. Anthropological Journal of Canada 4(2):51-
           54.

    1966b Archaeological Traces at Fort Chimo, Quebec, 1964. Anthropologi-
           cal Journal of Canada 4(1):33-44.

1966c Payne Lake, Ungava Peninsula, Archaeology, 1964. Collection, Travaux Divers No. 12. Centre d'Etudes Nordiques. Universite Laval. Quebec.

1967 Fort Chimo and Payne Lake, Ungava Peninsula Archaeology, 1965. Collection, Travaux Divers No. 16. Centre d'Etudes Nordiques. Universite Laval. Quebec.

1968a Archaeological Discoveries, Payne Bay Region, Ungava, 1966. Collection, Travaux Divers No. 20. Centre d'Etudes Nordiques. Universite Laval. Quebec.

1968b A Summary of Norse Evidence in Ungava, 1968. Anthropological Journal of Canada 6(4):17-21.

1969 Archaeological Findings: Gyrfalcon to Eider Islands, Ungava, 1968. Collection, Travaux Divers No. 27. Centre d'Etudes Nordiques. Universite Laval. Quebec.

1970a The Ungava Norse: A Reply to Birgitta Wallace. Anthropological Journal of Canada 8(1):21-23.

1970b Pre-Columbian Traces in Ungava Peninsula. Arctic Circular 20(2): 32-36.

1971a Review: Eskimo Prehistory, by Hans-Georg Bandi. University of Alaska Press. College, 1969. Anthropological Journal of Canada 9(2):29-32.

1971b Review: The Arctic Small Tool Tradition in Manitoba, by Ronald J. Nash. Occasional Paper No. 2 of the Department of Manitoba, University of Manitoba. Winnipeg, 1969. Anthropological Journal of Canada 9(3):28-29.

1972 Archaeological Investigations of Long House, Pamiok, Ungava, 1970. Collection Nordicana, No. 33. Centre d'Etudes Nordiques. Quebec.

1973 Rebuttal to Dekin's Review. American Anthropologist 75(6):2037-2040.

1974a Comment on the Dekin Affair. Anthropological Journal of Canada 12(3):30-32.

1974b Archaeological Investigations of a Longhouse Ruin, Pamiok Island, Ungava Bay, 1972. Paleo-Quebec No. 2. Universite du Quebec a Trois Rivieres. Trois-Rivieres.

Leechman, J. Douglas

1935 Whence Came The Eskimo? Beaver 265(4):38-41.

1943a Two New Cape Dorset Sites. American Antiquity 4:363-375.

1943b A New Type of Adze Head. American Anthropologist 45:153-155.

1946   Prehistoric Migration Routes Through the Yukon.   Canadian
       Historical Review 29(4):383-390.

LeFebre, Charlene Craft

1956   A Contribution to the Archaeology of the Upper Kuskokwim.
       American Antiquity 21(3):268-274.

Leroi-Gourhan, A.

1946   Archeologie du Pacifique-Nord.   Travaux et Memoires de L'Institut
       d'Ethnologie, No. 47.   Paris.

Lethbridge, T. C.

1939   Archaeological Data from the Canadian Arctic.   Journal of the
       Royal Anthropological Institute 69(2):187-233.

Levin, M. G. and D. A. Sergeev

1960   Contributions to the Problem of the Date of Arrival of Iron in the
       Arctic.   Sovietskaia Etnografia 3:116-122.   (in Russian)

Lewis, B. W.

1966   Inukshuks and Inunguaks on Foxe Peninsula and the North Quebec
       Coast.   Canadian Geographical Journal 73(3):84-87.

Linnamae, Urve

1973   Dorset Culture in Newfoundland and the Arctic.   Ph.D. disserta-
       tion.   University of Calgary.

1975   The Dorset Culture, a Comparative Study in Newfoundland and the
       Arctic.   Technical Papers of the Newfoundland Museum, No. 1.   St.
       John's, Newfoundland.

Lippold, Lois K.

1966   Chaluka: The Economic Base.   Arctic Anthropology 3(2):84-124.

1972   Mammalian Remains from Aleutian Sites: A Preliminary Report.
       Arctic Anthropology 9(2):113-114.

Lloyd, T. G. B.

1874   Notes on Indian Remains Found on the Coast of Labrador.   Journal
       of the Royal Anthropological Institute of Great Britain and
       Ireland 4:39-43.

Lotz, Jim

1970   Review: Aghvook, White Eskimo: Otto Geist and Alaskan Archaeology,
       by Charles J. Keim.   University of Alaska Press, College, 1969.
       Arctic 23(2):140-141.

Lotz, Pat and Jim Lotz

1971 Pilot Not Commander--Essays in Memory of Diamond Jenness. Anthropologica 13(1&2; Special Issue). (Eds.)

Lowdon, J. A., R. Wilmeth and W. Blake, Jr.

1972 Geological Survey of Canada Radiocarbon Dates XII. Department of Energy, Mines and Resources Bulletin 71(7). Ottawa.

Lowther, Gordon R.

1962 An Account of an Archaeological Site on Cape Sparbo, Devon Island. Contributions to Anthropology, 1960. National Museum of Canada Bulletin 180(1):1-19.

1965 Review: The Cultural Affinities of the Newfoundland Dorset Eskimo, by Elmer Harp, Jr. National Museum of Canada Bulletin, No. 200. Ottawa, 1964. Anthropologica 7:152-153.

Luth, Dietrich

1974 Further Evidence of Early Norse Settlement in the Americas. Journal of Indo-European Studies 2(1):47-56.

Lutz, Bruce J.

1969 Archaeological Investigations Near Unalakleet, Alaska. Expedition 11(2):52-54.

1970 Variations in Checked Pottery from an Archaeological Site Near Unalakleet, Alaska. Anthropological Papers of the University of Alaska 15(1):33-48.

1972 A Methodology for Determining Regional Intracultural Variation Within the Norton, an Alaskan Culture. Ph.D. dissertation. University of Pennsylvania.

1973a Review: Reconnaissance Archeologique dans la Region de la Baie de Wakeham (Nouveau-Quebec), by Georges Barre. Societe d' Archeologie Prehistorique du Quebec. Montreal, 1970. American Anthropologist 75(2):515.

1973b An Archaeological Karigi at the Site of Ungalaqliq, Western Alaska. Arctic Anthropology 10(1):11-118.

Lutz, H. J.

1951 The Concentration of Certain Chemical Elements in the Soils of Alaskan Archaeological Sites. American Journal of Science 249: 925-928.

McCartney, Allen P.

1967 An Analysis of the Bone Industry from Amaknak Island, Alaska.
Master's thesis. University of Wisconsin.

1969 Prehistoric Aleut Influence at Port Moller. Anthropological
Papers of the University of Alaska 14(2):1-16.

1970a Thule Eskimo Prehistory Along Northwestern Hudson Bay. Ph.D.
dissertation. University of Wisconsin. Madison.

1970b "Pottery" in the Aleutian Islands. American Antiquity 35(1):105-
107.

1971a A Proposed Western Aleutian Phase in the Near Islands, Alaska.
Arctic Anthropology 8(2):92-142.

1971b Preliminary Report of an Archaeological Reconnaissance in the
Izembek National Wildlife Refuge, Alaska. University of
Arkansas. Manuscript.

1972a Dorset Artifacts from Northwestern Hudson Bay. The Musk-Ox
10:21-25.

1972b An Archaeological Site Survey and Inventory for the Aleutian
Islands National Wildlife Refuge, Alaska, 1972. Report submitted
to the Wilderness Studies Branch, U. S. Fish & Wildlife Service.
Anchorage.

1973 An Archaeological Site Survey and Inventory for the Alaska Peninsula, Shumagin Islands and Other Islands South of the Alaska
Peninsula, 1973. Report submitted to the Refuge Branch, U. S. Fish
and Wildlife Service. Anchorage.

1974a Prehistoric Culture Integration Along the Alaska Peninsula. Anthropological Papers of the University of Alaska 16(1):59-84.

1974b Maritime Adaptations on the North Pacific Rim. Arctic Anthropology 11(Suppl.):153-162.

1974c 1972 Archaeological Site Survey in the Aleutian Islands, Alaska.
In: International Conference on the Prehistory and Paleoecology
of Western North American Arctic and Subarctic. Scott Raymond
and Peter Schledermann, eds. pp. 113-126. University of Calgary
Archaeological Association. Alberta.

1975 Maritime Adaptations in Cold Archipelagoes: An Analysis of Environ-
ment and. Culture in the Aleutian and Other Island Chains. In:
Prehistoric Maritime Adaptations of the Circumpolar Zone. William
W. Fitzhugh, IV, ed. pp. 281-338. Mouton and Company. Paris.

McCartney, A. P. and D. J. Mack

1973 Iron Utilization by Thule Eskimos of Central Canada. American
Antiquity 38(3):328-339.

McCartney, Allen P. and Christy G. Turner II

 1966 Stratigraphy of the Anangula Unifacial Core and Blade Site.
    Arctic Anthropology 3(2):23-40.

McClellan, Catherine

 1953 The Inland Tlingit. Memoirs of the Society for American
    Archaeology, No. 9.

 1970 Indian Stories About the First Whites in Northwestern America.
    In: Ethnohistory in Southwestern Alaska and Southern Yukon:
    Method and Content. Margaret Lantis, ed. pp. 103-133. Studies
    in Anthropology No. 7. University of Kentucky Press. Lexington.

MacFadyen, Annette M.

 1966 Koyukuk River Culture of the Arctic Woodlands: A Preliminary
    Study of Material Culture, with an Analysis of Hostility and
    Trade as Agents of Cultural Transmission. Master's thesis.
    George Washington University. (See A.M. Clark)

McGhee, Robert J.

 1968 Copper Eskimo Origins. Ph.D. dissertation. Department of
    Archaeology. University of Calgary.

 1969 An Archaeological Survey of Western Victoria Island, N.W.T.,
    Canada. National Museum of Canada Bulletin in Anthropology
    232(7):158-191. Ottawa.

 1970a Excavations at Bloody Falls, N.W.T., Canada. Arctic Anthro-
    pology 6(2):53-73.

 1970b A Quantitative Comparison of Dorset Culture Microblade Samples.
    Arctic Anthropology 7(2):89-96.

 1970c Speculations on Climatic Change and Thule Culture Development.
    Folk 11-12:172-184.

 1971a Current Research: Far North. American Antiquity 36(4):489-493. (Ed.)

 1971b Excavation at Kittigazuit. The Beaver Outfit 302(2):34-39.

 1972a Climatic Change and the Development of Canadian Arctic Cultural
    Traditions. In: Climatic Changes in Arctic Areas During the
    Last Ten Thousand Years. Y. Vasari, H. Hyvarinen and S. Hicks,
    eds. University of Oulu Symposium Series A 3(1):39-60.
    Oulu, Finland.

 1972b Copper Eskimo Prehistory. Publications in Archaeology.
    National Museum of Man Bulletin No. 2. National Museum of Man.
    Ottawa.

 1973 Preliminary Paper and Discussion. School of American Research
    Advanced Seminar on Pre-Dorset--Dorset Problems. Santa Fe.

1974a   Beluga Hunters: An Archaeological Reconstruction of the History and
         Culture of the Mackenzie Delta Kittegaryumiut. Newfoundland Social
         and Economic Studies, No. 13. Institute of Social and Economic Re-
         search. Memorial University of Newfoundland. St. John's,
         Newfoundland.

1974b   The Early Arctic Small Tool Tradition: A Prediction from Arctic
         Canada. In: International Conference on the Prehistory and Paleo-
         ecology of Western North American Arctic and Subarctic. Scott
         Raymond and Peter Schledermann, eds. pp. 127-132. University of
         Calgary Archaeological Association. Alberta.

1974c   The Peopling of Arctic North America. In: Arctic and Alpine
         Environments. Jack D. Ives and Roger G. Barry, eds. pp. 831-855.
         Methuen and Co., Ltd. London.

1975a   Late Dorset Art from Dundas Island, Arctic Canada. Folk 16-17:
         133-146.

1975b   Review: Labrador Eskimo Settlements of the Early Contact Period,
         by J. Garth Taylor. National Museums of Canada. Ottawa, 1974.
         Arctic 28(4):301-302.

1976   Paleoeskimo Occupations of Central and High Arctic Canada. In:
         Eastern Arctic Prehistory: Paleoeskimo Problems. Moreau S.
         Maxwell, ed. pp. 15-39. Memoirs of the Society for American
         Archaeology, No. 31.

McGhee, Robert and James Tuck

1973   Preliminary Paper and Discussion. School of American Research
         Advanced Seminar on Pre-Dorset--Dorset Problems. Santa Fe.

1975   An Archaic Sequence from the Strait of Belle Isle, Labrador.
         Mercury Series. Archaeological Survey of Canada Paper No. 34.
         National Museums of Canada. Ottawa.

1976   Un-Dating the Canadian Arctic. In: Eastern Arctic Prehistory:
         Paleoeskimo Problems. Moreau S. Maxwell, ed. pp. 6-14. Memoirs
         of the Society for American Archaeology No. 31.

McHugh, William P.

1961   Archaeological Evidence of the Occupation of Kodiak Island.
         Science in Alaska, Proceedings of the 12th Alaskan Science
         Conference. pp. 4-5. College.

1962   Archaeological Investigations on Kodiak Island. Arctic Anthro-
         pology 1(1):113-115.

McKennan, Robert A.

1970   Review: Eskimo Prehistory, by Hans-Georg Bandi. University of
         Alaska Press. College, 1969. Arctic 23(1):65-66.

1971   Review: An Historic Tanaina Indian Settlement, by James W.
         VanStone and Joan B. Townsend. Fieldiana Anthropology, Vol. 59.
         Chicago: Field Museum of Natural History, 1970. Arctic 24(3):237-238.

McKennan, Robert A. and John P. Cook

    1968   Prehistory of Healy Lake, Alaska. Proceedings of the 8th Inter-
               national Congress of Anthropological and Ethnological Sciences
               3:182-184. Japan, September.

    1970   The Athapaskan Tradition: A View from Healy Lake in the Yukon-
               Tanana Upland. Paper presented at the 10th Annual Meeting of the
               Northeastern Anthropological Association. Ottawa, May.

MacDonald, George F.

    1971   Research Report No. 1 - 1971. Archaeological Survey of Canada.
               National Museums of Canada. Ottawa. (Ed.)

    1973   Archaeological Survey of Canada Annual Review 1972. Mercury Series.
               Archaeological Survey of Canada Paper No. 10. National Museums of
               Canada. Ottawa. (Ed.)

    1974   Archaeological Survey of Canada, Annual Review, 1973. Mercury
               Series. Archaeological Survey of Canada Paper, No. 21. National
               Museums of Canada. Ottawa. (Ed.)

    1975   Archaeological Survey of Canada Annual Review 1974. Mercury Series.
               Archaeological Survey of Canada Paper, No. 31. National Museums of
               Canada. Ottawa. (Ed.)

MacDonald, Robert

    1971   The Romance of Canadian History. Canada 1. Years and Years Ago.
               The Ballantrae Foundation. Calgary.

MacKay, J.R., W.H. Mathews and Richard S. MacNeish

    1961   Geology of the Engigstciak Archaeological Site, Yukon Territory.
               Arctic 14(1):25-52.

MacNeish, Richard S.

    1951   An Archaeological Reconnaissance in the Northwest Territory.
               Annual Report for the National Museum of Canada, 1949-1950.
               National Museum of Canada Bulletin 123:24-41. Ottawa.

    1952   A Possible Early Site in the Thunder Bay District, Ontario.
               Annual Report for the National Museum of Canada, 1950-1951.
               National Museum of Canada Bulletin 126:23-47. Ottawa.

    1953   Archaeological Reconnaissance in the Mackenzie River Drainage.
               Annual Report for the National Museum of Canada, 1951-1952.
               National Museum of Canada Bulletin 128:23-40. Ottawa.

1954a Archaeological Investigations in the Yukon Territory. Arctic
8(3):195.

1954b The Pointed Mountain Site Near Fort Liard, N.W.T., Canada.
American Antiquity 19(3):234-253.

1956a The Engigstciak Site on the Yukon Arctic Coast. Anthropological
Papers of the University of Alaska 4(2):91-111.

1956b Archaeological Reconnaissance of the Delta of the Mackenzie River
and the Yukon Coast, Canada. Department of Northern Affairs and
Natural Resources. National Museum of Canada Bulletin 142:46-81.

1956c Two Archaeological Sites on Great Bear Lake, N.W.T., Canada.
Annual Report for the National Museum of Canada, 1953-1954.
National Museum of Canada Bulletin 136:54-84. Ottawa.

1957 Archaeological Investigations in the Arctic and Subarctic, 1957.
Arctic 10(3):189-190.

1958 An Introduction to the Archaeology of Southeastern Manitoba.
National Museum of Canada Bulletin, No. 157. Ottawa.

1959a A Speculative Framework of Northern North American Prehistory as
of April 1959. Anthropologica 1:1-17.

1959b Men Out of Asia: As Seen from Northwest Yukon. Anthropological
Papers of the University of Alaska 7(2):41-70.

1960a The Callison Site in the Light of Archaeological Survey of Southwest Yukon. Contribution to Anthropology, 1957. National Museum
of Canada Bulletin 162:1-51. Ottawa.

1960b Problems of Circumpolar Archaeology as Seen from Northwest Canada.
Circumpolar Conference, 1958. pp. 17-26.

1962a Recent Finds in the Yukon Territory of Canada. In: Prehistoric
Cultural Relations Between the Arctic and Temperate Zones of North
America. John M. Campbell, ed. pp. 20-26. Arctic Institute of
North America, Technical Paper No. 11. Montreal.

1962b A Discussion of the Relationships from the Great Lakes to the
Barren Lands. In: Prehistoric Cultural Relations Between the
Arctic and Temperate Zones of North America. John M. Campbell,
ed. pp. 140-142. Arctic Institute of North America, Technical
Paper No. 11. Montreal.

1963 The Early Peopling of the New World as Seen from Southwestern
Yukon. Anthropological Papers of the University of Alaska 10(2):
93-106.

1964 Investigations in Southwest Yukon: Archaeological Excavations,
Comparisons and Speculations. Papers of the Robert S. Peabody
Foundation for Archaeology 6(2).

1974 Review: The Development of North American Archaeology: Essays in the History of Regional Traditions, by James E. Fitting, ed. Anchor Press/Doubleday. Garden City, N.Y., 1973. American Anthropologist 76:462-463.

Magnusson, M., and H. Palsson

1965 English Translation of the Vinland Sagas: The Norse Discovery of America. Penguin Books. Harmondsworth.

Malaurie, Jean

1964 Le Nouveau Quebec--Contribution a l'Etude de l'Occupation Humaine. Bibliotheque Arctique et Antarctique. (Tome 2) Publication de l'Ecole Practique des Hautes Etudes. Sorbonne.

Manning, Thomas H.

1946 Ruins of Eskimo Stone Houses on the East Side of Hudson Bay. American Antiquity 11(3):201-202.

1948 Eskimo Stone House Ruins on the East Side of Hudson Bay: A Correction. American Antiquity 13(3):250-251.

1950 Eskimo Stone Houses in Foxe Basin. Arctic 3(2):108-112.

1951 A Mixed Cape-Dorset--Thule Site on Smith Island, East Hudson Bay. Annual Report for the National Museum of Canada for 1949-50. National Museum of Canada Bulletin 123:64-71. Ottawa.

Markham, A. H.

1865 On the Origin and Migrations of the Greenlander Eskimaux. Journal of the Royal Geographical Society, No. 35. London.

Marsh, Gordon H.

1956 A Stone Lamp from Yukon Island, Alaska. Anthropological Papers of the University of Alaska 4(2):113-115.

Marsh, Gordon H. and William S. Laughlin

1954 The Lamellar Flake Manufacturing Site on Anangula Island in the Aleutians. American Antiquity 20:27-39.

Marsh, Gordon H., William S. Laughlin and J. W. Leach

1952 Supplementary Note on the Aleutian Core and Blade Industry. American Antiquity 18:69-70.

Martijn, Charles A. and Edward S. Rogers

1969 Mistassini-Albanel, Contributions to the Prehistory of Quebec. Collection, Travaux Divers No. 25. Centre d'Etude Nordiques. Universite Laval. Quebec.

Mary-Rousseliere, Guy

1955 Report on Archaeological Excavations at Baker Lake and Chester-
field Inlet, Summer 1955. Manuscript on file at the National
Museum of Canada. Ottawa.

1964 The Paleo-Eskimo Remains in the Pelly Bay Region, N.W.T. National
Museum of Canada Contributions to Anthropology 1961-62. National
Museum of Canada Bulletin 193:62-183. Ottawa.

1968 Reconnaissance Archaeologique dans la Region de Pond Inlet. Collection, Travaux Divers No. 21. Centre d'Etudes Nordiques.
Universite Laval. Quebec.

1973 Preliminary Paper and Discussion. School of American Research
Advanced Seminar on Pre-Dorset--Dorset Problems. Santa Fe.

1976 The Paleoeskimo in Northern Baffinland. In: Eastern Arctic Prehistory: Paleoeskimo Problems. Moreau S. Maxwell, ed. pp. 40-57.
Memoirs of the Society for American Archaeology, No. 31.

Mason, J. Alden

1928 A Remarkable Stone Lamp from Alaska. University of Pennsylvania
Museum Journal 19(2):170-194.

1930 Excavations of Eskimo Thule Culture Site at Point Barrow Alaska.
Proceedings of the 23rd International Congress of Americanists.
pp. 383-394.

Mason, Otis T.

1891 The Ulu, or Woman's Knife of the Eskimo. Annual Report of the U.S.
National Museum for 1890. pp. 411-416.

1902 Aboriginal American Harpoons: A Study in Ethnic Distribution and
Invention. Annual Report of the U. S. National Museum for 1900.
pp. 189-304.

Mathiassen, Therkel

1925 Preliminary Report of the Fifth Thule Expedition: Archaeology.
Proceedings of the 21st International Congress of Americanists.
Goteborg, 1924. pp. 206-215.

1927 Archaeology of the Central Eskimos, the Thule Culture and Its
Position Within the Eskimo Culture. Report of the Fifth Thule
Expedition, 1921-1924 4(1&2).

1928a Eskimo Relics from Washington Land and Hall Land. Meddelelser om
Grønland 71:3.

1928b Norse Ruins in Labrador? American Anthropologist 30:569-579.

1929 Some Specimens From the Bering Sea Culture. Museum of the American Indian, Heye Foundation, New York. Indian Notes 6:33-56.

1930a The Archaeological Collection of the Cambridge East Greenland Expedition, 1926. Meddelelser om Grønland 74:137-166.

1930b An Old Eskimo Culture in West Greenland: Report of an Archaeological Expedition to Upper Navik. Geographical Review 20:605-614.

1930c Notes on Knud Rasmussen's Archaeological Collections from the Western Eskimos. Proceedings of the 23rd International Congress of Americanists, 1928 23:395-399.

1930d Archaeological Collections from the Western Eskimos. Report of the 5th Thule Expedition, 1921-24 10(1).

1930e The Question of the Origin of Eskimo Culture. American Anthropologist 32(4):591-607.

1930f Inugsuk, A Mediaeval Eskimo Settlement in Upernivik District, West Greenland. Meddelelser om Grønland 77:4.

1931a Ancient Eskimo Settlements in the Kangamiut Area. Meddelelser om Grønland 91:1.

1931b The Present Shape of Eskimo Archaeology. Acta Archaeologica 2:185-199.

1932 Bidrag til Angmagssalik-Eskimoernes for Historie. Geografisk tidsskrift, 1932 35:129-136.

1933 Prehistory of the Angmagssalik Eskimos. Meddelelser om Grønland 92(4).

1934a Eskimo Finds from the Kangerdlussuaq Region. Meddelelser om Grønland 104(4):1-25.

1934b Contributions to the Archaeology of Disko Bay. Meddelelser om Grønland 93(3).

1935a Eskimo Migrations in Greenland. Geographic Review 25:408-422.

1935b Archaeology in Greenland. Antiquity 9:195-203.

1937 The Eskimo Archaeology of Greenland. Smithsonian Institution Annual Report for 1936. Smithsonian Institution Bulletin. pp. 397-404.

1939 The Former Eskimo Settlements on Frederik VI's Coast. Meddelelser om Grønland 109(2).

1944-45 The Archaeology of the Thule District. Geografisk tidsskrift 47:43-71. Kjobenhavn.

1948   Aeldre Stenalder. Danske Oldsager, I. Copenhagen.

1958   The Sermermiut Excavations, 1955. Meddelelser om Grønland 161(3): 52.

Mathiassen, Therkel and Erik Holtved

1936   The Eskimo Archaeology of Julianehaab Distrikt, with a Brief Summary of the Prehistory of the Greenlanders. Meddelelser om Grønland 118(1).

Matthews, Barry

1975   Archaeological Sites in the Labrador-Ungava Peninsula: Cultural Origins and Climatic Significance. Arctic 28(4):245-262.

Mauger, Jeffrey Edward

1970   A Study of Donnelly Burins in the Campus Archaeological Collection. Master's thesis. Washington State University.

Maxwell, Moreau S.

1960a The Movement of Cultures in the Canadian High Arctic. Anthropologica N.S. 2(2):177-189.

1960b An Archaeological Analysis of Eastern Grant Land, Ellesmere Island, N.W.T. National Museum of Canada Bulletin 170(14). Ottawa.

1962   Pre-Dorset and Dorset Sites in the Vicinity of Lake Harbour, Baffin Island, N.W.T. Contributions to Anthropology, 1960. National Museum of Canada Bulletin 180(1):20-55.

1963a Change and Continuity in Dorset Culture. Paper Presented at the 62nd Annual Meeting of the American Anthropological Association, San Francisco.

1963b Review: A Contribution to the Human Osteology of the Canadian Arctic, by James E. Anderson and C. F. Merbs. In: Art and Archaeology Division of the Royal Ontario Museum Occasional Paper, No. 4. University of Toronto. Toronto, 1962. American Antiquity 28(4):564-565.

1963c Review: An Archaeological Collection from Somerset Island and Boothia Peninsula, N.W.T., by James W. VanStone. In: Art and Archaeology Division of the Royal Ontario Museum Occasional Paper, No. 4. University of Toronto. Toronto, 1962. American Antiquity 28(4):564-565.

1967   The Origin and Development of Dorset Culture. Paper Presented at the 32nd Annual Meeting of the Society for American Archaeology. Ann Arbor, 4 May.

1972   Diamond Jenness, 1886-1969. American Antiquity 37(1):86-88.

239

1973a Archaeology of the Lake Harbour District, Baffin Island. Mercury Series. Archaeological Survey of Canada Paper, No. 6. National Museums of Canada. Ottawa.

1973b Preliminary Paper and Discussion. School of American Research Advanced Seminar on Pre-Dorset--Dorset Problems. Santa Fe.

1975 An Early Dorset Harpoon Complex. Folk 16-17:125-132.

1976a Eastern Arctic Prehistory: Paleoeskimo Problems. Memoirs of the Society for American Archaeology, No. 31. (Ed.)

1976b Pre-Dorset and Dorset Artifacts: The View From Lake Harbour. In: Eastern Arctic Prehistory: Paleoeskimo Problems. Moreau S. Maxwell, ed. pp. 58-78. Memoirs of the Society for American Archaeology, No. 31.

May, Alan G.

1951 Mummies from Alaska. Natural History 60(3):114-119.

Mayer-Oakes, William J.

1966 Review: Investigations in Southwest Yukon: Geobotanical and Archaeological Reconnaissance, by Frederick Johnson and Hugh M. Raup (No. 1) and Investigations in Southwest Yukon: Archaeological Excavations, Comparisons and Speculations, by Richard S. MacNeish (No. 2). In: Papers of the Robert S. Peabody Foundation for Archaeology, Vol. 6, Nos. 1&2. Andover, 1964. American Antiquity 31(4):596-597.

1977 Review: Archaeological Investigations in the Transitional Forest Zone: Northern Manitoba, Southern Keewatin, N.W.T., by Ronald J. Nash. Manitoba Museum of Man and Nature. Winnipeg, 1975. American Antiquity 42(1):143-145.

Mazees, Richard B.

1966 Bone Density in Sadlermiut Eskimo. Human Biology 38(1):42-49.

Meany, Edmond S.

1906 Alaskan Mummies. Washington Magazine 1:459-468. Seattle.

Meier, Robert J. and William B. Workman

1963 Preliminary Report on a Surface Collection from Southwest Anchorage, Chirikof Island, Alaska. Manuscript.

Meldgaard, Jørgen

1952 A Paleo-Eskimo Culture in West Greenland. American Antiquity 17(3):222-230.

1955 Dorset Culture. The Danish-American Expedition to Arctic Canada, 1954. pp. 158-177. Kmul, Arbog Jysk Arkaeol. Selskab.

1960a Prehistoric Culture Sequences in the Eastern Arctic as Elucidated by Stratified Sites at Igloolik. Selected Papers of the 5th International Congress of Anthropological and Ethnological Sciences, 1956. pp. 588-595. University of Pennsylvania Press. Philadelphia.

1960b Origin and Evolution of Eskimo Cultures in the Eastern Arctic. Canadian Geographical Journal 60(2):64-75.

1960c Eskimo Sculpture. Methuen & Co. London.

1962 On the Formative Period of the Dorset Culture. In: Prehistoric Cultural Relations Between the Arctic and Temperate Zones of North America. John M. Campbell, ed. pp. 92-95. Arctic Institute of North America, Technical Paper No. 11. Montreal.

1973 The Lost Vikings of Greenland. Natural History 82(5):36-43,74,76, 77.

1975 Helge Larsen--Ipiutak and Other Arctic Adventures. Folk 16-17: 5-11.

Melville, Evolyn

1958 Discovery of the Site of Old Fort Yukon. Anthropological Papers of the University of Alaska 6(2):119-121.

Merbs, Charles F.

1963a The Sadlermiut Eskimo Vertebral Column. Master's thesis. University of Wisconsin.

1963b Patterns of Pathology in Eskimos and Aleuts. American Journal of Physical Anthropology n.s. 31:425.

1968 Anterior Tooth Loss in Arctic Populations. Southwestern Journal of Anthropology 24(1):20-32.

1969 The Northwest Hudson Bay Thule Project. Arctic Circular 19(3).

1971 An Island of the Dead: Sir Thomas Roe's Welcome. The Beaver Outfit 30.

1974 The Effects of Cranial and Caudal Shift in the Vertebral Columns of Northern Populations. Arctic Anthropology 11(Suppl.):12-19.

Merbs, Charles F. and W. H. Wilson

1962 Anomalies and Pathologies of the Sadlermiut Eskimo Vertebral Column. Contributions to Anthropology, 1960. National Museum of Canada Bulletin 180(1):154-180.

Merritt, M. L.

    1972   Cannikin: Effects on Archaeological Sites. Research Report SC-RR-72 0359. Sandia Laboratories/Sandia Corporation. Albuquerque.

Meyer, David A.

    1970   Pre-Dorset Settlements at the Seahorse Gully Site. Master's thesis. Department of Anthropology. University of Manitoba.

Michea, J. P.

    1950   Exploration in Ungava Peninsula. Annual Report to the National Museum of Canada, 1948-49. National Museum of Canada Bulletin 118:54-58.

Mikkelesen, Esnar

    1944   The East Greenlanders Possibilities of Existence, Their Production and Consumption. Meddelelser om Grønland 134(2).

Millar, James F. V.

    1968   Archaeology of Fisherman Lake, N.W.T. Ph.D. dissertation. Department of Anthropology. University of Calgary.

    1970   The Hughes and McLeod Complexes. Paper Presented to the 35th Annual Meeting of the Society for American Archaeology. Mexico City, 1970.

Minni, Sheila J.

    1975   Prehistoric Occupations of Black Lake, Northern Saskatchewan. Master's thesis. University of Saskatchewan.

Mitchell, B. W.

    1966   Inukshooks and Etigaseemautes; Mysterious Beacons of the North. Canadian Fisheries Research Board Journal 23(12):1897-1911.

Mitchell, Donald H.

    1970   Archaeological Investigations on the Chilcotin Plateau, 1968. Syesis 3(1-2):45-65.

Moore, G. W.

    1960   Recent Eustatic Sea-Level Fluctuations Recorded by Arctic Beach Ridges. United States Geological Survey Professional Paper, No. 400-B:B335-7.

Moore, G. W. and J. Louis Giddings, Jr.

1962 Record of 5000 Years of Arctic Wind Direction Recorded by Alaskan
      Beach Ridges. Geological Society of America Special Paper, No. 68.

Moorrees, Coenraad F. A.

1957 The Aleut Dentition. Harvard University Press. Cambridge.

Morgan, H. Morris

1965 An Archaeological Survey of Mount McKinley National Park. Report
      to the National Park Service.

Morice, A. G.

1897 Notes on Archaeological, Industrial and Sociological on the
      Western Dene. Transactions of the Royal Canadian Institute
      4(1892-93):1-222.

Morlan, Richard E.

1970a Symposium on Northern Athabaskan Prehistory: Introductory Remarks.
      Canadian Archaeological Association Bulletin 2:1-2. (English
      Edition)

1970b Toward a Definition of a Prehistoric Athabascan Culture.
      Canadian Archaeological Association Bulletin 2:24-33. (English
      Edition)

1970c Wedge-Shaped Core Technology in Northern North America. Arctic
      Anthropology 7(2):17-37.

1970d Toward the Definition of a Prehistoric Athabaskan Culture. Paper
      Presented at the 3rd Annual Meeting of the Canadian Archaeological
      Association. Ottawa.

1970e Review: Kijik: An Historic Tanaina Indian Settlement, by James W.
      VanStone and J. B. Townsend. Fieldiana Anthropology, Vol. 59.
      Chicago: Field Museum of Natural History, 1970. Man 5(4):709.

1971 The Later Prehistory of the Middle Porcupine Drainage, Northern
      Yukon Territory. Ph.D. dissertation. University of Wisconsin.

1972a The Cadzow Lake Site (MjVi-1): A Multi-Component Historic Kutchin
      Camp. Mercury Series. Archaeological Survey of Canada Paper, No.
      2. National Museum of Man. Ottawa.

1972b NbVk-1: An Historic Fishing Camp in Old Crow Flats, Northern Yukon
      Territory. Mercury Series. Archaeological Survey of Canada Paper,
      No. 5. National Museum of Man. Ottawa.

1972c Some Archaeological Problems Bearing Upon the Origins of Historic Brooks Range Cultures. Paper Presented at the 37th Annual Meeting of the Society for American Archaeology. Bal Harbour, Florida, May.

1973a The Later Prehistory of the Middle Porcupine Drainage, Northern Yukon Territory. Mercury Series. Archaeological Survey of Canada Paper, No. 11. National Museum of Man. Ottawa.

1973b A Technological Approach to Lithic Artifacts from Yukon Territory. Mercury Series. Archaeological Survey of Canada Paper, No. 7. National Museum of Man. Ottawa.

1974a Archaeological Resource Management in Yukon Territory. In: International Conference on the Prehistory and Paleoecology of Western North American Arctic and Subarctic. Scott Raymond and Peter Schledermann, eds. pp. 143-152. University of Calgary Archaeological Association. Alberta.

1974b Gladstone: An Analysis of Horizontal Distributions. Arctic Anthropology 11(Suppl.):82-93.

Morrow, Phyliss and Toby Alice Volkman

1975 The Loon With the Ivory Eyes: A Study in Symbolic Archaeology. Journal of American Folklore 88(348):143-150.

Müller-Beck, Hansjurgen

1966 Paleo-hunters in America: Origins and Diffusion. Science 152 (3726):1191-1210.

1967 On Migrations of Hunters Across the Bering Land Bridge in the Upper Pleistocene. In: The Bering Land Bridge. David M. Hopkins, ed. (Pt. 2) pp. 373-408. Stanford University Press. Stanford.

Müller-Beck, Hansjurgen, Wolfgang Torke and Wighart V. Koenigswald

1971 Die Grabungen des Jahres 1970 in der Pre-Dorset-Station Umingmak auf Banks Island (Arktisches Kanada). Quartar, Bd. 22. Bonn, Germany.

Murdoch, John

1887 The East Greenlanders. American Naturalist 21:133-138.

1888 On the Siberian Origin of Some Customs of the Western Eskimos. American Anthropologist 1:325-336.

Nash, Ronald J.

1969a The Arctic Small Tool Tradition in Manitoba. Occasional Paper of the Department of Anthropology, No. 2. University of Manitoba. Winnipeg.

1969b Dorset Culture in Northeastern Manitoba. Paper Presented to the 2nd Annual Meeting of the Canadian Archaeological Association. Toronto.

1970 The Prehistory of Northern Manitoba. In: Ten Thousand Years: Archaeology in Manitoba. Walter Hlady, ed. pp. 77-92. Manitoba Archaeological Society. Winnipeg.

1972 Dorset Culture in Northeastern Manitoba, Canada. Arctic Anthropology 9(1):10-16.

1973 Preliminary Paper and Discussion. School of American Research Advanced Seminar on Pre-Dorset--Dorset Problems. Santa Fe.

1975 Archaeological Investigations in the Transitional Forest Zone: Northern Manitoba, Southern Keewatin, N.W.T. Manitoba Museum of Man and Nature. Winnipeg.

1976 Cultural Systems and Culture Change in the Central Arctic. In: Eastern Arctic Prehistory: Paleoeskimo Problems. Moreau S. Maxwell, ed. pp. 150-155. Memoirs of the Society for American Archaeology, No. 31.

Nelson, Edward W.

1899 The Eskimo About Bering Strait. Eighteenth Annual Report of the Bureau of American Ethnology, Pt. 1.

Nelson, Nels C.

1935 Early Migrations of Man to America. Natural History 35:356.

1937 Notes on Cultural Relations Between Asia and America. American Antiquity 2:267-272.

Nelson, Willis H. and Frank Barnett

1955 A Burial Cave on Kanaga Island, Aleutian Islands. American Antiquity 20(4):387-392.

Newell, Raymond R. and Albert A. Dekin, Jr.

in preparation. An Integrative Strategy for the Definition of Behaviorally Meaningful Archaeological Units.

Newell, Raymond R. and Wayne E. Wiersum

in preparation. Reports on Archaeological Excavations Conducted at the Fish Creek Site (GUL-065), Paxson, Alaska, for the Alyeska Pipeline Service Company by the University of Alaska, ed. by John P. Cook.

Nielson, Niels

1936 Evidence of Iron Extraction at Sandes, in Greenland's West Settlement. Meddelelser om Grønland, Bd. 88.

Nissen, Karen and Margaret Dittemore

    1974   Ethnographic Data and Wear Pattern Analysis: A Study of Socketed
            Eskimo Scrapers. Tebiwa 17(1):67-87.

Noble, William C.

    1969   Comments on the Application of the Direct Historic Approach in
            Central District of Mackenzie, N.W.T. Paper Presented to the 2nd
            Annual Meeting of the Canadian Archaeological Association.
            Toronto.

    1971   Archaeological Surveys and Sequences in Central District of
            Mackenzie, N.W.T. Arctic Anthropology 8(1): 102-135.

    1974   The Tundra--Taiga Ecotone: Contributions from the Great Slave--
            Great Bear Lake Region. In: International Conference on the Pre-
            history and Paleoecology of Western North American Arctic and Sub-
            arctic. Scott Raymond and Peter Schledermann, eds. pp. 153-172.
            University of Calgary Archaeological Association. Alberta.

Noice, Harold

    1922   The Copper Eskimos. Science 55(1432):611-12.

Nörland, Poul

    1924   Buried Norsemen at Herjolfsnes. An Archaeological and Historical
            Study. Meddelelser om Grønland 67(1).

Nörland, Poul and Aage Roussell

    1929   Norse Ruins at Herjolfsnes. An Archaeological and Historical
            Study. Meddelelser om Grønland 67(1).

Nörland, Poul and Marten Stenberger.

    1934   Brattahlid. (App., No. 1: Animal Bones from the Norse Ruins at
            Brattahlid, by Magnus Degerbøl; and App., No. 2: Samples of Slag
            from Brattahlid.--List of Ruin Sites at Brattahlid, by Niels
            Nielson.) Meddelelser om Grønland, Bd. 88.

Nowak, Michael

    1968   Archaeological Dating by Means of Volcanic Ash Strata. Ph.D. dis-
            sertation. Department of Anthropology. University of Oregon.

    1970   A Preliminary Report on the Archaeology of Nunivak Island, Alaska.
            Anthropological Papers of the University of Alaska 15(1):19-32.

    1971   Review: Akulivikchuk: A Nineteenth Century Eskimo Village on the
            Nushagak River, Alaska, by James W. VanStone. Fieldiana Anthro-
            pology, Vol. 60. Chicago: Field Museum of Natural History, 1970.
            Arctic 24(2):136-147.

O'Bryan, Deric

 1953 Excavation of a Cape Dorset Culture Site, Mill Island, West Hudson Strait. Annual Report of the National Museum of Canada, 1951-52. National Museum of Canada Bulletin 128:40-57.

 1958 Ancient Cultures of Siberia and the Problems. of the First Relatives of the Old World with the New World. Revista de Cultura 3: 153-158. Univ. Mayor de San Simone. (in Spanish)

Oefteking, B.

 1945 Skeletal Remains from Prince William Sound, Alaska. American Journal of Physical Anthropology 3(1):57-96; 3(2):177-205; 3(3):277-311.

Osborne, Douglas

 1952 Late Eskimo Archaeology in the Western Mackenzie Delta Area. American Antiquity 18(1):30-39.

Oschinsky, Lawrence.

 1960 Two Recently Discovered Human Mandibles from Cape Dorset Sites on Sugluk and Mansel Islands. Anthropologica n.s. 2(2):212-227.

 1964 The Most Ancient Eskimos. Canadian Research Centre for Anthropology. University of Ottawa. Ottawa.

Osgood, Cornelius

 1971 Review: Ethnohistory in Southwestern Alaska and the Southern Yukon by Margaret Lantis, ed. Studies in Anthropology No. 7. University of Kentucky Press. Lexington, 1970. Science 173:804-805.

Oswalt, Wendell H.

 1949 Dated Houses at Squirrel River Alaska. Tree Ring Bulletin 16(1): 7-8.

 1950 Spruce Borings from the Lower Yukon River, Alaska. Tree Ring Bulletin 16(4):26-30.

 1951 The Origin of Driftwood at Hooper Bay, Alaska. Tree Ring Bulletin 18(1).

 1952a Pottery from Hooper Bay Village, Alaska. American Antiquity 18(1): 18-29.

 1952b The Archaeology of Hooper Bay Village, Alaska. Anthropological Papers of the University of Alaska 1(1):47-91.

 1952c Spruce Samples from the Copper River Drainage, Alaska. Tree Ring Bulletin 19(1).

1953a Recent Pottery from the Bering Strait Region, Alaska. Anthropological Papers of the University of Alaska 2(1):5-18.

1953b The Saucer Shaped Eskimo Lamp. Anthropological Papers of the University of Alaska 1(2):15-23.

1953c Northeast Asian and Alaskan Pottery Relationships. Southwestern Journal of Anthropology 9(4):394-407.

1954 Regional Chronologies in Spruce of the Kuskokwim, Alaska. Anthropological Papers of the University of Alaska 2(2):203-214.

1955a Prehistoric Sea Mammal Hunters at Kaflia, Alaska. Anthropological Papers of the University of Alaska 4(1):23-61.

1955b Alaskan Pottery: A Classification and Historical Reconstruction. American Antiquity 21(1):32-43.

1956 Review: Chugach Prehistory, by Frederica deLaguna. University of Washington Publications in Anthropology. Pullman, 1956. American Antiquity 22(2):201.

1957 A New Collection of Old Bering Sea I Artifacts. Anthropological Papers of the University of Alaska 5(2):91-96.

1962 Historical Populations in Western Alaska and Migration Theory. Anthropological Papers of the University of Alaska 11(1):1-14.

1965 The Kuskokwim River Drainage, Alaska: An Annotated Bibliography. Anthropological Papers of the University of Alaska 13(1).

1967 The Alaskan Eskimo. Chandler Publishing Co. San Francisco.

Oswalt, Wendell and James W. VanStone

1967 The Ethnoarchaeology of Crow Village, Alaska. Smithsonian Institution Bureau of American Ethnology Bulletin, No. 199.

Oxenstierna, E.

1967 The Vikings. Scientific American 216:67-78.

Patton, William W., Jr., and Thomas P. Miller

1970 A Possible Bedrock Source for Obsidian Found in Archaeological Sites in Northwestern Alaska. Science 169:760-761.

Pedersen, P. O.

1949 The East Greenland Eskimo Dentition. Meddelelser om Grønland 142(3).

Peterson, Lana

    1971   Ancient Aleut Rock Painting. The Alaska Journal 1(4):49-51.

Peterson, Robert

    1975   Some Considerations Concerning the Greenland Longhouse. Folk
           16-17:171-188.

Pierard, Jean

    1975   Archeologie du Nouveau-Quebec: Etude de Materiel Osteologique
           Provenant des Sites Ung.11 et Dia. 1. Collection Paleo-Quebec,
           No. 6. L'Universite du Quebec a Montreal.

Pinart, Alphonse

    1875   La Caverne d'Aknanh, Ile d'Ounga (Archipel Shumagin, Alaska).
           E. Leroux. Paris.

Plaskett, David C.

    1976   The Nenana River Gorge Site, HEA-62. Preliminary Report on
           Archaeological Investigations 1975. Report to Geist Fund, Uni-
           versity of Alaska Museum.

Plumet, Patrick

    1969   Archaeologie de l'Ungava: Le Probleme des Maisons Longues a Deux
           Hemicycles et Separations Interieures. Ecole Practique des
           Hautes Etudes, Sorbonne. Contributions du Centre d'Etude
           Arctiques et Finno Scandiennes, No. 7. Paris.

    1970   Recherches Archaeologiques dans la Baie Ungava Nouveau Quebec.
           Societe des Americanistes de Paris N.S. 57:127-233. Paris.

    1974   L'Archeologie et le Relevement Glacio-Isostatique de la Region
           de Poste-de-la-Baleine, Nouveau-Quebec. Revue de Geographie de
           Montreal 28(4):443-447.

    1976   Archeologie du Nouveau-Quebec: Habitats Paleo-Esquimaux a Poste de
           la Baleine. Paleo-Quebec, No. 7. Centre d'Etudes Nordiques.
           Universite Laval. Quebec.

Porsild, Morten P.

    1911   Une Arme Ancienne de Chasse des Esquimaux et Son Analogue de la
           Culture Prehistorique de France. Meddelelser om Grønland, Bd. 47.

    1914   Studies on the Material Culture of the Eskimo in West Greenland.
           Meddelelser om Grønland 51:113-200.

    1920   On Eskimo Stone Rows in Greenland Formerly Supposed to be of Norse
           Origin. The Geographical Review 10(5):297-309.

Porter, Stephen C.

    1964   Antiquity of Man at Anaktuvuk Pass, Alaska. American Antiquity
            29(4):493-496.

Potosky, Romayne, with Norman Potosky

    1947   A Unique Specimen of Pressure-flaked Pyrite from Saint Lawrence
            Island, Alaska. American Antiquity 13(2):181-182.

Powers, W. Roger

    1973   Palaeolithic Man in Northeast Asia. Arctic Anthropology 10(2):
            1-106.

    1974   The Pleistocene and Early Holocene Archaeology of Mainland North-
            east Asia. Ph.D. dissertation. University of Wisconsin.

Quimby, George I.

    1940   The Manitunik Eskimo Culture of East Hudson's Bay. American
            Antiquity 6(2):148-165.

    1945a Periods of Prehistoric Art in the Aleutian Islands. American
            Antiquity 11(2):76-79.

    1945b Pottery from the Aleutian Islands. Fieldiana: Natural History
            Museum Publication 36(1):1-13.

    1946a The Sadiron Lamp of Kamchatka as a Clue to the Chronology of the
            Aleut. American Antiquity 11(3):202-203.

    1946b Toggle Harpoon Heads from the Aleutian Islands. Fieldiana:
            Natural History Museum Publication 36(2):15-23.

    1948   Prehistoric Art of the Aleutian Islands. Fieldiana: Natural
            History Museum Publication 36(4):72-92.

    1954   Cultural and Natural Areas Before Kroeber. American Antiquity
            19:317-333.

Rainey, Froelich G.

    1936   Eskimo Chronology. Proceedings of the National Academy of Sciences
            22(6):357-362.

    1937   Old Eskimo Art. Natural History 40(3):603-607.

    1939   Archaeology in Central Alaska. Anthropological Papers of the
            American Museum of Natural History 36(4):351-405.

    1940   Archaeological Investigations in Central Alaska. American
            Antiquity 5(4):399-408.

1941a The Ipiutak Culture at Point Hope Alaska. American Anthropologist N.S. 43:364-375.

1941b A New Form of Culture on the Arctic Coast. Proceedings of the National Academy of Sciences 27:141-144.

1941c Culture Changes on the Arctic Coast. Transcripts of the New York Academy of Science (Ser. II) 3(6):148-155. Baltimore.

1941d Mystery People of the Arctic. Natural History 47(3):148-155.

1941e Eskimo Prehistory: The Okvik Site on the Punuk Islands. Anthropological Papers of the American Museum of Natural History 36(4).

1942a Discovering Alaska's Oldest Arctic Town. National Geographic Magazine 82:319-336.

1942b Review: Outline of Eskimo Prehistory, by Henry B. Collins, Jr. Smithsonian Miscellaneous Collection, Vol. 100, pp. 533-592. Smithsonian Institution. Washington, D.C., 1940. American Antiquity 7(3):336.

1947 The Whale Hunters of Tigara. Anthropological Papers of the American Museum of Natural History 41(2).

1953 The Significance of Recent Archaeological Discoveries in Inland Alaska. In: Asia and North America: Transpacific Contacts. Marian W. Smith, ed. Society for American Archaeology Memoirs, No. 9. American Antiquity 18(3:2):43-46.

1965 J. Louis Giddings, Jr., 1909-1964. American Anthropologist 67(6): 1503-1507.

1971 The Ipiutak Culture: Excavations at Point Hope, Alaska. Addison-Wesley Modular Publications 8:1-32.

1975 Speculations on the Future of Archaeology. Folk 16-17:25-32.

Rainey, Froelich G. and Elizabeth Ralph

1959 Radiocarbon Dating in the Arctic. American Antiquity 24(4):365-374.

Ray, Dorothy Jean

1964 Nineteenth Century Settlement and Subsistence Patterns in Bering Strait. Arctic Anthropology 2(2):61-94.

1966 Pictographs Near Bering Strait, Alaska. Polar Notes: Occasional Publication of the Stefansson Collection 6:35-40. Dartmouth College Library.

Ray, Patrick H. (Lieut.)

1885　Report of the International Polar Expedition to Pt. Barrow, Alaska, in response to the resolution of the House of Representatives of December 11, 1884. Washington, D. C.

Raymond, Scott and Peter Schledermann

1974　International Conference on the Prehistory and Paleoecology of Western North American Arctic and Subarctic. University of Calgary Archaeological Association. Alberta. (Eds.)

Reger, Douglas R.

1969　Report of Investigations in the Power Creek Power Dam Site and Impoundment Area near Cordova, Alaska. Manuscript.

1973　An Eskimo Site Near Kenai, Alaska. Master's thesis. Department of Anthropology. University of Washington.

Reger, Douglas R. and Richard D. Reger

1972　An Archaeological Survey in the Utopia Area, Alaska. Anthropological Papers of the University of Alaska 15(2):23-37.

Reger, Richard D., Troy L. Pewe, F. Hadleigh-West and I. Skarland

1964　Geology and Archaeology of the Yardang Flint Station. Anthropological Papers of the University of Alaska 12(2):92-100.

Richter, S.

1934　A Contribution to the Archaeology of North-East Greenland. Norsk Polarinstitutt. Skrifter, No. 63.

Ridley, Frank

1964　Burins, Indian or Eskimo? Anthropological Journal of Canada 2(4): 19-21. Ottawa.

Rink, Hinrich J.

1887　The Eskimo Tribes; Their Common Origin, Their Dispersion and Their Diversities in General. (The Eskimo Tribes, 1887-91. Vol. 1, Pt. 1). Meddelelser om Grønland 11:1-34.

Ritchie, William A.

1951　Ground Slates: Eskimo or Indian? Pennsylvania Archaeologist 21(3&4):46-52.

1962　Northeastern Crossties with the Arctic. In: Prehistoric Cultural Relations Between the Arctic and Temperate Zones of North America. John M. Campbell, ed. pp. 96-99. Arctic Institute of North America, Technical Paper No. 11. Montreal.

1969 Ground Slate: East and West. American Antiquity 34(4):385-391.

Roberts, F. H. H., Jr.

1943 A New Site. American Antiquity 8:300.

Rogers, E. S. and R. A. Bradley

1953 An Archaeological Reconnaissance in South Central Quebec, 1950.
      American Antiquity 19(2):138-144.

Rogers, E. S. and M. H. Rogers

1950 Archaeological Investigations in the Region about Lakes Mistassini
      and Albanel, Province of Quebec, 1948. American Antiquity 15(4):
      322-337.

Rogers, Edward S., Donald Webster and James Anderson

1972 A Cree Burial, Moose Factory, Ontario. Arctic Anthropology 9(1):
      37-34.

Ross, Richard E.

1971 The Cultural Sequence at Chagvan Bay, Alaska: A Matrix Analysis.
      Ph.D. dissertation. Washington State University.

Rouse, Irving

1976 Peopling of the Americas. Quaternary Research 6(4):597-612.

Roussell, Aage

1936 Sandes and the Neighboring Farms. (App., No. 1: Greenland Runic
      Inscriptions, by Erik Moltke.) Meddelelser om Grønland, Bd. 88.

1941 Farms and Churches in the Mediaeval Norse Settlements of Green-
      land. (App., No. 1: The Osseous Material from Austmannadal and
      Tungmeralik, by Magnus Degerbøl.) Meddelelser om Grønland, Bd. 89.

Rowley, Graham

1940 The Dorset Culture of the Eastern Arctic. American Anthropolo-
      gist N.S.: 42:490-499.

1950 An Unusual Archaeological Specimen from Foxe Basin. Arctic 3(1):
      63-65.

Rudenko, S. I.

1961   The Ancient Culture of the Bering Sea and the Eskimo Problem. In:
Anthropology of the North. Arctic Institute of North America,
Technical Paper No. 1. (Translated from the Russian Sources by
Paul Tolstoy; Henry M. Michael, ed.). Montreal. (Original
Russian Publication: Moscow and Leningrad, 1947).

Ruffman, Alan

1976   An Archaeological Site on Karluk Island in Crozier Strait, N.W.T.
Arctic 29(3):165-167.

Ryder, C.

1895   Om den tidligere eskimoiske Bebyggelse af Scoresby Sund.
Meddelelser om Grønland, Bd. 17.

Saladin d'Anglure, Bernard

1962   Decouverte de Petroglyphes a Qajartalik sur l'ile de Qikertaaluk.
North, novembre-decembre, 1962. pp. 34-39. Ottawa.

1963   Discovery of Petroglyphs Near Wakeham Bay. Arctic Circular 15(2):
6-13.

Salter, E.

1976   Burial Investigations at Kingnait Fjord Baffin Island (Niutang
site MbDc-1). The Calgary Archaeologist 4:23-24. University of
Calgary.

Sanger, David

1965   Review: Early Man in the Western Arctic: A Symposium, by Frederick
Hadleigh-West, ed. Anthropological Papers of the University of
Alaska, Vol. 10, No. 2. College, Alaska, 1963. American
Antiquity 30(4):517-518.

1967   Prehistory of the Pacific Northwest Plateau as Seen from the
Interior of British Columbia. American Antiquity 32(2):186-197.

1968   Prepared Core and Blade Traditions in the Pacific Northwest.
Arctic Anthropology 5:92-120.

1970a   Mid-Latitude Core and Blade Traditions. Arctic Anthropology 7(2):
106-114.

1970b   Introduction: Papers from a Seminar on Northern North American
Blades and Cores, National Museum of Man, Ottawa, Ontario,
November 25-27, 1969. Arctic Anthropology 7(2):1.

Sanger, David, Robert McGhee and David Wyatt

    1970 Appendix I: Blade Description. Arctic Anthropology 7(2):115-117.

Sarafian, Winston L. and James W. VanStone

    1972 The Records of the Russian-American Company.as a Source for the Ethnohistory of the Nushagak River Region, Alaska. Anthropological Papers of the University of Alaska 15(2):53-78.

Schaller, George B.

    1957 Some Artifacts from Ninilchik, Alaska. Manuscript.

Schimber, Dave and Peter Schledermann

    1967 Additional Material from Two Sites in Mt. McKinley National Park. Department of Anthropology. University of Alaska. Manuscript.

Schledermann, Peter

    1971a The Thule Tradition in Northern Labrador. Master's thesis. Department of Anthropology. Memorial University of Newfoundland.

    1971b 1971 Site Survey in Cumberland Sound, Baffin Island: Preliminary Report. In: Canadian Archaeological Association Bulletin, No. 3. Richard E. Morlan, ed. pp. 56-99. Canadian Archaeological Association.

    1975a A Late Dorset Site on Axel Heiberg Island. Arctic 28(4):300.

    1975b Thule Eskimo Prehistory of Cumberland Sound, Baffin Island, Canada. Ph.D. dissertation. University of Calgary.

    1976a Thule Eskimo Prehistory of Cumberland Sound, Baffin Island, Canada. Mercury Series. Archaeological Survey of Canada Paper, No. 38. National Museums of Canada. Ottawa.

    1976b The Effect of Climatic/Ecological Changes on the Style of Thule Culture Winter Dwellings. Arctic and Alpine Research 8(1):37-47.

    1976c Thule Culture Communal Houses in Labrador. Arctic 29(1):27-37.

Schledermann, Peter and Wallace Olson

    1969 Archaeological Survey of C. O. D. Lake Area, Minto Flats. Anthropological Papers of the University of Alaska 14(2):67-76.

Schlesier, Karl Heinz

    1965 Vorbericht uber die Erste Deutsche Archaeologische Brooks-Range Expedition, Nord Alaska. 1964. Anthropos 59:911-917.

1966   Sedna Creek: Abschlussbericht uber eine Archaeologische Felderbeit in Nord Alaska. Zeitschrift fur Ethnologie 91(1):5-39.

1967   Sedna Creek: Report on an Archaeological Survey on the Arctic Slope of the Brooks Range. American Antiquity 32(2):210-222.

1971   The Archaeology of Sedna Creek. Wichita State University Bulletin. University Studies, No. 8-9.

1972   Ice Age Hunters. The Beaver Outfit 203(4):30-35.

Schweger, Charles

1974   Forest History and Dynamics of the Fisherman Lake Area, N.W.T. and Implications to Human Ecology. In: International Conference on the Prehistory and Paleoecology of Western North American Arctic and Subarctic. Scott Raymond and Peter Schledermann, eds. pp. 173-186. University of Calgary Archaeological Association. Alberta.

Seltzer, C. C.

1933   The Anthropometry of the Western and Copper Eskimos, Based on Data of Vilhjalmur Stefansson. Human Biology 5(3):315-370.

Shapiro, H. L.

1934   Some Observations on the Origin of the Eskimo. Proceedings of the 5th Pacific Science Congress 4:2723-2732. Victoria and Vancouver, B.C.

Shinkwin, Anne Dolores

1964   Early Man in the Brooks Range: The Tuktu-Naiyuk Sequence. Master's thesis. George Washington University.

1974   Dakah De'nin's Village: An Early Historic Atna Site. Arctic Anthropology 11(Suppl.):54-64.

1975   Dakah De'nin's Village and the Dixthada Site: A Contribution to Northern Athapaskan Prehistory. Ph.D. dissertation. University of Wisconsin.

Shutler, Richard, Jr.

1971   Papers from a Symposium on Early Man in North America, New Developments: 1960-1970. Arctic Anthropology 8(2):1-91. (Ed.)

Simmons, William S.

1960a   Faunal Remains from Prehistoric Sites, Alaska. Honors thesis, Human Biology. Brown University.

1960b Faunal Remains from the Newly Discovered Choris Site, Alaska.
Paper Presented at the Annual Meeting of the Society for
American Archaeology, May.

Skarland, Ivar

1954 The Bering Land-bridge Re-evaluated. Proceedings of the Alaskan
Science Conference, 1952. pp. 125-127.

1956 Review of Early Alaskan Prehistory. Proceedings of the Alaskan
Science Conference, 1953. pp. 197-200.

1964a Climate and Culture Change in the Western American Arctic. Paper
Presented at the 7th International Congress of Anthropological and
Ethnological Sciences. Moscow, U.S.S.R., August.

1964b Otto William Geist, 1888-1963. American Antiquity 29(4):484-485.

Skarland, Ivar and J. Louis Giddings, Jr.

1948 Flint Stations in Central Alaska. American Antiquity 14(2):116-
120.

Skarland, Ivar and Charles J. Keim

1958 Archaeological Discoveries on the Denali Highway, Alaska. Anthropological Papers of the University of Alaska 6(2):79-88.

Slobodin, Richard

1966 Review: The Chandalar Kutchin, by Robert A. McKennan. Arctic
Institute of North America, Technical Paper No. 17. Montreal,
1965. American Antiquity 31(6):892-893.

Smith, George S. and Michael R. Zimmerman

1975 Tattooing Found on a 1600 Year Old Frozen, Mummified Body from
St. Lawrence Island, Alaska. American Antiquity 40(4):433-437.

Smith, Jason W.

1971 The Ice Mountain Microblade and Core Industry, Cassiar District,
Northern British Columbia, Canada. Arctic and Alpine Research
3(3):199-214.

1974a The Northeast Asian--Northwest American Microblade Tradition and
the Ice Mountain Microblade and Core Industry. Ph.D. dissertation.
Department of Archaeology. University of Calgary.

1974b The Northeast Asian--Northwest American Microblade Tradition
(NANAMT). Journal of Field Archaeology 1(3/4):347-364.

Smith, Jason W. and James Calder

1972 The Microtool Industry of the Ice Mountain Microblade Phase.
Northwest Science 46:90-107.

Smith, Marion W.

1953 Asia and North America: Transpacific Contacts. Memoirs of the Society for American Archaeology, No. 9. American Antiquity 18(3):2. (Ed.)

Smith, Philip S.

1937 Certain Relations Between Northwestern America and Northeastern Asia. In: Early Man. McCurdy, ed. pp. 85-92. International Symposium on Early Man in the Academy of Natural Sciences. Philadelphia, 1937.

Smith, Philip S. and J.B. Mertie, Jr.

1930 Geology and Mineral Resources of Northwestern Alaska. Geological Survey Bulletin, No. 815.

Smith, R.A. and J.W. Smith

1970 Early Man and Environments in Northwest North America. Proceedings of the 2nd Annual Paleo-Environmental Workshop of the University of Calgary Archaeological Association. Students' Press. Calgary. (Eds.)

Smith, Timothy Alan

1977 Obsidian Hydration as an Independent Dating Technique. Master's thesis. University of Alaska.

Solberg, Ole Martin

1907 Beitrage zur Vorgeschichte der Ost-Eskimo. Steinerne Schneidergerate und Waffenschärfen aus Grønland 2(1).

Solecki, Ralph, S.

1950a New Data on the Inland Eskimo of Northern Alaska. Journal of the Washington Academy of Sciences 40(5):137-157.

1950b Archaeology and Geology in Northwestern Alaska. Earth Science Digest 4(7):3-7.

1950c A Preliminary Report of an Archaeological Reconnaissance of the Kukpowruk and Kokolik Rivers in Northwest Alaska. American Antiquity 16(1):66-69.

1951a Notes on Two Archaeological Discoveries in Northern Alaska, 1950. American Antiquity 17(1):55-57.

1951b Archaeology and Ecology of the Arctic Slope of Alaska. Annual Report of the Smithsonian Institution. pp. 469-495.

1951c How Man Came to North America. Scientific American 184(1):11-15.

1952   A Petroglyph in Northern Alaska. American Antiquity 18(1):63-64.

1955   Lamellar Flakes Versus Blades: A Reappraisal. American Antiquity
       20(4):393-394.

Solecki, Ralph S. and R.J. Hackman

1951   Additional Data on the Denbigh Flint Complex in Northern Alaska.
       Journal of the Washington Academy of Sciences 41(3):85-88.

Solecki, Ralph S., Bert Salwen and Jerome Jacobson

1973   Archaeological Reconnaissance North of the Brooks Range in North-
       eastern Alaska. University of Calgary Department of Archaeology
       Occasional Paper, No. 1.

Sorenson, C.J. and J.C. Knox

1974   Paleosols and Paleoclimates Related to Late Holocene Forest/Tundra
       Border Migrations: Mackenzie and Keewatin, N.W.T., Canada. In:
       International Conference on the Prehistory and Paleoecology of
       Western North American Arctic and Subarctic. Scott Raymond and
       Peter Schledermann, eds. pp. 187-204. University of Calgary
       Archaeological Association. Alberta.

Spaulding, Albert C.

1946   Northwestern Archaeology and General Trends in the Northern Forest
       Zones. In: Man in Northeastern North America, Frederick Johnson,
       ed.· pp. 143-146. Papers of the Robert S. Peabody Foundation for
       Archaeology, Vol. 3. Andover, Mass.

1953   The Current Status of Aleutian Archaeology. In: Asia and North
       America: Transpacific Contacts. Marian W. Smith, ed. Society for
       American Archaeology Memoirs, No. 9. American Antiquity 18(3):2:
       29-31.

1962   Archaeological Investigations on Agattu, Aleutian Islands. Anthro-
       pological Papers of the Museum of Anthropology, No. 18. University
       of Michigan.

n.d.   Notes on the Archaeology of the Boreal Forest Zone. Ph.D. disser-
       tation. Columbia University.

Speck, Frank G.

1924a Eskimo Collection from Baffin Land and Ellesmere Land. Museum of
       the American Indian, Heye Foundation. Indian Notes 1(3):143-149.

1924b Collections from Labrador Eskimos. Museum of the American Indian,
       Heye Foundation. Indian Notes 1(4).

1931   Montagnais-Naskapi Bands and Early Eskimo Distribution in the
       Labrador Peninsula. American Anthropologist 33:557-600.

1963   Inland Eskimo Bands of Labrador. In: Essays in Anthropology.
       Papers Presented to A.L. Kroeber. pp. 313-330. Berkeley.

1941 Art Processes in Birchbark of the River Desert Algonquin, a Circumboreal Trait. Anthropological Papers of the Bureau of American
Ethnology 128(17):231-274.

Spence, Michael

1974 The Study of Residential Practices Among Prehistoric Hunters and
Gatherers. World Archaeology 5(3):346-357.

Spencer, Robert F.

1965 Arctic and Sub-Arctic in Native America. In: The Native Americans,
by Robert F. Spencer, Jesse D. Jennings, et. al. pp. 119-167.
Harper & Row. New York.

Spiess, Arthur

1976 Determining Season of Death of Archaeological Fauna by Analysis of
Teeth. Arctic 29(1):53-55.

Sproull, Jane

1976 Thule Swimming Figurines in the National Museum, Ottawa. In:
Primitive Art and Technology. J. S. Raymond, B. Loveseth, C.
Arnold and G. Reardon, eds. pp. 129-134. Archaeological
Association of the University of Calgary. Alberta.

Spurr, Josiah E.

1900 A Reconnaissance in Southwestern Alaska in 1898. Twentieth Annual
Report of the United States Geological Survey 7:31-244.

Stanford, Dennis J.

1971 Evidence of Paleo-Eskimos of the North Coast of Alaska. Paper
Presented to the 36th Annual Meeting of the Society for American
Archaeology. Norman, Oklahoma, May.

1972 The Origins of Thule Culture. Ph.D. dissertation. Department
of Anthropology. University of New Mexico.

Steensby, H. P.

1910 Contributions to the Ethnology and Anthropogeography of the Polar
Eskimos. Meddelelser om Grønland 34:255-405.

1917a An Anthropogeographical Study of the Origin of Eskimo Culture.
Meddelelser om Grønland 53:39-288.

1917b Norsemen's Route from Greenland to Wineland. Meddelelser om
Grønland, Bd. 56.

Steer, Donald N.

    1973 History and Archaeology of the Historic Site of LaLoche House.
           The Musk Ox 12:13-31.

Stefansson, Vilhjalmur

    1906 The Icelandic Colony in Greenland. American Anthropologist
           N.S.(8):262-270.

    1914 Prehistoric and Present Commerce Among the Arctic Coast Eskimo.
           National Museum of Canada Anthropological Series 3(6).

    1939 The Disappearance of the Greenland Colony. Natural History
           Magazine 43(7-12):34-37.

Stefansson, Vilhjalmur and C. Wissler

    1914 The Stefansson-Anderson Arctic Expedition of the American Museum:
           Preliminary Ethnological Report. Anthropological Papers of the
           American Museum of Natural History 14(1).

Stewart, T. Dale

    1939 Anthropometric Observations on the Eskimos and Indians of
           Labrador. Fieldiana Anthropology: Field Museum of Natural
           History 31(1).

Stothers, David M. and Marlene A. Dullabaun

    1975 A Bibliography of Arctic and Sub-Arctic Prehistory and Proto-
           history. Toledo Area Aboriginal Research Bulletin. Supple-
           mentary Monograph, No. 2. Toledo Area Aboriginal Research Club.

Stringer, W. J. and J. P. Cook

    1974 Feasibility Study for Locating Archaeological Village Sites by
           Satellite Remote Sensing Techniques. Final Report (Contract
           NAS5-21833 Task 110N) to National Aeronautics and Space Admini-
           stration. University of Alaska.

Strong, W. D.

    1930 A Stone Culture from Northern Labrador, and Its Relation to the
           Eskimo-Like Culture of the Northeast. American Anthropologist
           32(1):126-143.

Stuckenrath, Robert Jr., William Coe and Elizabeth Ralph

    1966 University of Pennsylvania Radiocarbon Dates IX. Radiocarbon
           8:348-385.

Swindler, Daris R.

1964 Skull Fragments from Norton Levels at Iyatayet. In: The
Archaeology of Cape Denbigh (Appendix #2), by J. Louis Giddings,
Jr. pp. 304-310. Brown University Press. Providence.

Sykes, Egerton

1966 Review: Payne Lake, Ungava Peninsula, Archaeology 1964, by Thomas
E. Lee. Centre d'Etudes Nordiques, Travaux Divers No. 12.
Quebec: Universite Laval. New World Antiquity 13(9-10):96-99.
London.

Syncrude Canada, Ltd.

1974 The Beaver Creek Site--A Prehistoric Stone Quarry on Syncrude
Lease No. 22. Environmental Research Monograph, No. 22.
Syncrude Canada, Ltd. Edmonton.

Taylor, J. Garth

1968 An Analysis of the Size of Eskimo Settlements on the Coast of
Labrador during the Early Contact Period. Ph.D. dissertation.
University of Toronto.

1974 Labrador Eskimo Settlements of the Early Contact Period.
National Museum of Man, Publications in Ethnology, No. 9.
National Museums of Canada. Ottawa.

1975 Demography and Adaptations of Eighteenth-Century Eskimo Groups in
Northern Labrador and Ungava. In: Prehistoric Maritime Adaptations of the Circumpolar Zones. William W. Fitzhugh, IV, ed.
pp. 169-180. Mouton and Company. Paris.

Taylor, William E. Jr.

1958a Archaeology in the Canadian Arctic. Canadian Geographic Journal
57(3):92-95. Ottawa.

1958b Archaeological Work in Ungava, 1957. Arctic Circular 10(2)25-27.

1959a Review and Assessment of the Dorset Problem. Anthropologica
1(1&2):24-26. University of Ottawa.

1959b Archaeological Work in Ungava and Mansel Island. Arctic
Circular 11(4):66-68.

1960a Archaeological Work, Ivugivik and Mansel Island. Arctic
Circular 13(1):1-4.

1960b A Description of Sadlermiut Houses Excavated at Native Point,
Southhampton Island, N.W.T. National Museum of Canada Contribution to Anthropology, 1957. National Museum of Canada Bulletin
62:53-99.

1962a Pre-Dorset Occupations at Ivugivik in Northwestern Ungava. In: Prehistoric Cultural Relations Between the Arctic and Temperate Zones of North America. John M. Campbell, ed. pp. 80-91. Arctic Institute of North America, Technical Paper No. 11. Montreal.

1962b A Distinction Between Blades and Microblades in the American Arctic. American Antiquity 27(3):425-426.

1962c Comments on the Nature and Origin of the Dorset Culture. In: Problems of the Pleistocene and Arctic. G. R. Lowther, ed. Publication of the McGill University Museum 2(2):56-67.

1963a Archaeological Collections from the Jay Bay Region, Ungava Peninsula. Arctic Circular 15(2):24-36.

1963b Implications of a Pre-Dorset Lance Head from the East Canadian Arctic. Arctic 16(2):129-133.

1963c Hypotheses on the Origin of Canadian Thule Culture. American Antiquity 28(4):456-464.

1963d Review: An Archaeological Collection from Somerset Island and Boothia Peninsula, N.W.T.; A Contribution to the Human Osteology of the Canadian Arctic, by James W. VanStone, James Anderson and Charles Merbs. Art and Archaeology Division of the Royal Ontario Museum Occasional Paper, No. 4. Toronto, 1962. Arctic 16(2):144-145.

1964a Interim Account of an Archaeological Survey in the Central Arctic, 1963. Anthropological Papers of the University of Alaska 12(1): 46-55.

1964b The Prehistory of the Quebec-Labrador Peninsula. In: Le Nouveau Quebec. J. Malaurie, ed. pp. 181-210. Bibliotheque Arctique et Antarctique. (Tome 2) Publication de l'Etude Practique des Hautes Etudes, Sorbonne. Paris.

1964c Archaeology of the McCormick Inlet Site, Melville Island, N.W.T. Arctic 17(2):125-128.

1965a The Arnapik and Tyara Sites: An Archaeological Study of Dorset Culture Origins. Ph.D. dissertation. Department of Anthropology. University of Michigan.

1965b The Fragments of Eskimo Prehistory. The Beaver Outfit 195:4-17.

1966a . . . and then came Man. In: People of Light and Dark. M. Van Steensel, ed. pp. 1-5. Department of Indian Affairs and Northern Development. Queen's Printer. Ottawa.

1966b An Archaeological Perspective on Eskimo Economy. Antiquity 40:114-120.

1967   Summary of Archaeological Field Work on Banks and Victoria Islands, Arctic Canada, 1965. Arctic Anthropologist 4(1):221-243.

1968a The Arnapik and Tyara Sites: An Archaeological Study of Dorset Culture Origins. Memoirs of the Society for American Archaeology, No. 22. American Antiquity 33(4:2):1-129.

1968b Prehistory of Hudson Bay, Part I, Eskimos of the North and East Shores. In: Science, History and Hudson Bay. C. S. Beals, ed. pp. 1-26. Queen's Printer. Ottawa.

1968c Review: Ancient Men of the Arctic, by J. Louis Giddings, Jr. Alfred A. Knopf, Inc. New York, 1967. Science 160:675-676.

1968d An Archaeological Overview of Eskimo Economy. In: Eskimo of the Canadian Arctic. V. F. Valentine and F. G. Valley, eds. pp. 3-17. Carleton Library, D. Van Nostrand Co., Inc. Princeton, New Jersey.

1969a Archaeology in Canada's Arctic: Past and Future. Canadian Journal of Science and Technology, Science Forum 2(2):23-26. Toronto.

1969b L'Art Esquimau Canadien Prehistorique. Prehistoric Canadian Eskimo Art. In: Chefs-d'oeuvre des arts indiens et esquimaux du Canada. Masterpieces of Indian and Eskimo Art from Canada. unpaginated (9 pages). National Gallery of Canada. Ottawa.

1971   Taisumanialuk--Prehistoric Canadian Eskimo Art. Taisumanialuk--L'Art Prehistorique des Eskimo du Canada. In: Sculpture/Inuit. Sculpture of the Inuit: Masterworks of the Canadian Arctic. pp. 23-35. Canadian Eskimo Arts Council. University of Toronto Press.

1972a An Archaeological Survey Between Cape Parry and Cambridge Bay, N.W.T., Canada in 1963. Mercury Series. Archaeological Survey of Canada Paper, No. 1. National Museum of Man. Ottawa.

1972b Found Art--and Frozen. Artscanada December 1971/January 1972:32-47.

1975   Speculations and Hypotheses on Shamanism in the Dorset Culture of Arctic Canada. Valmonica Symposium '72. Actes du Symposium International Sur les Religions de la Prehistoire, Capo Di Ponte (Ed. Del Centro). pp. 473-482.

Taylor, William E., Jr., and G. Swinton

1967   Prehistoric Dorset Art. The Beaver Outfit 298:32-47.

Teilhard de Chardin, P.

1939   On the Presumable Existence of a World-Wide Sub-Arctic Sheet of Human Culture at the Dawn of the Neolithic. Bulletin of the Geological Society of China 19:333-339. Peking.

Thalbitzer, William

1904   A Phonetical Study of the Eskimo Language. Meddelelser om
       Grønland, Bd. 31.

1909   Ethnological Description of the Amdrup Collection from East Green-
       land Comprising Objects Found in Eskimo House-Ruins and Graves
       North of Angmagsalik Between 68° and 75° Lat. Meddelelser om
       Grønland 28(7):329-542.

1914   The Ammassalik Eskimo. Meddelelser om Grønland, Bd. 39.   (Ed.)

1951   Two Runic Stones from Greenland and Minnesota. Smithsonian
       Miscellaneous Collections 116(3).

Thompson, Raymond M.

1948   Notes on the Archaeology of the Utukok River, Northwest Alaska.
       American Antiquity 14(1):62-65.

Thomsen, Thomas

1917   Implements and Artifacts of the North East Greenlanders.
       Meddelelser om Grønland 44:5.

1928a Eskimo Archaeology, Greenland. Meddelelser om Grønland 2:271-329.

1928b Eskimo Archaeology. In: Greenland: The Past and Present Popula-
       tion of Greenland (Vol. II). M. Vahl, Chief ed. pp. 271-330.
       C. A. Reitzl. Copenhagen.

Thorsteinsson, R. and E. T. Tozer

1957   Geological Investigations in Ellesmere and Axel Islands, 1956.
       Arctic 10(1):2-31.

Thostrup, C. B.

1911   Ethnographic Description of the Eskimo Settlement and Stone Remains
       in North-East Greenland. Meddelelser om Grønland 44:183-355.

Tolstoy, Paul

1953   Some Amerasian Pottery Traits in North Asian Prehistory.
       American Antiquity 19(1):25-39.

1958   The Archaeology of the Lena Basin and Its New World Relationships.
       Part I. American Antiquity 23(4):397-418. Part II. American
       Antiquity 24(1):63-81.

Tourville, Elsie A.

1974   Alaska, A Bibliography: 1570-1970. G. K. Hall and Co. Boston.

Townsend, Joan B.

1965 Ethnohistory and Culture Change of the Pedro Bay Tanaina. Ph.D.
      dissertation. Department of Anthropology. University of
      California at Los Angeles.

1969 Review: Chugach Prehistory: The Archaeology of Prince William
      Sound, Alaska, by Frederica de Laguna. University of Washington
      Publication in Anthropology, No. 13. 1956. Man 4(2):299.

1970a Tanaina Archaeology in the Iliamna Lake Region, Alaska.
      Canadian Archaeological Association Bulletin 2:34-41. (English
      Edition)

1970b Tanaina Ethnohistory: An Example of Method for the Study of
      Cultural Change. In: Ethnohistory in Southwestern Alaska and the
      Southern Yukon: Method and Content. Margaret Lantis, ed. pp. 71-
      102. Studies in Anthropology No. 7. University of Kentucky
      Press. Lexington.

1970c Review: The Archaeology of the Glacier Bay Region, Southeastern
      Alaska, by Robert E. Ackerman. Laboratory of Anthropology,
      Report of Excavations, No. 44. Washington State University,
      1968. American Anthropologist 72(1):176-177.

1971 Review: Historic Site Archaeology in Canada, by Kenneth Kidd.
      Anthropological Papers of the National Museum of Canada, No. 22.
      Ottawa, 1969. American Anthropologist 73(2):415.

1972 Review: Akulivikchuk: A Nineteenth Century Eskimo Village on the
      Nushagak River, Alaska, by James W. VanStone. Fieldiana
      Anthropology, Vol. 60. Chicago: Field Museum of Natural History,
      1970. and Historic Settlement Patterns in the Nushagak River
      Region, Alaska, by James W. VanStone. Fieldiana Anthropology.
      Vol. 61. Chicago: Field Museum of Natural History, 1971.
      American Anthropologist 74(4):960-962.

1973 Review: A Summary of Archaeology in the Katmai Region, South-
      western Alaska, by Don E. Dumond. University of Oregon Anthro-
      pological Papers, No. 2. 1971. Arctic 26(1):85-87.

1974 Review: V. S. Khromchenko's Coastal Explorations in Southwestern
      Alaska, 1922, by James W. VanStone, ed. (Translated by David H.
      Kraus) Fieldiana Anthropology, Vol. 64. Chicago: Field Museum
      of Natural History, 1973. Arctic 27(4):314-315.

Townsend, Joan B. and Sam-Joe Townsend

1961 Archaeological Investigations at Pedro Bay, Alaska. Anthropolo-
      gical Papers of the University of Alaska 10(1):25-58.

1964 Additional Artifacts from Iliamna Lake, Alaska. Anthropological
      Papers of the University of Alaska 12(1):14-16.

Treganza, Adan E.

1964 Archaeological Survey in Mount McKinley National Park, 1964.
Report to the National Park Service.

Tuck, James A.

1968 Aboriginal Inhabitants of Newfoundland and Labrador. In: Historic
Newfoundland. L.E.F. English, ed. pp. 68-71. Department of
Economic Development. St. John's (4th Edition, 1971)

1971a Newfoundland Prehistory Since 1950: Some Answers and Questions.
Man in the Northeast 1:27-33.

1971b An Archaic Cemetery at Port Au Choix, Newfoundland. American
Antiquity 36(3):343-358.

1972 Report from Northern Labrador. Man in the Northeast 3:56-58.

1973 Preliminary Paper and Discussion. School of American Research
Advanced Seminar on Pre-Dorset--Dorset Problems. Santa Fe.

1975a Maritime Adaptation on the Northwestern Atlantic Coast. In: Prehistoric Maritime Adaptations of the Circumpolar Zone. William W.
Fitzhugh, IV, ed. pp. 255-268. Mouton and Company. Paris.

1975b Prehistory of Saglek Bay, Labrador: Archaic and Palaeo-Eskimo
Occupations. Mercury Series. Archaeological Survey of Canada
Paper, No. 32. National Museums of Canada. Ottawa.

1976a Ancient People of Port au Choix: The Excavation of an Archaic
Indian Cemetery in Newfoundland. Newfoundland Social and Economic
Studies, No. 17. Institute of Social and Economic Research.
Memorial University of Newfoundland. St. John's, Newfoundland.

1976b Paleoeskimo Cultures of Northern Labrador. In: Eastern Arctic
Prehistory: Paleoeskimo Problems. Moreau S. Maxwell, ed. pp. 89-
102. Memoirs of the Society for American Archaeology, No. 31.

Turner, Christy G., II

1965 Aleut Dental Evolution. Abstract. American Journal of Physical
Anthropology 23(3):328-329.

1967 The Dentition of Arctic Peoples. Ph.D. dissertation. Department
of Anthropology. University of Wisconsin.

1970 Archaeological Reconnaissance of Amchitka Island, Alaska. Arctic
Anthropology 7(2):118-128.

1972 Preliminary Report of Archaeological Survey and Test Excavations
in the Eastern Aleutian Islands, Alaska. Arctic Anthropology
9(2):32-35.

1974 The Use of Prehistory for Direct Comparative Baselines in the Study of Aleut Microevolution and Adaptation. In: International Conference on the Prehistory and Paleoecology of Western North American Arctic and Subarctic. Scott Raymond and Peter Schledermann, eds. pp. 205-216. University of Calgary Archaeological Association. Alberta.

1976 The Aleuts of Akun Island. The Alaska Journal 6(1):125-31.

Turner, Christy G., II, Jean S. Aigner and Linda R. Richards

1974 Chaluka Stratigraphy, Umnak Island, Alaska. Arctic Anthropology 11(Suppl.):125-142.

Turner, Christy G., II, and James D. Cadien

n.d. Dental Chipping in Aleuts, Eskimos and Indians. Mimeographed manuscript.

Turner, Christy G., II, Linda R. Richards and Jacqueline A. Turner

1974 The Relation of Aleut Population Size to Seasonality of Marine Fauna. Proceedings of the 41st International Congress of Americanists. Mexico City, September.

Turner, Christy G., II, and Jacqueline A. Turner

1974 Progress Report on Evolutionary Anthropological Study of Akun Strait District, Eastern Aleutians, Alaska, 1970-71. Anthropological Papers of the University of Alaska 16(1):27-57.

n.d. Report of the 1972 Evolutionary Anthropology Field Investigations on Akun and Akutan Islands, Eastern Aleutians, Alaska. Mimeographed manuscript.

n.d. Akun. Mimeographed manuscript.

VanStone, James W.

1953a Notes on Kotzebue Dating. Tree Ring Bulletin 20:1.

1953b Carved Human Figures from St. Lawrence Island, Alaska. Anthropological Papers of the University of Alaska 2(1):19-29.

1953c Report of a Brief Archaeological Survey of the Copper River in the Chitina Region. Manuscript.

1954a Archaeological Excavations at Kotzebue, Alaska. Ph.D. dissertation. University of Pennsylvania.

1954b Pottery from Nunivak Island, Alaska. Anthropological Papers of the University of Alaska 2(2):181-193.

1955a Archaeological Excavations at Kotzebue, Alaska. Anthropological Papers of the University of Alaska 3(2):75-155.

1955b Exploring the Copper River Country. Pacific Northwest Quarterly
46(4):115-123.

1957 An Archaeological Reconnaissance of Nunivak Island, Alaska.
Anthropological Papers of the University of Alaska 5(2):97-117.

1961 Review: An Archaeological Analysis of Eastern Grant Land, Ellesmere
Island, N.W.T., by Moreau S. Maxwell. Contributions to Anthro-
pology, 1960. National Museum of Canada Bulletin, No. 170.
Ottawa, 1960. American Antiquity 27(2):251.

1962 Point Hope. An Eskimo Village Transition. University of
Washington Press. Seattle.

1963 Review: The Ancient Culture of the Bering Sea and the Eskimo
Problem, by S. I. Rudenko. In: Anthropology of the North. Arctic
Institute of North America, Technical Paper No. 1. Montreal,
1961. (Translated from the Russian Source by Paul Tolstoy; Henry
M. Michael, ed.) American Anthropologist 65:425.

1966 Review: Archaeology of the Yakutat Bay Area, Alaska, by Frederica
deLaguna. Bureau of American Ethnology Bulletin, No. 1972.
Smithsonian Institution, Washington, D.C., 1964. American
Antiquity 31(4):399.

1967 Eskimos of the Nushagak River. University of Washington Press.
Seattle.

1968a An Annotated Ethnohistorical Bibliography of the Nushagak River
Region, Alaska. Fieldiana Anthropology 54:2. Field Museum of
Natural History. Chicago.

1968b Tikchik Village: A Nineteenth Century Riverine Community in Southwestern Alaska. Fieldiana Anthropology 56:3. Field Museum of
Natural History. Chicago.

1970a Akulivikchuk: A Nineteenth Century Eskimo Village on the Nushagak
River, Alaska. Fieldiana Anthropology, Vol. 60. Field Museum of
Natural History. Chicago.

1970b Review: The Archaeology of the Glacier Bay Region, Southeastern
Alaska, by Robert E. Ackerman. Laboratory of Anthropology Report
of Investigations, No. 44. Washington State University. Pullman,
1968. American Antiquity 35(1):113.

1970c Ethnohistorical Research in Southwestern Alaska: A Methodological
Perspective. In: Ethnohistory in Southwestern Alaska and the
Southern Yukon: Method and Content. Margaret Lantis, ed. pp. 49-
70. Studies in Anthropology No. 7. University of Kentucky Press.
Lexington.

1971 Review: The Arnapik and Tyara Sites: An Archaeological Study of
Dorset Culture Origins, by William E. Taylor, Jr. Memoirs of the
Society for American Archaeology, No. 22. Arctic 24(4):311-312.

1972   Nushagak: An Historic Trading Center in Southwestern Alaska. Fieldiana Anthropology, Vol. 62. Field Museum of Natural History. Chicago.

1973a V. S. Khromchenko's Coastal Explorations in Southwestern Alaska, 1822. Fieldiana Anthropology, Vol. 64. Field Museum of Natural History. Chicago. (Ed.) (Translated by David H. Kraus.)

1973b Review: Modern Alaskan Native Material Culture, by Wendell Oswalt, ed. University of Alaska Museum, 1972. Arctic 26(3):265.

1977   Review: Archaeology of the Lake Harbour District, Baffin Island, by Moreau S. Maxwell. Mercury Series. Archaeological Survey of Canada Paper, No. 6. National Museums of Canada. Ottawa, 1973. American Antiquity 42(1):146.

VanStone, James W., James Anderson and Charles Merbs

1962   An Archaeological Collection from Somerset Island and Boothia Peninsula, N.W.T.; A Contribution to the Human Osteology of the Canadian Arctic. Art and Archaeology Division of the Royal Ontario Museum. Occasional Paper, No. 4. University of Toronto.

VanStone, James W., and Charles V. Lucier

1974   An Early Archaeological Example of Tattooing from Northwestern Alaska. Fieldiana Anthropology 66(1):1-9.

VanStone, James W., and Joan B. Townsend

1970   Kijik: An Historic Tanaina Indian Settlement. Fieldiana Anthropology, Vol. 59. Field Museum of Natural History. Chicago.

VanValin, William B.

1941   Eskimo Land Speaks. New York.

Vasilievsky, R. S.

1973   On the Problem of the Origin of the Ancient Cultures of the Sea Hunters on the North Pacific Coast. Paper Presented to the IXth International Congress of Anthropological and Ethnological Sciences. Chicago.

1975   Problems of the Origin of the Ancient Sea Hunters' Cultures in the Northern Pacific. In: Prehistoric Maritime Adaptations of the Circumpolar Zone. William W. Fitzhugh, IV, ed. pp. 113-122. Mouton and Company. Paris.

Vebaek, C. L.

1958   Ten Years of Topographical and Archaeological Investigations in the Medieval Norse Settlements in Greenland. Proceedings of the 32nd International Congress of Americanists. pp. 732-743. Copenhagen, 1956.

Veltre, Douglas and Jean S. Aigner

    1976 A Preliminary Study of Anangula Blade Tool Typology and Spatial
           Clusterings Using A Factor Analytic Approach. Arctic Anthropology
           13(2):60-70.

Vetter, John

    1970 Typological Analysis of the British Mountain Tradition in the
           North American Arctic. Master's thesis. New York University.
           New York.

Wallace, Birgitta L.

    1969 Review: Fort Chimo and Payne Lake, Ungava, Archaeology, 1965, by
           Thomas E. Lee. Collection Travaux Divers, No. 16. Centre d'Etude
           Nordiques, Universite Laval, Quebec, 1967. American Antiquity
           34(2):185-187.

    1971 Review: The Viking Achievement: A Survey of the Society and Culture
           of Early Medieval Scandinavia, by Peter G. Foote, and David M.
           Wilson. Praeger. New York, 1970. American Anthropologist 73(6):
           1419-1422.

Waugh, L. M.

    1937a Influence of Diet on the Jaws and Face of the American Eskimo.
           Journal of the American Dental Association 24:1640-1647.

    1937b Dental Observations among the Eskimos. Journal of Dental Research
           16:355-356.

West, Frederick Hadleigh, see Hadleigh-West, Frederick

Wettlaufer, B.

    1955 The Mortlach Site. Department of Natural Resources Anthropology
           Series, No. 1. Regina, Saskatchewan.

Weyer, Edward M., Jr.

    1929 An Aleutian Burial. Anthropological Papers of the American Museum
           of Natural History 31(4):221-238.

    1930 Archaeological Material from the Village Site at Hot Springs, Port
           Moller Alaska. Anthropological Papers of the American Museum of
           Natural History 31(4):239-279.

    1945 Review: The Aleutian and Commander Islands and Their Inhabitants, by
           Ales Hrdlicka. Wistar Institute of Anatomy and Biology. Phila-
           delphia, 1945. and The Anthropology of Kodiak Island, by Ales
           Hrdlicka. Wistar Institute of Anatomy and Biology. Philadelphia,
           1944. The Geographical Review 35(3):511-514.

Wheeler, Marilyn E.

1976 Elemental Characterization of Archaeological Obsidian from Alaska
      by Atomic Absorption Spectrophotometry. International Institute
      of Conservation/Canada Group Bulletin, No. 1.

Wheeler, Marilyn E. and Donald W. Clark

1976 Elemental Characterization of Obsidian from the Koyukuk River,
      Alaska, by Atomic Absorption Spectrophotometry. Manuscript in
      Preparation.

Whitaker, Ian

1954 The Scottish Kayaks and the "Finn-Men." Antiquity 28(110):99-104.

Wilkinson, Paul F.

1972 Oomingmak: A Model for Man/Animal Relationships in Prehistory.
      Current Anthropology 13(1):23-44.

1975a The Relevance of Musk Ox Exploitation to the Study of Prehistoric
      Animal Economies. Ph.D. dissertation. Cambridge University.

1975b The Relevance of Musk Ox Exploitation to the Study of Prehistoric
      Animal Economies. In: Paleoeconomy. Being the Second Volume of
      Papers in Economic Prehistory by Members of the Associates of the
      British Academy Major Research Project in the Early History of
      Agriculture, E. S. Higgs, ed. pp. 9-53. Cambridge University
      Press.

Wilkinson, Paul F. and Christopher C. Shank

1975 Archaeological Observations in North Central Banks Island. Arctic
      Anthropology 12(1):104-112.

Willey, Gordon R.

1966 An Introduction to American Archaeology: Vol. One, North and
      Middle America. Prentice-Hall, Englewood Cliffs, N.J.

1968 One Hundred Years of American Archaeology. In: One Hundred Years
      of Anthropology. J. O. Brew, ed. pp. 29-53. Harvard University
      Press.

1969 James Alfred Ford, 1911-1968. American Antiquity 34(1):62-71.

Wilmeth, Roscoe

1971 Canadian Archaeological Radiocarbon Dates. Contributions to Anthro-
      pology VII: Archaeology and Physical Anthropology. National
      Museum of Canada Bulletin 232:68-126. Ottawa.

Wilmsen, Edwin N.

    1964   Flake Tools in the American Arctic: Some Speculations. American
            Antiquity 29(3):338-344.

    1965   Metrical Analysis of Paleo-Indian Flake Technologies. Year Book
            of the American Philosophical Society, 1965. pp. 646-648.

Wintemberg, William J.

    1929   Preliminary Report of Field Work in 1927. Annual Report to the
            National Museum of Canada for 1927. National Museum of Canada
            Bulletin 56:40-41. Ottawa.

    1930   Review: A Stone Culture from Northern Labrador, and its Relation to
            the Eskimo-Like Culture of the Northeast, by W. D. Strong.
            American Anthropologist 32(1):126-143. Menasha, 1930. Geographi-
            cal Review 20:673.

    1939   Eskimo Sites of the Dorset Culture in Newfoundland. (Part I)
            American Antiquity 5(2):83-102.

    1940   Eskimo Sites of the Dorset Culture in Newfoundland. (Part II)
            American Antiquity 5(4):309-333.

    1942   The Geographical Distribution of Aboriginal Pottery in Canada.
            American Antiquity 8(2):129-141.

    1943   Artifacts from Ancient Workshop Sites Near Tadoussac, Saguenay
            County, Quebec. American Antiquity 8(4):313-340.

Wissler, Clark

    1916   Harpoons and Darts in the Stefansson Collection. Anthropological
            Papers of the American Museum of Natural History 14(2).

    1918   Archaeology of the Polar Eskimo. Anthropological Papers of the
            American Museum of Natural History 22(3).

    1920   Arctic Geography and Eskimo Culture: A Review of Steensby's Work.
            Geographical Review 9(2):125-138.

    1924   The Relation of Nature to Man as Illustrated by the North American
            Indian. Ecology 5(4):311-318.

Witter, Dan C.

    1974   Nunamiut Caribou Processing, Categories of Faunal Analysis, and
            Organizational Measures of Subsistence Strategy. Paper Presented
            at the Annual Meeting of the Society for American Archaeology.
            Washington, May.

Witthoft, John

1948   Review: Man in Northeastern North America, by Frederick Johnson, ed. Papers of the Robert S. Peabody Foundation for Archaeology, Vol. 3. Andover, Mass., 1946. American Antiquity 13(4):332-334.

1968   Flint Arrowpoints: From the Eskimo of Northwestern Alaska. Expedition 10:2:30-37.

Workman, Karen Wood

1972   Alaskan Archaeology: A Bibliography. Miscellaneous Publications in History and Archaeology Series, No. 1. Alaska Division of Parks. Anchorage. (Second edition, 1974)

Workman, William B.

1966a Prehistory at Port Moller, Alaska Peninsula; in Light of Fieldwork in 1960. Arctic Anthropology 3(2):132-153.

1966b Archaeological Reconnaissance on Chirikof Island, Kodiak Group: A Preliminary Report. Arctic Anthropology 3(2):185-192.

1969a Contributions to the Prehistory of Chirikof Island, Southwestern Alaska. Master's thesis. University of Wisconsin.

1969b Southwestern Alaskan Crossties with the Bering Sea Region: A Discussion Based on the Data from Chirikof Island, Southwestern Alaska. Paper Presented at the Annual Meeting of the Society for American Archaeology. Milwaukee, 1969.

1970   Report on an Archaeological Evaluation of the Southern Part of the Route of the Proposed Trans-Alaska Pipeline System: Valdez to Hogan's Hill. Manuscript.

1972   Review: A Summary of Archaeology in the Katmai Region, Southwestern Alaska, by Don E. Dumond. University of Oregon Anthropological Papers, No. 2. Eugene, 1971. American Anthropologist 74(6):1505-1506.

1974a Continuity and Change in the Prehistoric Record from the Aishihik-Kluane Region, Southwest Yukon, Canada. Paper Presented at the Annual Meeting, Canadian Archaeological Association. Whitehorse, Yukon Territory, 1974.

1974b First Dated Traces of Early Holocene Man in the Southwest Yukon Territory Canada. Arctic Anthropology 11(Suppl.):94-103.

1974c The Cultural Significance of a Volcanic Ash which Fell in the Upper Yukon Basin about 1400 Years Ago. In: International Conference on the Prehistory and Paleoecology of Western North American Arctic and Subarctic. Scott Raymond and Peter Schledermann, eds. pp. 239-261. University of Calgary Archaeological Association. Alberta.

1975 Research Reports. Newsletter, Alaska Anthropological Association 1(1):2-4. (Ed.)

1976 A Late Prehistoric Ahtna Site near Gulkana, Alaska. Paper Presented at the 3rd Annual Conference of the Alaska Anthropological Association.

Wormington, Hannah M.

1953 Origins. Program of the History of America 1(1):110. Comision de Historia. Mexico.

1957 Ancient Man in North America. The Denver Museum of Natural History. Popular Series, No. 4. Fourth Edition (Revised).

1962 A Survey of Early American Prehistory. American Scientist 50(1): 230-242.

Wright, James V.

1965 A Regional Examination of Ojibwa Culture History. Anthropologica 7:189-227. Ottawa.

1969 Current Research: Boreal Forest. American Antiquity 34(3):346-347.

1970a The Shield Archaic in Manitoba--A Preliminary Statement. In: Ten Thousand Years: Archaeology in Manitoba. Walter Hlady, ed. pp. 29-45. Manitoba Archaeological Society. Winnipeg.

1970b Current Research, Boreal Forest. American Antiquity 34(2):244-246.

1972a The Aberdeen Site, Keewatin District, N.W.T. Mercury Series. Archaeological Survey of Canada Paper, No. 2. National Museums of Canada. Ottawa.

1972b The Shield Archaic. Publications in Archaeology, No. 3. National Museums of Canada. Ottawa.

1975 The Prehistory of Lake Athabasca: An Initial Statement. Mercury Series. Archaeological Survey of Canada Paper, No. 29. National Museums of Canada. Ottawa.

1976 The Grant Lake Site, Keewatin District, N.W.T. Mercury Series. Archaeological Survey of Canada Paper, No. 47. National Museums of Canada. Ottawa.

Wyatt, David J.

1968 Microblades from the Arctic Small Tool Tradition. Master's thesis. Brown University. Providence.

1970a Statistical Analysis of Lochnore-Nesikep Locality Microblades. In: The Archaeology of the Lochnore-Nesikep Locality, British Columbia: Final Report. (Appendix I). Syesis 3(Suppl.). Victoria.

1970b Microblade Attribute Patterning: A Statistical Examination. Arctic Anthropology 7(2):97-105.

Yarborough, Michael R.
1974 Analysis of Pottery from the Western Alaska Peninsula. Anthropological Papers of the University of Alaska 16(1):85-89.

1975 The People of the East--The Aleut of the Alaska Peninsula. Paper Presented at the 2nd Annual Meeting of the Alaska Anthropological Association. Fairbanks.

Yesner, Donald R.

1973 The Southwest Umnak Settlement System. Paper presented to the Annual Meeting of the Society for American Archaeology. San Francisco.

1975 Nutrition and Population Dynamics of Hunter-gatherers. Paper presented at the Annual Meeting of the American Anthropological Association. San Francisco.

1976 Aleutian Island Albatrosses: A Population History. Auk 93(2): 263-280.

n.d. Comparative Biomass Estimates and Prehistoric Cultural Ecology of the Southwest Umnak Region, Aleutian Islands. Manuscript.

Yesner, David R. and Jean S. Aigner

1976 Comparative Biomass Estimates and Prehistoric Cultural Ecology of the Southwest Umnak Region, Aleutian Islands. Arctic Anthropology 13(2):91-112.

Yesner, David R. and Alan M. Beiber, Jr.

1974 Application of Multivariate Analysis to Regional Faunal Assemblages. Manuscript.

Zimmerman, Michael R. and George S. Smith

1975 A Probable Case of Accidental Inhumation of 1600 Years Ago. Bulletin of the New York Academy of Medicine, Second Series 51(7): 828-837.

Zolotariv, A.

1938 The Ancient Culture of North Asia. American Anthropologist, N.S.: 40:1:13-23.

Appendix 1 - Additional Sources of Information

la. Libraries with Unusually Good Collections of Arctic Materials

University of Alaska Fairbanks, Alaska	The Elmer Rasmuson Library, Skinner Collection, Library of the Institute of Arctic Biology
University of Alberta Edmonton, Alberta	Library of the Boreal Institute
University of Calgary Calgary, Alberta	Library of the Arctic Institute of North America
University of Colorado Boulder, Colorado	Library of the Institute for Arctic and Alpine Research
Dartmouth College Hanover, New Hampshire	Dartmouth College Libraries, Stefansson Collection
Cambridge University Cambridge, England	Library of the Scott Polar Institute
Universite de la Sorbonne Paris, France	Bibliotheque du Centre d'Etudes Arctiques
University of Toronto Toronto, Ontario	Library of the Department of Anthropology
University of Washington Seattle, Washington	Library of the Quaternary Research Center

Any of the libraries of the larger universities or research institutes would have above average collections, especially if their staff have been involved in Arctic studies. These include the University of Wisconsin, Michigan State University, Brown University, Harvard University, University of Oregon, Washington State University, Ohio State University and the University of New Mexico.

1b. Museums with Extensive Collections of Arctic Archaeological Materials

The University of Alaska Museum
Fairbanks, Alaska

Danish National Museum
Copenhagen, Denmark

The Dartmouth College Museum
Hanover, New Hampshire

Field Museum of Natural History
Chicago, Illinois

The Haffenreffer Museum
Brown University
Providence, Rhode Island

Maxwell Museum of Anthropology
University of New Mexico
Albuquerque, New Mexico

National Museum of Man
National Museums of Canada, Ottawa

Royal Ontario Museum
Toronto, Ontario

The Smithsonian Institution
Washington, DC

Active researchers in the Arctic may retain research collections in
the laboratories and museums of the institution with which they are
affiliated. Universities may house such collections, especially if
their staff have been involved in Arctic studies.

1c. Serial Publications with Significant Content on Arctic Archaeology

Acta Arctica

The Alaska Journal

Anthropological Papers of the University of Alaska

Arctic

Arctic Anthropology

Arctic and Alpine Research

The Beaver

Bulletins, National Museum of Man

Fieldiana Anthropology

Meddelelser om Grønland

The Mercury Series, National Museum of Man

The Musk Ox

Paleo-Quebec

Quaternary Research

Smithsonian Contributions to Anthropology

Travaux Divers, Centre d'Etudes Nordiques

For access to these publications, consult the Union List of Periodicals or ask your librarian.

1d. Other Publications of Relevance

In addition to those bibliographies cited in the body of this volume, you might find the American Anthropological Association's "Guide to Departments of Anthropology" published annually useful to find the present location of Arctic researchers who are anthropologists in academic institutions.

Most doctoral dissertations are available from University Microfilms (if from US universities). Master's theses are more difficult to find, the best sources being interlibrary loan from the libraries where they were deposited. In Canada, most significant dissertations have been subsequently published in recent years. Master's theses are often available from the Public Archives of Canada in microform.